INTERNATIONAL ENVIRONMENTAL CONFLICT RESOLUTION

THE ROLE OF THE UNITED NATIONS

Jon Martin Trolldalen

INTERNATIONAL ENVIRONMENTAL CONFLICT RESOLUTION

THE ROLE OF THE UNITED NATIONS

Jon Martin Trolldalen

WFED

World Foundation for
Environment and Development

Oslo • Washington D.C.

UNITAR

United Nations Institute for
Training and Research

Geneva • New York

NIDR

National Institute for
Dispute Resolution

Washington D.C.

International support for the research programme *International Environmental Conflict Resolution* is being co-ordinated by the World Foundation for Environment and Development (WFED). WFED is an independent and nonpartisan organization that has been established to encourage collaborative international efforts to advance the peaceful resolution of international environmental conflicts (with special focus on the economic burdens and environmental challenges facing developing countries).

* * *

The cover illustrations are based on photographs of
sculptures by Gustav Vigeland (1869—1943)
Frognerparken, Oslo, Norway.
WFED gratefully acknowledges permission
from Vigeland-museet to reproduce the images
© Vigeland-museet / BONO, 1992
Cover design by Colin H.F. Dobinson

* * *

WFED gratefully acknowledges permission to reprint the diagram 'The UN System' (page 15) from 'The United Nations: International Organization and World Politics', by Robert E. Riggs and Jack C. Plano, published by Wadsworth Publishing Co., 1988.

Photo credits appear in the list on page xvi.

The denominations used and the line boundaries shown on the maps do not imply on the part of WFED, UNITAR, and NIDR any judgement on the legal status of any territory or any endorsement or acceptance of such boundaries.

Production Manager / Designer: Colin H.F. Dobinson
Typeset with an Apple Macintosh™ and a Linotronic™ 300 in Oslo, Norway.
Set in Goudy and Frutiger type families.

Printing Consultant: Stephen Wilson Design, Inc. (Washington)
Printed by: C & R Printing, Inc. (Virginia)
Printed in the United States on recycled paper.

ISBN 0-9635465-0-3
UN sales no. E.92.III.K.PS./13

Foreword

INTERNATIONAL ENVIRONMENTAL CONFLICTS that come to the attention of the United Nations and other international organizations typically reflect an aggregation of unresolved local, national and regional resource-based problems and disputes. Because the nature of conflict changes and often becomes more complex as it moves from local to international levels, analysts suggest that such conflicts might be managed more effectively if intercepted for resolution before reaching multilateral stages.

International Environmental Conflict Resolution: The Role of the United Nations examines the issues and problems relating to international environmental conflicts from the perspective of many disciplines, and pays particular attention to theoretical and analytical as well as empirical issues. The case studies presented in the book highlight the variety of resource-based conflicts that are emerging throughout the world. The causes of such conflicts are as varied as their effects and complexity underscores the difficult challenges to the world community to find satisfactory ways to respond to the scientific, economic and political problems presented.

The book also focuses on the fact the nations have developed different ways for managing competition for natural resource utilization as well as for responding to the effects of environmental degradation. Evidence suggests, however, that many such ways are being strained by accelerating competition for increasingly scarce resources and the resulting conflicts that are emerging. Existing resource management policies at many local, national and international levels simply do not meet the demands of rapidly growing populations and sustainable development needs.

This perspective also was taken by the World Commission on Environment and Development, which expressed great concern over the increase in international conflicts due not only to political and military threats, but also to environmental degradation and the preemption of development options. The stakes are high for governments everywhere—whether they represent affluent industrialized countries with powerful economies or developing countries in need of economic growth simply to meet the most basic needs of life.

Against such a background, the role of the United Nations is of particular interest, especially with regard to issues relating to the development of norms and procedures that recognize national sovereignty yet also accommodate transboundary environmental concerns. At a time when traditional sovereign interests are being challenged as never before by the demands and obligations of a greater global interdependence, the book is timely and a welcome contribution in an important field.

Mohamed T. El-Ashry, Ph.D.

Director, Environment Department
The World Bank

Chairman, Global Environment Facility
UNDP / UNEP / The World Bank

Acknowledgements

This book was made possible through invaluable support from Kåre Bryn, Royal Norwegian Ministry of Foreign Affairs, and Oddmund Graham, Royal Norwegian Ministry of Environment.

I am greatly indebted to Mohamed El-Ashry, World Bank, and Marcel A. Boisard, UNITAR, for their support and acknowledgement of this book.

I would also like to express my appreciation to Gro Harlem Brundtland, Prime Minister of Norway, for her statement.

* * *

Various people have assisted me in the effort of writing this book. Ideas however, intermingle and refuse to sort themselves out so that the sources can be identified. Valuable comments and criticisms were offered, not all of which I was able to respond to adequately. Any errors or weaknesses remain my own.

To nobody am I more indebted than to Preston T. Scott—my partner in WFED—for his visions and insight in building WFED, as well as for his invaluable meticulous and constructive editing.

Colin Dobinson has made a great contribution by combining design and editing. Arlette Snyder's patient editorial work has been invaluable.

Considerable help has been received from my research assistants at the International Environmental Conflict Resolution (IECR) programme at the Resource Geography Group, Department of Geography, University of Oslo. My sincere appreciations go to: Nina M. Birkeland (land resources and environmental refugees), Nils P. Fjeld (process tools and international aquifers), Øyvind Hugsted (biodiversity), Mette Kristensen (forestry), Harald Nygaard (coastal areas), Fred Ivar Aasand (international river systems), and not at least, Lynn Parker Nygaard who provided administrative as well as professional assistance, particularly on regional organizations.

A close colleague over several years, Just Gjessing, has, as always, offered inspirations and comments.

Thomas Fee (NIDR) has been supportive and a source of inspiration, as well as broadening my perspective on process-tools and their applicability. Many thanks also to Gao Pronove (UNITAR) for productive collaborative efforts.

Larry Kohler's (ILO) constructive criticisms came at a very important stage in the writing process, and through his advice, the book is hopefully more concrete and applicable for international organizations. Rolf Selrod's (CICERO) insight in substantive and organizational matters related to

UNEP's role in conflict prevention and resolution was especially welcome. I have also benefitted from Carola Bjørklund's (Norwegian Ministry of Environment) thoughtful interpretation of international law and applicability to international environmental conflicts.

Jan Borgen's (Norwegian Refugee Council) insights in refugee matters have benefitted this book (as well as the joint effort in writing 'Environmental Refugees', May 1992). Valter Angell's (NUPI) thoughts on linkages between environment and economics have enhanced my understanding of important distinctions between competition and conflicts. Arne Dalfelt's (World Bank) comments were particularly challenging to respond to. I have benefitted from Gervase Coles' insights on refugee issues related to the environment. Terje Grøntoft and Gunnar Sandvik gave valuable contributions in the fields of international organisations and problems in the Horn of Africa, respectively.

Øyvind Trolldalen's assistance was highly appreciated at a critical step in the writing process.

Kristin Dobinson made an important contribution in proofreading and editing. Anne Sörensen's assistance with photo editing and clerical tasks has been very constructive.

Discussions with Stein W. Bie has been a great source of inspiration in developing this book.

Past work under Kenneth Piddington (World Bank) provided many ideas for this book, and his comments were most appropriate. A most stimulating past working relationship with Erik Arrhenius, Mohan Munasinghe, Leif Christoffersen (World Bank) gave many of the ideas for this programme.

I have also enjoyed most creative consultations on environmental conflicts with Mustafa Tolba, Bill Mansfield and Yusuf J. Ahmed (UNEP), as well as with Michael Gucovsky and Erik Hellan-Hansen (UNDP), and Peter Branner and Ruben Mendez (UNSO). Ricard C. Collins and Bill Street (Institute for Environmental Negotiations, University of Virginia) have both in their way contributed to the formation of the programme. A special thanks to Abby Arnold (former CMI, Harvard University, now WWF) and to Terry Barnett (CMI, Harvard University) for their introduction to alternative dispute resolution-approach 'Getting to Yes'.

Encouragement and support for the programme was offered by Michael Williams (WFED). Therese Myklebust's administrative support has been valuable.

My wife, Bente, was an active participant in the preparation of this book. She took on additional responsibilities to provide me extra time for travelling, consultations, and writing. In addition, Christina and Andreas were patiently waiting for their father. This book is dedicated to them.

I would like to acknowledge the following institutions for their funding of this book: Royal Norwegian Ministry of Foreign Affairs, Royal Norwegian Ministry of Environment, National Institute for Dispute Resolution (NIDR), United Nations Institute for Training and Research (UNITAR), and Norwegian Research Council for Science and the Humanities (NAVF).

J. Martin Trolldalen   November 1992, Oslo

Contents

Part One   Responses to international environmental conflicts

Chapter One   Environmental complexity and international environmental conflicts (IECs)

Chapter Two   Institutional responses to international environmental conflicts

Chapter Three   Ways of managing international environmental conflicts   3

Part Two   International environmental conflicts and how they generate

Chapter Four   Methodology and analysis   4

5

Chapter Five

International River Systems

Chapter Eight

8

Land Resources
—*Marginal lands, border landscapes, land-based effects of air pollution*

Chapter Nine — Secondary effects of degradation: environmental refugees

9

List of Tables

List of Figures

List of Boxes

List of Photographs

Statement

At a time when the United Nations is drawn to enhance its peacekeeping role, the book *International Environmental Conflict Resolution: The Role of the United Nations* makes a timely contribution. It identifies one of the most important sources of conflict in the post-cold war era - the use and misuse of the world's limited natural resources and fragile environment - and reminds us that the foundation for lasting peace is that kind of development which is also of a lasting quality. Indeed, the concept of sustainability as applied to development applies as well to conflict resolution and the promotion of peace. In this sense, by bringing the concept of sustainability to bear down on these two important concerns, the book is able to present a cohesive and perhaps new role for the United Nations. For this reason, UNITAR is pleased to contribute to the realization of this book and hopes it will stimulate more ideas in this growing and important field.

Marcel A. Boisard, Ph.D.

Acting Executive Director, UNITAR

Preface

TWENTY YEARS AFTER the United Nations Conference on the Human Environment in Stockholm—and in the wake of the 1992 United Nations Conference on Environment and Development (UNCED) in Rio de Janeiro—the world community continues to face the critical task of finding peaceful and effective ways to protect the environment as well as to promote desperately needed social and economic development.

The need to balance protection of the environment with improvement of human welfare through social and economic development triggers local, national, and international conflicts of interest. UNCED showcased the competing claims for both protection and development of the world's natural resources in a dramatic but not entirely satisfactory way.

This study focuses on the increased tensions and competing claims between national governments, non-governmental organizations, private companies, and local populations that relate to conflicts over utilization of even local resources which may have international implications, over shared natural resources (such as international rivers and atmospheric ozone) as well as transboundary externalities (such as water and air pollution) Although the terms 'environmental conflicts' and 'environmental diplomacy' have appeared previously, this study examines international environmental conflicts (IECs) as competing interests in efforts to balance protection of the environment with the impacts of various development decisions.

Before turning to a more in-depth presentation of IECs, I would like to give a sketch of how this book came about.

The experience gained—from working within the academic community; working at a local level through research and extensive fieldwork, particularly in West Africa; working in a non-governmental development organization, and subsequently working for the World Bank as well as participating in the United Nations General Assembly—suggested a gap in both academic approaches as well as in various organizations' and governments' ability to cope with emerging IECs. Accordingly, I decided to design this study to discuss possible ways to improve both the prevention and resolution of IECs. I began the study in the fall of 1990 just after leaving the World Bank. The work reflected here results from numerous consultations worldwide, various types of data collection, extensive literature reviews, and long discussions with the staff at the 'International Environmental Conflict Resolution' programme at the University of Oslo as well as numerous other observers.
The issues addressed by this study may be summarized as follows:

Nations have different ways of managing competition for natural resources and of preventing and resolving conflicts at local, national, regional, and global levels. Strong evidence suggests, however, that these ways are not always capable of handling new forms of competition, nor the resulting conflicts that emerge. A growing number of cases indicates that many present management systems are not equipped to handle the complexity and dynamics of new forms of resource utilization. Existing resource management policies at local, national, and international levels typically do not satisfy the fundamental quest for sustainable development.

To my knowledge, no studies have been carried out taking this particular integrative perspective. I also have paid considerable attention to development of a consistent conceptual, theoretical, analytical, and empirical framework for IEC evaluation. The cases outlined in the study attempt to test some of others reasonings. In light of the vast variety in types, scopes, and magnitude of IECs all over the world, this study simply provides an indication of how the international community might improve the prevention and resolution of IECs.

The perspective taken in this study is derived from the World Commission on Environment and Development (WCED)[1] which expressed great concern over the increase in international conflicts due not only to political and military threats to national sovereignty, but also to environmental degradation and pre-emption of development options. The Commission suggested that the idea of national sovereignty is being challenged by growing international interdependence in the realms of economics, environment and security, because regional and global commons simply cannot be managed from any single national centre.

Against the background of such observations, the UN General Assembly specifically requested that the United Nations Conference on Environment and Development (UNCED):[2]

"...(a)ssess the capacity of the United Nations system to assist in the prevention and settlement of disputes in the environmental sphere and to recommend measures in this field, while respecting existing bilateral and international agreements that provide for the settlement of such disputes."[3]

Understanding IECs

Local, national, regional, and global resources are being stressed at an unprecedented rate which is destabilizing the world's ecological balance. This trend is likely to increase and create additional 'ecological surprises' (such as depletion of the ozone layer, sudden loss of species and change in the quality of vital resources as well as other unexpected environmental deteriorations). The challenge is to create and improve means for international cooperation and environmental conflict management.

One might argue that IECs should be resolved along the same lines as economic, social, and military or security conflicts.[4] As the study reveals, however, most existing institutions lack the specific mandate and competence to deal with the dimensions of conflicts particular to IECs: tensions between environment and development interests, negative externalities and questions of compensation.

Although IECs are intersectoral and should be dealt with accordingly, most institutions are not set up for this purpose. Neutrality, legitimacy, effectiveness, credibility and membership commitment should ideally be the attributes of entities involved in the prevention and resolution of IECs. It is unlikely that any single institutional body acting alone can encompass all of these attributes. Because many IECs are at a regional or global level, they represent a particular challenge to world bodies such as the United Nations (UN).

The term IEC may be applied to any situation where the utilization of natural resources in one country has negative environmental impacts for another country or group of countries. It is important to make a distinction between real and perceived IECs, as well as manifest and potential IECs. IECs occur on various institutional, political, and geographical levels that transcend national borders. It also is impossible to define these conflicts in terms of one country versus another nation or group of nations, since many IECs start at a local level, and subsequently develop into international conflicts with implications for many different parties.

The Challenge

The challenge is to help define the role of international institutions in preventing and resolving IECs. It is commonplace to say that, in an age of global interdependence, international cooperation is imperative for all nations. Perhaps the greatest challenge relates to the integration of developing countries into the international system. It is clear that no single nation or groups of nations now dominates this era in history. The UN system,[5] the Bretton Woods institutions,[6] and the international trading systems are all being challenged to address new international environmental problems. For example, as stated by the South Commission, it is crucial to enhance institutional capacity building through multilateral organizations and regimes backed by a strengthened UN system.[7] This need is particularly acute because many of the means to resolve IECs involve difficult but crucial questions concerning the transfer of additional funds (in addition to traditional development assistance[8]) and 'environmentally sound technology' to developing countries and the conditions governing such transfers. With an increasing number of participants, the conflict resolution process is becoming more complex.

Seeking Vehicles for Conflict Resolution

International environmental problems and conflicts often reflect traditional political positions. Because the UN is the mirror—not the shaper—of world politics, it often reflects such alliances and blocs. Nonetheless, IECs within a region may call for collective actions for which familiar political blocs are not applicable. Some argue that the traditional modes of cooperation in the UN are not particularly useful. Accordingly, regional arrangements are often advocated as the more appropriate vehicles for conflict resolution (as discussed in Chapter Two).

In dealing with IECs, the UN has many opportunities to cooperate with regional organizations and NGOs, the Bretton Woods institutions and development banks—particularly when compensation for damage and the transfer of additional[9] funds are an issue. The disadvantage, however, may be that existing UN institutional setups are not appropriate to address these challenges. Despite institutional changes and improvements, the UN is not able to achieve more than what individual governments are willing to subscribe to. Although the UN should be able to assist in the prevention and resolution of IECs through utilization of its vast institutional, technical, and political resources (as discussed in Chapter Three), the difficulties of identifying the most critical remedial institutional changes leading to satisfactory resolution of IECs should not be underestimated.

Organization of this study

The study is organized in two parts. Part One introduces some conceptual and analytical reasonings, and discusses the role of several international organizations in the prevention and resolution of IECs. This analysis is to a large extent based on Part Two, which is comprised principally of IEC case studies.

Part One

Chapter One: *Environmental complexity and international environmental conflicts.* As an introduction to the study, this chapter provides a framework for analysing IECs as a basis for preventing and resolving IECs at regional and global levels. Some fundamental conceptual and theoretical reasonings are discussed.

Chapter Two: *Institutional response to international environmental conflicts.* From an historical perspective, the UN possesses important attributes necessary for effective prevention and resolution of international environmental conflicts (IECs). The chapter briefly outlines the role of the following UN organs, organizations, and agencies in prevention, avoidance, settlement and resolution of IECs: the Security Council, Economic and Social Council (ECOSOC), Trusteeship Council, International Court of Justice, Permanent Court of Arbitration, Secretary General, United Nations Environment Programme, and Bretton Woods Institutions. Some observations about the Vatican, the International Committee of Red Cross, and various regional organisations and their role in preventing and resolving IECs also are briefly outlined.

Chapter Three: *Ways of managing international environmental conflict.* Various non-legal and legal approaches to prevent, avoid, settle, and resolve IECs are examined in this chapter. Certain mechanisms are applicable for different organizations. The main focus is on such mechanisms rather than organizational capacities (as discussed in the previous chapter). Special emphasis is on prevention and resolution of IECs of a legal character.

Part Two

Part Two deals with IECs related to international river systems, coastal areas, forestry and biodiversity, land resources, and secondary effects of environmental degradation and disruptions—environmental refugees. The main focus is put on why IECs generate and escalate at an international level. This provides a basis for an assessment of means to prevent and resolve IECs at regional and global levels.

Chapter Four: *Methodology and analysis.* This chapter explores the development of a Systems Approach in order to link traditional conflict analysis with ecosystem analysis.[10] The purpose of this chapter is to outline an analytical framework for analysing IECs applied on the various themes and case-studies selected.

Chapter Five: *International river systems.* This chapter assesses the driving forces behind IECs related to international river systems and illustrates some of their main components through brief case studies, such as the Indus, Jordan, Nile, and Ganges river systems. A more in-depth case study focuses on IECs and how they have been managed in relation to the Zambezi River System in Southern Africa.

Chapter Six: *Coastal areas.* Coastal areas, as transitional zones between land and sea, are increasingly affected by aquatic and terrestrial human activities. The many national and international interests associated with the use of these areas make them particularly interesting to study in the light of IECs. A case study from the Mediterranean which is shared by 18 nations, is discussed in the light of the origins and management of coastal IECs.

Chapter Seven: *Forestry and biodiversity.* This chapter examines some of the driving forces behind IECs related to forestry and biodiversity, and assesses some of their main components through several case studies. A more in-depth case-study focuses on conflicts related to the tropical forest shared by Cameroun, the Congo, and the Central African Republic in Central and West Africa.

Chapter Eight: *Land resources.* This chapter outlines systemic linkages between land resources and economic, political, social and other environmental factors related to IECs. The main conflicts are between development and environmental requirements (in particular, how to satisfy human needs while at the same time protecting land resources for future use).

IECs associated with 'air pollution' as a cause of land degradation is of particular interest since there are some lessons learned in prevention and resolution of such conflicts in Europe.

Chapter Nine: *Secondary effects of degradation—environmental refugees.* This chapter deals with environmental refugees as sources of IECs caused by secondary effects of environmental degradation or disruptions. The causal linkages between degradation of natural resources and cross border movement of people are complex, but of great interest in the context of IECs.

The endnotes for this section, as well as for the other chapters, appear at the end of the book.

Part One

Responses to international environmental conflicts (IECs)

Chapter One

1

Environmental complexity and international environmental conflicts

THIS CHAPTER introduces some concepts for analysing international environmental conflicts (IECs). The concepts are used to develop a framework to aid understanding of regional and global IECs. The concepts and framework introduced in the chapters are based on an examination of IECs and their relationship to environmental complexity and the management of natural resources.[1]

Quite often, current ways of managing and allocating natural resources do not pay enough attention to environmental side-effects of resource utilization. A growing number of approaches to resource management do not fulfil basic criteria of sustainable development. If sustainable development practices are not introduced, however, the goals of resource users at local, national and international levels are likely to become increasingly incompatible. Generally, increasing pressure on natural resource management systems results directly from development and population growth. Inevitably, if a dwindling natural resource base is required to provide an ever-increasing stream of goods and services, then competition between resource-users will increase. Such competition may result in IECs.

In this study, emphasis is put on factors that can cause competition for resources to escalate into IECs, especially in those cases where IECs result from negative environmental effects. This study also focuses on prevention and resolution of IECs, and considers new roles that could be played by the UN and other international institutions.

1.1 The nature of IECs

Many nations (and in some cases, groups of nations) perceive that they have mutually incompatible goals when it comes to dealing with the negative impacts on the environment that arise from utilizing natural resources. 'Incompatible goals' in this sense means 'consciously desired future outcomes, conditions or end stages, which have intrinsic (but different) values', for those nations or groups of nations. IECs may appear elsewhere on a spectrum of incompatible goals, ranging from unsustainable natural resource utilization to insufficient protection of the environment. Conflicts of interests that relate to incompatible goals over utilization of natural resources can provide the basis for a working definition of IECs:

> International environmental conflicts (IECs) are conflicts of interest that arise from the utilization of natural resources in one country which has negative environmental consequences for another country or group of countries.

Definition of IECs

Manifest and potential IECs

This study also differentiates between various stages in the escalation of IECs. For example, a **manifest** conflict is one which is recognized and could lead to actual conflict behaviour (as in the conflict between Turkey and Iraq, where Turkey's Ataturk dam is upstream of Iraq—see Chapter Five). Adversaries in manifest conflicts often consider the potential costs of pursuing their goals further to be too high to be worth attempting (such situations can be termed 'suppressed conflicts'). In contrast, a **potential** conflict is one which may not yet be fully recognized by the parties; nevertheless, their goals are mutually incompatible. Conflict behaviour could follow (as in the conflict between nations over pollution of the Mediterranean Sea—see Chapter Six).

Manifest & potential IECs

Manifest conflict
—is recognized and could lead to conflict behaviour

Potential conflict
—not yet recognized by the adversaries, although their goals are mutually incompatible

1.2 IECs at local, regional and global levels

Because the world's natural resources are not evenly distributed according to political boundaries, IECs have many characteristics which extend beyond national borders. Accordingly, it is difficult to define IECs simply in terms of one nation versus another. Many IECs start at a local level, but then escalate into international conflicts involving more that one nation. Some IECs may have a regional or even global dimension. The three main geographical levels of IECs can be categorized as follows:

■ **Local.** If resources at the local level are poorly managed, the productive capacity of the resource base may be reduced (which in turn hinders their sustainable development). For example, local indigenous people's historical use of a tropical rain forest may trigger many conflicts with a national government's need for revenue through logging.

Local Resource Management— hunting in the Ituri forest, Africa

Damming of international rivers: fisheries development in southern Zimbabwe

■ **Regional.** Regional IECs often involve one country's national interests being at odds with those of other nations, especially concerning:
— activities within national borders which have regional environmental consequences (for example, cross-border air pollution)
— activities which affect shared resources (such as damming of international rivers)
■ **Global.** Global IECs involve management of international commons, such as atmospheric ozone or the oceans. Increasingly, such conflicts are linked to other industrialized and developing countries (often in a North–South context).

Additionally, **Transnational Corporations** (TNCs) may be at odds with local and / or international interests, leading to IECs. To simplify the analysis in this study, however, only the first three levels will be treated.

The case studies in Part Two illustrate some of the causal links between the levels and the escalation of IECs as well as the nature of the conflicts.

The relationship between demand and availability of resources is central to the question of how natural resource systems should be managed. This apparent opposition has implications for environmental, economic and energy policies on both a national and international scale. Failure to manage natural resource systems successfully can be seen as a major cause of environmental degradation.

Approaches to resource management

The way in which a society or state views the natural resource system will determine its policies and management practices. The case studies in Part Two show that at least three perspectives can be identified, with each leading to different policies.[2]   These are:
■ **The Nature Benign Approach** considers the absorption capacity ('resilience') of natural resource systems as a safeguard against stress—for example pollution or extractive activities from natural resources—to continue the existing management practice with a 'business as usual' policy (for example, as advocated by some states in the negotiations for the Global Climatic Convention).[3]
■ **The Nature Linear Approach** assumes that the absorption capacity of resource systems acts as a safeguard against irreversible response to stress, even though the resource systems are sometimes signalling the need for intervention (for example, the attitude among the European Mediterranean states regarding the initial sea pollution). This often results in a 'wait and see' approach to natural resource management.
■ **The Nature Non-Linear Approach** recognizes that resource systems absorb stress through absorption capacities, conceal responses, and then

sometimes generate 'environmental surprises'. This reflects a more cautious approach that can be characterized as a blend of the approaches above.

A critical issue is the degree to which nations regard scientific proof as a prerequisite for a policy response, or alternatively, the degree to which they regard science as only one element in the issue. The effect of the latter view is that if the scientific proof is uncertain, this element becomes less important than other considerations, such as equity and insurance. A good illustration might be the position adopted by the small island states (such as the Maldives) in the negotiations for a Framework Convention on Climate Change (signed in Rio in 1992). They felt they did not need any further scientific proof that action is needed now, and therefore concentrated on compensatory mechanisms related to equity and insurance issues.

1.3 Reciprocal and collective obligations

IECs can also be understood in terms of disputes arising out of the reciprocal and collective obligations among and between states. Reciprocal obligations typically result from negotiated agreements between two or more states and relate to specifically identified resources or fields of activity. Collective obligations are less clearly defined, and typically relate to commons and other widely shared resources.[4]

Equity is an important principle that can be used to define the obligations between states. It is also clear that the costs and benefits from the utilization of natural resources need to be shared equitably. The Brundtland Commission noted that developing countries should be able to derive benefit from economic growth through utilization of their natural resources (which also include shared resources).[5]

1.4 Natural resource scarcity and distribution

IECs also arise because of the gap between demand and availability of natural resources. As population increases, demand too can be expected to increase. Two distinct approaches to resource management can be identified.

■ One view argues that shortage of resources is the major barrier to continued economic development—which can have severe implications for the economies of developing countries.[6] This approach has been criticized because it overlooks human response mechanisms (particularly the effects of technological development and the influence of culture).

■ Another approach relies on market mechanisms as the primary tool for optimal regulation of resource use. This approach assumes that since the price of a dwindling resource is forced to rise, the market acts to avoid worldwide resource shortage problems.[7]

Some of the difficulties with this approach arise because of uneven spatial distribution of resource reserves, and because of consumption and production patterns.

Alternative views of resource management

■ **Resource scarcity**
—scarcity of resources is a major barrier to development (has severe implications for developing countries' economies)

■ **Market forces**
—reliance on market mechanisms as the primary tool for resource management. Prices rise to protect dwindling resources

Box 1

Externalities

—the uncompensated side effects of economic and social activity

Reciprocal externalities

All users of a common property resource impose costs on all, including themselves

Transfer unidirectional externalities

The costs are imposed by one economic unit (for example, a state) on other users (for example, another state) of the same resource, such as effluent discharge to a river, (where external costs are imposed on users downstream)

Market mechanisms alone also cannot guarantee that the rate of resource extraction will not prevent physical exhaustion of semi-renewable and stock resources. Economic systems which have been allowed to operate unchecked by democratic government activity or by other agencies have had significant negative impacts on the environment. Until now, such impacts have been treated as free goods with little or no market value. There is a growing understanding that the effects of unchecked environmental destruction threaten the prospects for sustainable development for both North and South, as individual nations and groups of nations become increasingly unwilling to overlook the 'externalities' of using the resource base (see Box 1).[8]

The argument that the physical resource base is diverse enough to sustain production of a full range of essential goods and services can also be challenged. Resource scarcity occurs at local, national, and regional levels because some nations are unable to import or gain access to the required materials or production technology and management skills, due to global economic structures. The degree to which a nation exerts control over its own natural resources varies, but is affected by its developmental level and future intentions.

1.5   The dynamics of IECs

The IECs examined in the case studies in Part Two point to two interesting observations: one related to the escalation of local conflicts into international conflicts; and the other related to the way in which the number of parties involved tends to increase as the conflict becomes more polarized. Because only limited studies are available, the particular characteristics of IECs cannot be directly compared to other international conflicts.[9]

The dynamics of IECs and the conflict management tools associated with them share certain common features. Figure 1 illustrates general escalation patterns of IECs. Remedial efforts at the different stages of one such pattern are shown.

IECs can be approached in various ways, ranging from *prevention* and *avoidance* to *settlement* and *resolution*. Each approach must be applied differently according to whether the conflict is in an *incipient, latent,* (that is, potential) stage, or *acknowledged* and *overt behaviour* (i.e., manifest) stage (see Box 2 about escalation of conflicts for further discussion).

■ *Prevention* is defined as an active planning attempt to identify areas of conflict, and to remove or minimize their causes. Preventive measures can include legal arrangements; policy charges and other activities at local, regional, and global levels (including awareness-raising and public participation—which may, however, also generate IECs under certain circumstances); environmental impact assessments and exchange of environmental data).

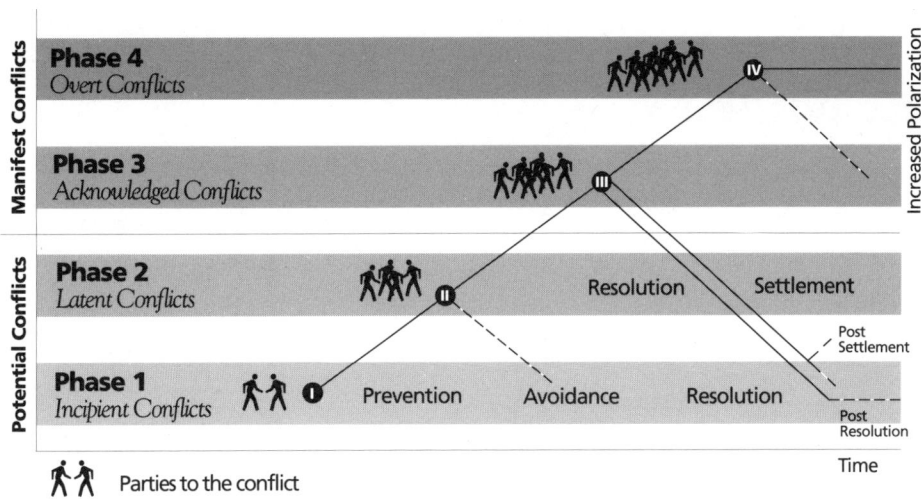

Figure 1. Escalation Model. See pages 8–12 for detailed discussion

■ *Avoidance* is a reaction made in a situation where incompatible goals have emerged.

■ *Settlement* aims primarily to alter the symptoms of the conflict, and is often a non-sustainable agreement that retains the possibility of re-emergence of the conflict.

■ *Resolution* is a mutually acceptable, sustainable agreement that eliminates the root causes of the conflict. There are distinctions between conflict resolution within the realm of legal obligations and conflicts which are resolved through less formal channels. The term **conflict management** embraces all four stages identified above.

These introductory concepts provide a basis for studying the ways in which the various organizations are involved in preventing and resolving IECs (See Chapters Two and Three). Additional theoretical reasonings are developed in Chapter Four (Methodology and Analysis).

Box 2

The Escalation Model

The model has two dimensions—the vertical axis, which is divided into four phases, depicts the level of polarization of the conflict; the horizontal axis depicts the passage of time. The polarization phases are separated by the degree of resource utilization and awareness among the parties, the number of parties involved in the conflict, the complexity level of the conflict, and the behaviour of the parties involved.

The Nature Benign Approach (taken by some governments—see page 4) can help explain why some IECs may escalate from one phase to another. A conflict will escalate if stress on natural resources is absorbed and later generates 'ecological surprises' such as negative environmental effects on other countries (for example, acid rain's damage to forests).[10] The case studies help to provide an empirically-based explanation of the conflict escalation process by focusing on transnational externalities of resource management practices.

An important feature of this model is that utilization of disputed resources takes place in all phases. This is why Phase 1 has been labelled **incipient conflict**, in recognition of the fact that any utilization of a resource may cause conflicts among actual and potential users of the resource. Also typical of the escalation pattern is that the number of parties involved in the conflict tends to increase as the conflict escalates, and as time passes.[11] This is illustrated by the number of parties in each phase. However, not all of the case studies support this observation. (Some features of the model are derived from Carpenter & Kennedy, 1990).

The phases are more continuous than discrete, and they suggest a likely path of progress rather than a strict analytical model. Based on the case studies, the following phases can be identified:

Situation I: Incipient phase—prevention

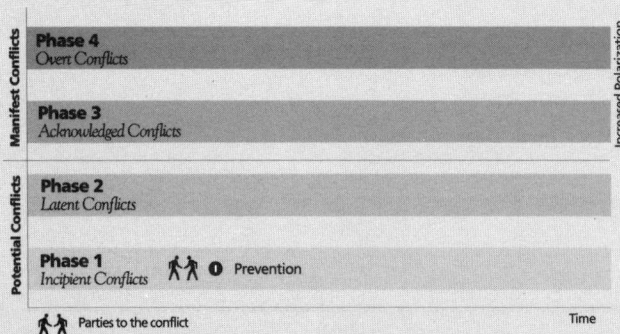

The incipient phase is characterized by a low degree of tension between the users of a resource. Because resource utilization is taking place, however, the potential for conflict exists. Most natural resources can be used in several ways, and if competition between these alternatives is not properly managed, negative environmental impacts may occur and conflicts may arise. In order to avoid the development of conflicts, competent authorities may develop a resource management strategy to reduce the environmental externalities. This kind of approach can be described as **prevention** and defined as an active planning attempt to identify possible areas of contention, and to remove or minimize the basis of conflict. Preventive measures include legal arrangements, policy initiatives, and other activities at local, national and international levels.

Many of the preventive measures at national, regional and even global levels are informal or voluntary initiatives and programmes of a non-treaty character. In recent years, a variety of resolutions, recommendations and standards (often called 'soft laws' so as to distinguish them from formal legal agreements) have been established. Environmental soft laws are often provided in the form of guidelines. They may also constitute a first step towards the actual establishment of legally-binding instruments, or facilitate their application.

National institution building is considered to be another important way of preventing conflict (also discussed in Chapter Three).

Some IECs begin as demands for protecting certain resources (such as tropical rainforests), or for covering increasing costs related to the reduction of negative environmental effects due to resource utilization. There is an increasing demand for such economic mechanisms, particularly in North-South contexts. An arrangement such as the Global Environment Facility may be able to function as a preventive tool and eventually serve as a mechanism for conflict resolution.[12]

Licensing and authorization practices are also found in some contexts. Such instruments have been used for a number of years, as in the case of the Convention on International Trade of Endangered Species (CITES), which authorizes the issuing of permits to designated entities in member countries for the import and export of plants and animals covered by the convention.

Awareness raising and public participation are also important in the context of developing preventive measures. Environmental impact assessments, monitoring procedures, exchange of data, prior notification and fact-finding procedures are increasingly considered important elements when defining preventive measures in environmental treaties.

Situation II: Latent phase—avoidance

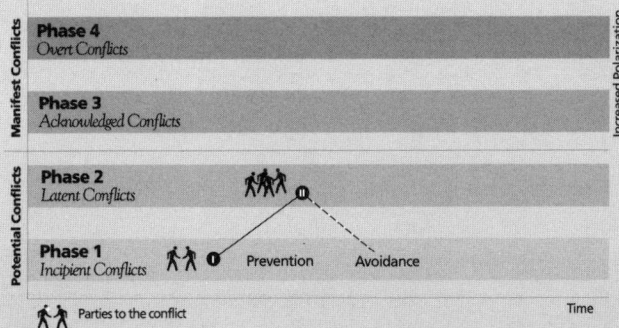

In many instances, preventive measures turn out to be inadequate as competition over the use of resources becomes more intense, resulting in escalation of the conflict to Phase 2. This occurs when one resource user realizes that its goals are incompatible with the goals of other users, or when it is realized that other parties are exposed to negative environmental effects. In such a situation, one party may try to increase the rate of its resource utilization in order to maximize the gain while the resource is still abundant. This may lead to an increase in the negative environmental impacts and to the involvement of other parties (either as competitors for the existing resources, or as supporters. In Situation II, it is clear that intervention from a third party may be required to keep the conflict from escalating further. Such an approach can be termed **avoidance**, and may be defined as: 'A reactive effort taken in situations where incompatible goals have emerged'.

Situation III: Acknowledged phase— settlement and resolution

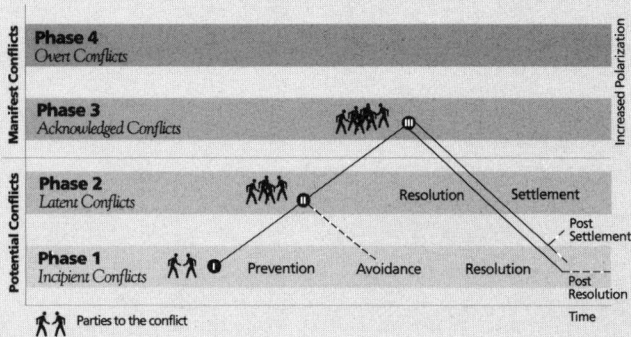

If the avoidance attempt fails, or if no attempts are made to prevent or avoid conflicts (for example, in situations where one party clearly holds most of the power) the situation is likely to become a manifest, acknowledged conflict. The incompatible goals associated with the negative environmental impacts of the resulting resource utilization rate will then become apparent to all utilizing parties.

At this stage, the following sequence of events may take place: the utilizing parties become aware of the competition and perceive it as a threat to their own interests, and they may make their position clear to neighbouring parties. In some instances, additional parties may become involved, motivated either by concerns for the environment (international NGOs, for example), or because other interests are threatened. This may motivate one or more third parties to intervene. Once this stage has been reached, the parties are likely to advocate and defend their positions. Three approaches to handle such a situation include:

■ **Conflict Settlement** is aimed at altering the symptoms of the conflict (the conflict behaviour) and positions. Little effort is made to change the adversaries' goals, so settlement techniques tend to leave the underlying goal structure, as well as the conflicting attitudes and perceptions of the actors, unchanged. Any compromise settlement, whether arranged bilaterally or through the action of intermediaries (such as the UN), is likely to leave at least one party with the impression that important goals remain unattained. Although conflict settlement may be the only realistic option in a given case, it provides no guarantee that the conflict will not re-escalate at a later stage. However, settlements may prevent conflicts from escalating, thereby allowing the parties or a third party to address the underlying interests. **Conflict Settlement** may therefore be referred to as a non-sustainable agreement that contains a possibility for a re-escalation of the conflict.

Preventive measures combined with public participation are important when developing new environmental instruments; indeed, they represent the most effective tools aimed at the avoidance of conflicts. They will be even more effective if environmental agreements have compulsory stipulations on dispute settlements.

■ **Conflict Resolution** refers to acceptable agreements which eliminate the root causes of the conflict. Conflict Resolution also contemplates sustainable use of the disputed resource. The condition of sustainability implies that a conflict resolution must also include some kind of prevention or avoidance measures. Sustainable use involves financial, technical, institutional and ecological sustainability. Conflict Resolution normally means that a set of preconditions are fulfilled such as: the third party is mutually accepted by the adversaries; the conflict resolution process itself is considered by the adversaries to be legitimate and constructive; and, the parties are willing and able to address their underlying interests. Accordingly, *Conflict Resolution* can be referred to as *a mutually acceptable, sustainable agreement that eliminates the root causes of the conflict.*

A distinction should be made between conflict resolution within the realm of legal obligations, and in unregulated areas. Multilateral agreements are binding only on those countries which are parties; the effectiveness of such agreements is therefore largely dependent on the identity of the signatories and their collective willingness to comply as individual sovereign states. Such compliance is ordinarily dependent on the enactment of national implementing legislation to carry out the obligations of specific international environmental agreements, which depends largely on *domestic* political will.

Legally recognized international rights and obligations also arise from customary practice. However, the fact that different states frequently have different perceptions of the nature of rights and obligations that are established by custom poses significant problems for reaching international consensus on a particular course of action or code of conduct.

■ **Use of Incentives** is necessary in recognition of the fact that environmental problems often reflect international political realities, and are closely linked to *economic development*. Accordingly, global environmental problems must be addressed and resolved in North-South contexts. The complex role that environmental law plays in balancing economic growth with protection of the environment underlines the need to find new ways of addressing IECs. The case studies reveal the need for *transfer of financial assistance and technology* to developing countries, in order to facilitate all states' participation and ability to comply with international obligations for the protection of the global environment (see Chapter Three).

Situation IV: Incipient phase— post-settlement / post-resolution

The case studies in Part Two indicate that many conflicts may eventually return to an incipient phase. Although the causal relationships between the driving forces have not been fully analysed, the conditions are likely to be similar to the conditions found in Situation I.

To reach this phase, the process might go through three or four stages: (1) Situation I (Prevention); (2) Situation II (Avoidance) (3) Situation III (Conflict Settlement or Resolution).

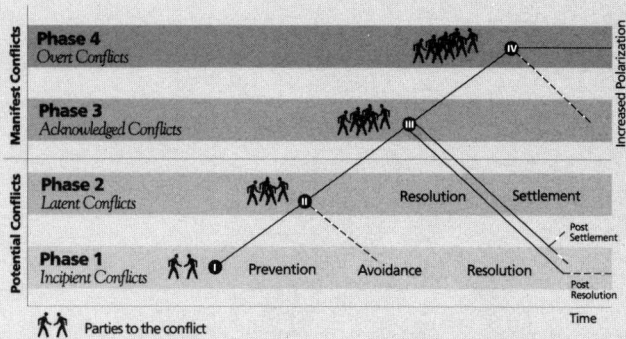

If Situation IV has been reached by Prevention, Avoidance or Conflict Resolution, the development path may become **post resolution**. If Situation IV has been reached by conflict settlement, the conflict is likely to re-escalate and the development path can be characterized as **post settlement**.

Obviously, an IEC escalation pattern such as this is only a representation of the complex development of these conflicts. The Escalation Model offers a conceptual approach which will be applied later in the book.

Chapter Two

Institutional responses to international environmental conflicts

2

THIS CHAPTER examines ways in which international organizations, and especially the United Nations, can participate in the prevention and resolution of IECs. Many organizations have responded to IECs, including UN organizations and agencies, Bretton Woods institutions, regional organizations, and non-governmental organizations (NGOs). Existing institutional arrangements are clearly challenged by the difficult international decision-making initiatives that are required to address IECs effectively. Ways in which existing arrangements might be improved to respond to IECs are also considered in this chapter.

2.1 The United Nations

For several decades, the UN system has been building structures and institutions to manage many types of conflicts between nations. However, the UN's record in dealing with these issues has unfortunately not been very encouraging. UN military efforts often address only the visible manifestations of conflict and not the underlying causes. Although the UN's record in conflict settlement has been modest, attempts at stopping hostilities have been more effective. However, attributing 'failure' to the UN or to other intergovernmental organizations is a common mistake that implies that these organizations have an autonomy which in fact they do not possess.

If the history of conflict management is examined, three major diplomatic roles in which the UN plays a part can be indentified: (1) the UN provides a convenient forum for general diplomacy; (2) the UN legitimizes diplomacy; and (3) the UN mediates. What is questionable, however, is the extent to which these roles can promote sustainable development and international environmental conflict management procedures. In spite of the UN resolutions and declarations that result from such diplomatic roles, recognition of liability and responsibility for transboundary environmental degradation—as an example—remains undefined. Such issues are also considered in the next chapter's discussion of some of the legal aspects of managing IECs.

The role of the UN: an historical perspective

Initially established to deal with the prevention and removal of threats to peace, the UN system has been working increasingly with social, economic, and developmental issues rather than security and conflict resolution. Its founders intended the system to help prevent conflicts between states and to be able to react to transgressions of peaceful co-existence between states through collective security measures before actual armed conflicts broke out.

With the decline of East–West tensions, the importance of the Security Council is increasing. As political systems continue to change, however, in the next decade and beyond, the Security Council will depend not only on developments in the independent states of the former East Bloc but also on China's role in world politics. Much of the role of the Security Council may therefore depend on the strained *status quo* of the North-South relationship.

Diplomatic roles played by the UN

■ Provides a convenient forum for general diplomacy
■ Legitimizes diplomacy
■ Mediates

The United Nations General Assembly

Figure 2. The United Nations System

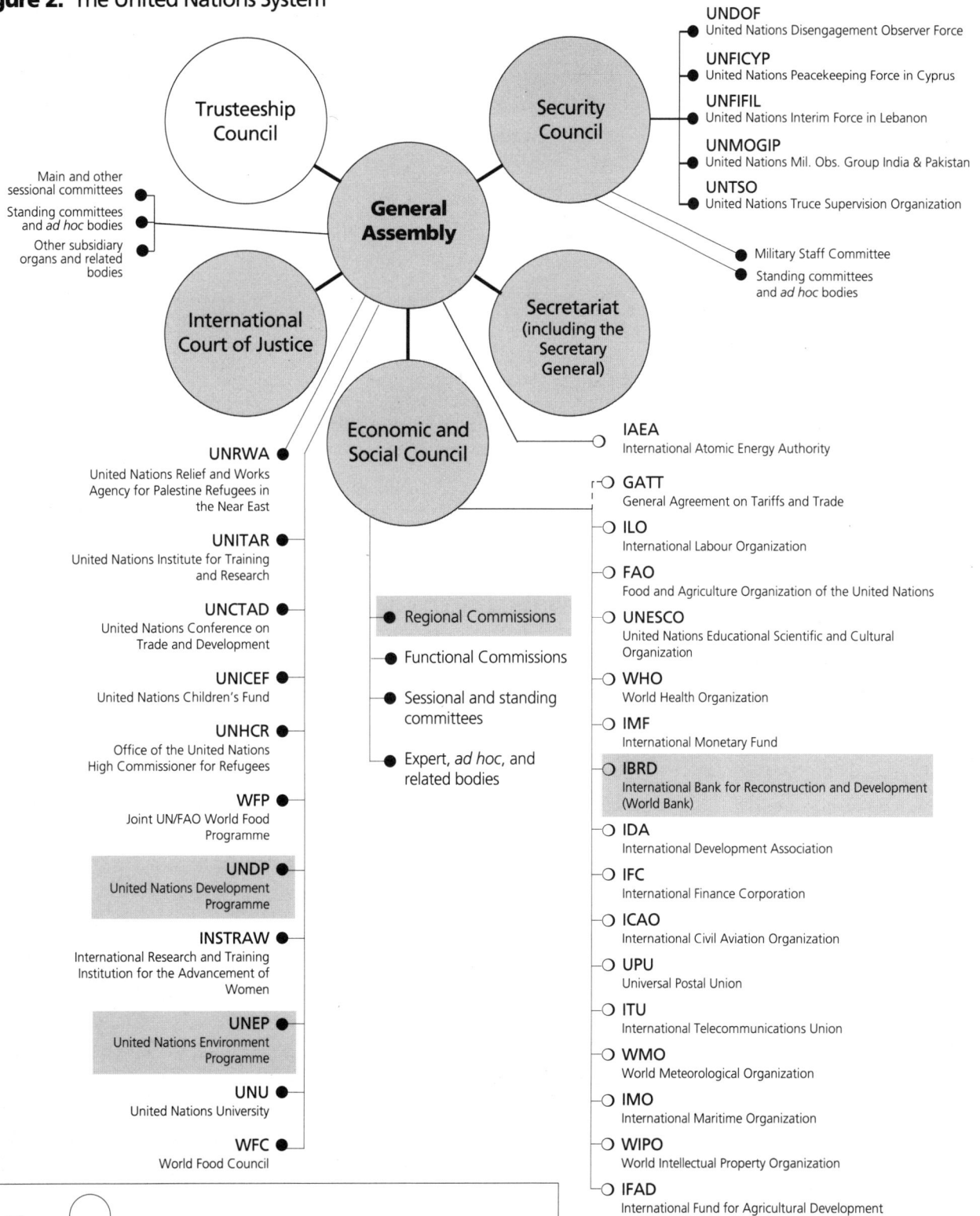

Trusteeship Council

Security Council

- UNDOF
  United Nations Disengagement Observer Force
- UNFICYP
  United Nations Peacekeeping Force in Cyprus
- UNFIFIL
  United Nations Interim Force in Lebanon
- UNMOGIP
  United Nations Mil. Obs. Group India & Pakistan
- UNTSO
  United Nations Truce Supervision Organization

- Military Staff Committee
- Standing committees and *ad hoc* bodies

General Assembly

- Main and other sessional committees
- Standing committees and *ad hoc* bodies
- Other subsidiary organs and related bodies

International Court of Justice

Secretariat (including the Secretary General)

Economic and Social Council

- UNRWA
  United Nations Relief and Works Agency for Palestine Refugees in the Near East
- UNITAR
  United Nations Institute for Training and Research
- UNCTAD
  United Nations Conference on Trade and Development
- UNICEF
  United Nations Children's Fund
- UNHCR
  Office of the United Nations High Commissioner for Refugees
- WFP
  Joint UN/FAO World Food Programme
- UNDP
  United Nations Development Programme
- INSTRAW
  International Research and Training Institution for the Advancement of Women
- UNEP
  United Nations Environment Programme
- UNU
  United Nations University
- WFC
  World Food Council

- Regional Commissions
- Functional Commissions
- Sessional and standing committees
- Expert, *ad hoc*, and related bodies

- IAEA
  International Atomic Energy Authority
- GATT
  General Agreement on Tariffs and Trade
- ILO
  International Labour Organization
- FAO
  Food and Agriculture Organization of the United Nations
- UNESCO
  United Nations Educational Scientific and Cultural Organization
- WHO
  World Health Organization
- IMF
  International Monetary Fund
- IBRD
  International Bank for Reconstruction and Development (World Bank)
- IDA
  International Development Association
- IFC
  International Finance Corporation
- ICAO
  International Civil Aviation Organization
- UPU
  Universal Postal Union
- ITU
  International Telecommunications Union
- WMO
  World Meteorological Organization
- IMO
  International Maritime Organization
- WIPO
  World Intellectual Property Organization
- IFAD
  International Fund for Agricultural Development

Key

○ Principal Organs of the United Nations

◓ Specialized agencies and other autonomous organizations

● Other United Nations programmes and organs whose governing bodies report directly to the principal organs

Institutions marked with a grey background are focused on in this book (especially Chapter Two)

In the period since 1945, the UN system has developed an elaborate array of special- and under-agencies to deal with social and economic development.[1] These agencies owe their existence to UN mandates to relieve human suffering and to resolve a multitude of problems occurring in all regions of the world. Many of their programmes have been designed to resolve problems facing developing states. A large proportion of the UN budget is therefore being allocated to various projects in developing countries, partly as a result of the growing number of developing nations becoming UN members and the new majority of developing countries in the General Assembly.

East-West tensions in the UN that emerged in the 1950s were complicated by the subsequent emergence of North-South tensions in the 1960s. In the late 1980s, as East-West tensions declined, North-South tensions tended to affect many contentious issues. The alteration in the balance of voting power, resulting from increased UN membership by independent developing countries, shifted voting blocs in favour of developing countries and this also served to spur new debates and new conflicts between states over how the UN system should be managed—particularly the Secretariat. The Group of 77 at the UN (also known as the G–77, which originally was a coalition of 77 developing countries) promoted their agenda in various forums. Their influence reached a peak in the mid 1970s (represented by the New International Economic Order (NIEO) programme initiatives).

Throughout this period, the influence of the industrialized Organization for Economic Co-operation and Development (OECD) countries declined dramatically in the UN (particularly in the General Assembly). Accordingly, OECD countries began to focus their efforts on institutions in which they continued to wield significant influence and authority (such as the Bretton Woods institutions and the General Agreement on Tariffs and Trade (GATT)). They also increasingly criticized G–77 initiatives.

The UN System now appears slowly to be becoming revitalized and regaining its influence in industrialized and developing countries alike. This is resulting from UN initiatives in security matters as well as because of threats to the global environment and other long-term security matters which require global co-operation.

The Security Council

Preeminent among UN organs in conflict settlement and resolution, the Security Council recently re-emerged as the central security organ of the UN. The re-emergence of the Security Council can be attributed to several advantages it has over the General Assembly—its smaller size, a capacity to function continuously, and the primacy assigned to the Security Council by the UN Charter.[2]

The 15-member Security Council is primarily responsible for main-

The Security Council is primarily responsible for maintaining peace and security

taining peace and security. Through the collective security system, the UN Charter intended to restrict the unilateral right to use force in international relations as much as possible. More recently, the question of the meaning of the term 'security' has been raised and some have argued that 'ecological security' could become part of the Security Council's mandate. This could prove to have serious implications, since the UN Charter recognizes the right of self-defence in the event of Security Council deadlocks.[3] In recent years, Security Council actions have been frequently blocked by lack of unanimity among its permanent members. If a threat to environmental security were to arise, certain states might exploit the chance to take unilateral action. The term itself is relatively vague for purposes of international decision-making.[4]

The General Assembly

Traditionally, the General Assembly has been a forum for a broad spectrum of important political, economic and social issues. Increasingly, environmental issues have come onto the agenda, and, like the Security Council, the General Assembly has been extensively involved in conflicts among UN members. Because it is a large forum, its debate- and decision-making processes are more inclined to bolster the position of one side or another than they are to promote negotiated settlements.

The General Assembly's security role came to be strengthened largely because of an American-led reaction to Soviet vetoes in the Security Council, with the General Assembly tending to legitimize the positions of the developing countries rather than those of OECD countries on social and economic issues.

Occasionally, the General Assembly has been able to initiate third

Negotiations at the General Assembly

Occasionally, the General Assembly has been able to initiate third party roles beyond legitimization

party roles beyond legitimization.[5] The services of the President or one of the General Assembly's officers can be provided as a way of assisting negotiations among the adversaries. The General Assembly may also appoint a UN mediator as a third party (although mediation is now more likely to be undertaken by the Secretary General or the Security Council).

The Economic and Social Council (ECOSOC)

The Economic and Social Council (ECOSOC) is a principal organ of the UN and has wide-ranging responsibilities, including co-ordination of social and economic issues (especially the International Monetary Fund (IMF), the World Bank Group and the Food and Agricultural Organization (FAO)).[6] However, ECOSOC, with its 54 members, has only played a minor role, since the other institutions actually formulate and implement policy, without ECOSOC being able to carry out its intentions of effective co-ordination. Furthermore, the developing countries have always used the plenary (Second and Third) Committees of the General Assembly and the UN Conference on Trade and Development (UNCTAD) rather than ECOSOC as a forum for discussing economic questions.[7]

Considerable effort is needed to restore ECOSOC's effectiveness

Several proposals have been made to revitalize ECOSOC, and it is clear that considerable effort is needed to restore its effectiveness.[8] Although the reform of ECOSOC has been the subject of many discussions, no significant results have been produced. At the moment, conditions may be more conducive to reforming and strengthening the Council. Pending proposals include many general policy decisions, which (although useful) are more procedural than substantive. The institutional changes outlined in UNCED's Agenda 21 give ECOSOC a co-ordinating role on environmental matters, but the implications for its role in IEC prevention are yet to be defined.

The Trusteeship Council

The Trusteeship Council was established to supervise the administration of trust territories carried over from the League of Nations. However, because many of these territories have since gained their independence, the Trusteeship Council has lost much of its relevance. Although the Charter designates the Trusteeship Council as a principal organ of the UN, it is (like ECOSOC) subordinate to the General Assembly. In its primary function of supervising non-strategic trust territories for the General Assembly and strategic trusts for the Security Council, the Trusteeship Council provides only recommendations. Although there have been proposals to turn the Trusteeship Council into an Ecological Security Council,[9] the present functions of the Trusteeship Council have very little to do with environmental issues; it has limited powers without the legitimacy or credibility of the Security Council; and is viewed by many developing countries as stigmatized by its colonial origins.[10]

Alternative proposals have been made to reconstruct the Trusteeship Council as a Humanitarian Council. This arrangement would seem more appropriate and closer to the original objectives of the trusteeship system. The Trusteeship Council does not play a major role in either mitigating or resolving IECs, and there are no reasons to anticipate that this will change in the future.

The Trusteeship Council does not play a major role in mitigating or resolving IECs, and there are no reasons to anticipate that this will change in the future

The International Court of Justice

The International Court of Justice (ICJ) at The Hague in the Netherlands is considered to be one of the few judicial institutions the world community can use for conflict resolution.[11] The ICJ is named in the UN Charter as one of the six principal organs of the UN. Its budget is included within the regular UN budget, and its 15 members are selected by the Security Council and the General Assembly. All UN members are *ipso facto* parties to the ICJ statute. Nevertheless, the ICJ carries out its judicial functions independently of the other UN organs, and its decisions are made on the basis of international law rather than international politics.[12]

In matters of international conflict resolution, the ICJ's role is weak. Of the contentious cases it has considered, about half went to adjudication on their merits. Apart from three cases pending, the remainder were dismissed either on grounds of lack of jurisdiction, lack of standing to raise the legal issues involved, at the request of the parties themselves, or because of other procedural issues. The ICJ also lacks effective procedures to ensure compliance with its judgements and has no direct application to private entities. While international courts and arbitration tribunals are prepared to interpret and apply international law, sovereign states are reluctant to accept compulsory jurisdiction over disputes that evade negotiated settlements.[13]

These issues illustrate weaknesses in the international legal system.

They cannot be remedied merely by calling for stronger institutions, which could not survive without a firm foundation in widely shared values. Judicial settlement and international law will continue to be heavily influenced by politics in the resolution of international environmental conflicts. It is likely that the ICJ's role will remain unchanged for the foreseeable future (see also Chapter Three).

Various proposals have been made—for instance, to establish a special International Environmental Court related to relevant environmental instruments for the purpose of conflict settlement; or the creation of a separate chamber in the ICJ specializing in environmental law. The Hague Declaration has suggested promoting a new institutional authority which could be created either by establishing a new institution, or by building on existing ones. The WCED advocated a more active role for the ICJ.[14]

Articles 92–96 of the UN Charter indicate that "the Court may from time to time form one or more chambers, composed of three or more judges as the Court may determine, for dealing with particular categories of cases; for example, labour cases and cases relating to transit and communications."[15] The ICJ has already indicated that it might establish a special chamber for environmental law.[16]

As mentioned above, a number of nations remain reluctant to accept the authority and legitimacy of the ICJ. Criticism has also been voiced about the ICJ's lack of speed and flexibility. Proposals to develop a new International Court with special competence in the field of environmental law is likely to experience the same lack of international support, especially concerning issues of compulsory jurisdiction. It would also require considerable time and effort to establish a new court system able to handle the dynamics of environmental law.

Many conflicts can be avoided or resolved if rights and responsibilities are reflected in national legislation. It also is more difficult for states to evade the legal provisions of environmental agreements which have established effective capacities for verifying the compliance of signatories.

The Permanent Court of Arbitration

Many of the disadvantages of the ICJ may be applied to the Permanent Court of Arbitration (PCA) which was established by the Hague Convention for the Pacific Settlement of International Disputes of 1899 and 1907.

The PCA, which comprises a list of arbitrators and an arbitration process for resolving international conflicts, continued to operate after the establishment of the ICJ in 1946. The arbitration process provides an alternative for nations who do not want to avoid international adjudication. Since 1970, no cases have been submitted to the PCA, but the process is still available for the settlement of conflicts (including IECs). The PCA has not been discussed as an active supplement to the ICJ.

Judicial settlement and international law will continue to be heavily influenced by politics in the resolution of international environmental conflicts

Many conflicts can be avoided or resolved if rights and responsibilities are reflected in national legislation

The Secretary General

The Secretary General and his staff have a wide range of responsibilities. These include preparing the agenda for major UN organs, drawing up the biennial budget of the organization, expanding funds, supervising day-to-day operations, taking the initiative on new programmes, offering political leadership when requested, serving as a diplomatic agent to work out difficulties among member delegations, and serving as the ceremonial head of the UN in formal affairs. The Secretary General is the sole person who can speak on behalf of the entire organization.

As a result of recent diplomatic successes, the role of the Secretary General is becoming increasingly important. The following excerpt from *The Washington Post* illustrates this growing expectation:

> "The Secretary General should ... lead the institution in its enhanced role to actively maintain international peace ... manage, motivate, root out ineptitude and cronyism and reorganize an institution in which the proliferation of jealous, independent agencies has created managerial chaos ... define a leading role for the UN in the intertwined economic and environmental concerns, from debt and development to global warming, that can only be dealt with at the global level and that will increasingly determine nations' security and well-being." [17]

The UN Charter makes provisions for the Secretary General to have a role in the settlement and resolution of international conflicts, which may include IECs.[18] Much depends on the political climate and its effect on the inter-governmental level at the UN, as well as the personal abilities of the Secretary General himself.

2.2 The United Nations Environment Programme (UNEP)

The mandate of the United Nations Environment Programme (UNEP) is to co-ordinate environmental action throughout the UN system. Its principal task is to exercise leadership and be a catalyst for the programmes and projects of other international organizations, principally within the UN system. UNEP has established an environmental programme called the System-Wide Medium-Term Environment Programme (SWMTEP), but this has not proved to be very successful due to lack of effective co-ordinating instruments, and shortages of financial resources.

UNEP's greatest strengths lie in the areas of monitoring, assessing, reporting, developing action plans, initiating new legal instruments and giving assistance to build environmental competence in developing coun-

UNEP's Mandate

■ to exercise leadership
■ to be a catalyst for the programmes and projects of other international organizations, principally within the UN system

tries. In a draft paper to the 16th Governing Council of UNEP, the secretariat pointed out that UNEP's mandate and wide experience make it well-suited to making a substantial contribution in the area of conflict resolution. The paper went on to say that the UN General Assembly empowers the Governing Council to assist in the resolution of environmental conflicts, to keep under review the world environmental situation in order to ensure that emerging environmental problems of wide international significance receive appropriate and adequate considerations by governments.[19]

The Manila Declaration on Peaceful Settlements of International Disputes also makes provision for UNEP having a role, referring to 'utilizing ... the subsidiary organs established by the General Assembly in the performance of its functions under the Charter' as an option for early peaceful settlement of disputes.[20]

For a number of years, UNEP has been involved in the prevention of environmental conflicts. Such activities as the UNEP Regional Seas Programme and the Action Plans for Shared Lake and River Basins are examples of programmes designed especially to anticipate and avoid potential environmental conflicts.

During UNCED, the Hexagonal countries proposed the establishment of an 'Inquiry Commission' for resolution of IECs. UNEP's experience could be valuable in conjunction with the support of such a commission. It has also been suggested that a framework should be created for a dispute prevention and settlement service under the UN.[21] The participation of a third party in the resolution of IECs has been supported in many substantive proposals.

Proposals have also been made for the Executive Director of UNEP to play conciliatory and mediatory roles.[22] If UNEP were strengthened and its Executive Director's role as mediator given higher status, it could work with IEC resolution (if assisted by experts) by monitoring, gathering information and making authoritative assessments. An entity within the secretariat also could be established to assist states in environmental conflict negotiations. This entity should be able to call upon a roster of credible domestic and international experts and institutions.

If UNEP were strengthened and its Executive Director's role as mediator given higher status, it could monitor, gather information and make authoritative assessments as a basis for IEC resolution

2.3 Bretton Woods Institutions

The Bretton Woods institutions include the International Monetary Fund (IMF) and the World Bank Group. The World Bank Group includes the International Bank for Reconstruction and Development (IBRD), the International Development Association (IDA), the International Finance Corporation (IFC), the Multilateral Investment Guarantee Agency (MIGA), and the International Centre for Settlement of Investment Disputes (ICSID).[23]

In the context of IECs, the IMF has less relevance than the World Bank Group (IMF's primary concern is financial and foreign exchange issues). As a special agency functioning within the framework of the UN system, the World Bank (IBRD) is involved in its own fund-raising and decision-making processes. The World Bank has assumed the leading role in the global effort to stimulate development through massive capital transfer, with the co-operation of its two affiliates (IFC and IDA).

Playing a crucial but controversial role in promoting sustainable development for its borrowers, the World Bank has become increasingly aware of the need for concerted action to safeguard the environment in harmony with social and economic development. Accordingly, the World Bank has taken several steps to develop a more environmentally-sound lending portfolio including environmental statement procedures and environmental policy guidelines relevant to important sectors like energy, forestry and transportation.[24]

One of the most important tasks for the World Bank is to make the management of the environment an integral part of its operational activities, particularly through project financing and economic and sector work. Although structural adjustment lending has not paid specific attention to environmental issues, it can have implications for environmental management and conflict prevention (for example, through reforms that reduce subsidies for energy or pesticides). The World Bank is making an effort to better anticipate the effects of adjustment policies on the environment, and therefore design interventions accordingly.[25]

Economic development is closely linked to environmental issues. It can be both a cause of IECs and a potential way of resolving them. The World Bank has played an important role in a number of cases by, for example, mediating in conflicts over international river systems (such as the Indus River Basin in the 1960s[26]) and through its active participation in regional programmes (as in the Mediterranean) and in the Global Environment Facility (GEF).[27]

While it is important to bear in mind that the Bank has no explicit mandate to actively settle or resolve IECs *per se*, it views resolving IECs as part of its traditional role.[28] It is also important to note that the Bank maintains an investment dispute settlement mechanism, (the ICSID) (see Box 3, overleaf).[29]

The World Bank has become increasingly aware of the need for concerted action to safeguard the environment

The World Bank and IECs

Can the World Bank play a more active role in resolving IECs? The Bank has legitimacy in the field of financial and economic affairs, but less so in the case of social and environmental issues. The international NGO community frequently questions the Bank's credibility, and this may weaken its potential role in the factual analysis of IECs.[30]

However, the Bank does have the necessary staff resources to gain access to appropriate scientific information and expertise, and is therefore

Box 3

The International Centre for Settlement of Investment Disputes (ICSID)

The World Bank's direct involvement in investment disputes takes the form of informal attempts to encourage settlement, either negotiated between parties or by conciliation, arbitration, or litigation before national courts. It attempts to improve communication between parties and impress upon them the desirability of reaching a settlement.

On a number of occasions, the Bank or its President has, at the request of both parties, participated more actively in resolving disputes. The Bank has sought to assist adversaries in agreeing on a method of solving disputes outside the framework of the Bank; it has offered advice and its good offices to help parties settle their disputes; the President has occasionally agreed to act as the appointed arbitrating authority; and instances of full-scale mediation or conciliation have been undertaken by the President in his personal capacity (as for example, during a dispute between Zaire and a Belgian mining company in 1968).

There seem to be several main reasons why ICSID has been successful: the system is truly international (that is, based exclusively on a treaty and rules); the Centre is a specialized forum; the system is based on consent; and the ICSID is in most respects independent of the national courts of all Contracting States.

able to separate the issues as a basis for efficient conflict resolution. This separation of issues is crucial, and helps explain the Bank's vital role alongside UNDP and UNEP in the tripartite co-operation that constitutes GEF.

The Bank could play an increasingly important role in the resolution of IECs involving compensation for transboundary negative externalities. With the capability to assist nations in reallocating funds, the Bank can arrange additional financial resources (as in the case of GEF) and develop compensation mechanisms. Nonetheless, the role of the Bank as a third party should not be overemphasized.

2.4   Regional Organizations

Regional organizations and their formal relationship to the UN can be identified under three main groupings: Independent Regional Organizations, UN Regional Economic Commissions, and Regional Projects Co-ordinated by UNEP. Regionally-based development banks are not included in this discussion.

Different regions experience different types of IECs—for example, East African countries may be plagued by land degradation issues, European countries may suffer air pollution, and other regions in Asia and South America are facing the implications of deforestation. Even where problems are similar from region to region—as, for example, in the case of shared water basins—socio-economic and cultural differences can preclude the use of similar solutions in different regions.

It appears that a regional approach focusing on a particular set of conflicts would be the most effective method of conflict resolution. And, since regions often include nations which share similar cultures, politics, economies, and often languages, many obstacles which typically hinder conflict resolution can be removed. This is particularly true for nations with a history of friendly relations.[31]

Regional approaches can take a variety of forms, with some more suited to IEC resolution than others. These approaches can be categorized by scale, scope and organizational structure.

Independent Regional Organizations

Most regional organizations today fall into the category of *Independent Regional Organizations* which includes all regional organizations with no formal institutional links with the UN. It is useful to consider the two main subdivisions of these organizations: security-oriented organizations (which come under the category of regional arrangements in Chapter VIII of the UN Charter), and those which do not.

Chapter VIII organizations include the Organization of American States (OAS), the Organization of African Unity (OAU), the Arab League, and the Council of Europe. Chapter VIII organizations are primarily concerned with security issues within regions, bringing the issues of autonomy and power to the forefront.

The UN Charter makes provision for regional arrangements and encourages the use of such arrangements in conflict resolution before the conflicts are brought to the Security Council. Article 52 (1) of the Charter operating under the Security Council states:

> "Nothing in the present Charter precludes the existence of regional arrangements or agencies for dealing with such matters relating to the maintenance of international peace and security as are appropriate for regional action provided that such arrangements or agencies and their activities are consistent with the Purposes and Principles of the United Nations".

This may severely hamper the autonomy and power of regional organizations. At the same time, it acts as a safeguard to ensure that no one regional organization will take steps to threaten global security. This is particularly important considering that, by nature, regional organizations are not microcosms of the UN and generally have a professed bias, be it political, economic, cultural or religious. Because one region cannot develop a role denied to another, unlimited regional autonomy is not achievable.[32]

Because of the tension between the broad, security-oriented mandate and somewhat reduced powers and autonomy, the role of most of the Chapter VIII organizations is rather weak. Security-oriented Organizations that are not actually Chapter VIII have therefore been created as a complement to the Chapter VIII regional organizations. Such organizations include, among a multitude of others: the European Community (EC); North Atlantic Treaty Organization (NATO); Organization of Economic Co-operation and Development (OECD); Economic Community of East Africa (ECEA); Association of South East Asian Nations (ASEAN); and South-Africa Development Co-ordinated Conference (SADCC). Because the UN Charter also allows organizations designed for 'self-defence,' which may have more autonomy and powers than Chapter VIII arrangements, many regional organizations, for instance, NATO, were created with this in mind.

These organizations vary considerably in terms of scope. Some are established to cover a fairly wide range of issues, while others focus on just one issue. Moreover, some cover an entire region (i.e., Africa, Europe) while others may be sub-regional in their geographical scope. Both because of their increased autonomy and their more specialized nature, these organizations have often been considered more effective than the Chapter VIII organizations (see box on ASEAN).

Few, if any, of these organizations exhibit explicit conflict settlement or resolution functions (as in the case of the Conference on Security and Co-operation in Europe), but the potential for them to play an active role in the management of IECs clearly exists.

Chapter VIII organizations

The Organization of American States (OAS)

The Organization of African Unity (OAU)

The Arab League

The Council of Europe

Box 4

The Association of South East Asian Nations (ASEAN)

ASEAN includes government repre-sentatives from Indonesia, Malaysia, the Philippines, Singapore, Thailand and Brunei. It was established in 1967 to encourage economic growth, cul-tural development and social progress; and to promote peace and security in the south east Asia region although economic development is in fact its main focus. (Since security is only a minor concern of ASEAN, it cannot properly be termed a Chapter VIII ar-rangement.)

Its main projects involve eco-nomic co-operation and development, and promotion of trade both within ASEAN countries and between ASEAN and the rest of the world. It has also excelled in developing programmes for joint research and technical co-opera-tion between member nations. For example, an ASEAN Workshop on Nature Conservation was held in Bali and was attended by representatives of FAO, UNDP, UNEP, IUCN and WWF.

ASEAN's organizational frame-work comprises summit meetings, where heads of state of member na-tions meet, and annual ministerial conferences held in each member country in rotation and attended by the foreign ministers of the member nations. In addition, there is the stand-ing committee, which conducts busi-ness between ministerial conferences

UN Regional Economic Commissions

Recognizing the success of a more specialized regional approach, particularly in areas not directly related to security, the UN created a number of regional economic commissions to be co-ordinated by ECOSOC. These include the Economic Commission of Europe (ECE), the Economic Commission for Latin America (ECLA), the Economic and Social Commission for Asia and the Pacific (ESCAP), the Economic Commission for Africa (ECA) and the Economic Commission for Western Asia (ECWA). These commissions are of special interest to the area of environmental conflict resolution because of the connections between environment, development and economics. This is further outlined in Part Two.

In general, the mandates of these commissions include areas to un-dertake studies of economic problems in the region; organize conferences among governments of the region in specialized fields; and draft commission reports. They are therefore generally better equipped to handle the task of studying problems than that of implementing solutions.

It is important to evaluate these commissions separately, particularly when it comes to environmental issues. For example, ECLA does not mention the environment in its mandate or in its policy work. Neither does ECA (although it has carried out environmental assessments and management specifically related to natural resource utilization). While ECWA also does not specifically mention the environment in its mandate, it *does* have an Environmental Co-ordination Unit. ESCAP specifically mentions the en-vironment, and has an Environmental Co-ordinating Unit, in addition to co-operating with UNEP and the Asian Development Bank. ECE is perhaps best equipped to resolve IECs; not only does it emphasize the environment in its mandate, but it also works closely with the Conference for Security and Co-operation in Europe (CSCE) as a specific conflict resolution mecha-nism (see CSCE box). ECE's work has contributed significantly to reducing air pollution in Europe (see Chapter Five for a more detailed discussion).

Regional projects co-ordinated by UNEP

IECs, although occurring in a specific region, may not occur in a region that falls under either the geographical scope, or the mandate of just one existing regional organization. For example, 47% of the global land area (excluding Antarctica) consists of shared river- and lake basins. In 44 countries, at least 80% of the total land area lies within international basins, and at least nine river and/or lake basins fall under the territory of six or more nations.[33] In such cases, it may be necessary to create new institutional arrangements focusing on and including the nations directly concerned.

Another reason to examine the possibilities of such arrangements is that the resolution of IECs often requires innovative approaches, which must overcome the tendency in many organizations to continue with 'business as usual' practices unless a significant impetus for change has been introduced.

UNEP's Regional Seas Programme provides an example of both innovation and the need for geographic specificity. As explained in Chapter Seven, the Mediterranean Region encompasses nations both under the EC and the Arab League, as well as a number of other nations not represented in either of these organizations. The Mediterranean Action Plan was created as part of the Regional Seas Programme because of these institutional considerations.

There are a number of other examples where UNEP has acted as a catalyst in regional programmes such as the 'Lake Chad Plan' and 'ZACPLAN' (see Chapter Six for further discussion). While these organizations tend to excel in defining problems and even in reaching agreements, they often fail to implement their objectives (see Chapter Three).

2.5 Independent Organizations

There are several independent organizations which can play a role in the prevention and resolution of IECs. Many bilateral agencies such as CIDA, GTZ, USAID and NORAD along with NGO constituencies do work in this field (particularly in the prevention of conflict). The Vatican State and the Red Cross/Red Crescent play a more specific role, and may exhibit functions which equip them to work on not only prevention, but also on avoidance and resolution of IECs.

Vatican State—The Holy See

The Vatican State has activities and representation in most nations around the world, through its clerical structure and its diplomatic missions. Historically, the Vatican exercised significant direct influence over social, cultural and even economic development (particularly in Europe). The character of the Church's influence has changed significantly during the last century; and, particularly since the Second Vatican Council in the early 1960s, the Church continues to refine its structural relations to national governments and international organizations.

In some regions (particularly Latin America), the Church has been playing an active role as facilitator of reconciliatory processes (often between national governments and local populations in disputes related to social, cultural and even economic, political and military issues). The Vatican also has been asked to participate in conflict resolution initiatives in the Middle East, South-East Asia, and increasingly in the countries of eastern Europe.

As outlined in Part Two, most IECs involve a complex set of social, economic and environmental issues. From this perspective, there may be opportunities where the Church can play an active role as convenor (particularly in situations where local populations are affected by national or international interventions physically (through resource utilization, or for

and consists of the foreign minister of the host country and the ambassadors of the other five. Then there is a permanent secretariat in Jakarta, headed by a secretary general; nine other committees; and several subcommittees and *ad hoc* groups.

Unlike many other organizations of its type, ASEAN does not shun co-operation with other organizations. Currently, because of the resistance from China, Taiwan and Vietnam, the initiative for instigating UNEP's Regional Seas Programme in the region has rested with ASEAN.

Following meetings in 1979 and 1980, the ASEAN states established regional environment priorities headed by a regional seas programme, and followed by environmental impact assessment, urban water and air quality monitoring, and pollution control technology. An Action Plan was adopted in 1981, but implementation has yet to be negotiated.

In 1980, UNEP sponsored a meeting organized by IMCO (IMO) and Indonesia, and attended by Malaysia and the Philippines to control oil pollution in the Celebe Sea: the plan adopted followed the procedures established by ASEAN.

In an area of political and economic instability where mutual antagonism obstructs co-operation, ASEAN's scientific capability and its ability to win commitments from its member nations and stimulate co-operation with other organizations (including UN organizations) have allowed it to achieve a considerable degree of success.

Box 5

The Conference on Security and Co-operation in Europe (CSCE) and the UN Economic Commission of Europe (ECE).

In the field of conflict resolution, the mandate of CSCE is as follows: "As laid down in the Helsinki Final Act (cf. Principle 5). Peaceful settlement of disputes and subsequent relevant documents, the participating States will endeavour in good faith and in a spirit of co-operation to reach a rapid and equitable solution of their disputes on the basis of international law, and will for this purpose use such means as negotiation, enquiry, good offices, mediation, conciliation, arbitration, judicial settlement or other peaceful means of their own choice, including any settlement procedure agreed to in advance of disputes to which they are parties." [34]

The *CSCE Dispute Settlement Mechanism* is an innovative approach. It offers a precise and well-elaborated set of rules to follow during a conflict-resolution process. The procedure is divided into 16 sections, all giving detailed instructions on what to do at different stages and situations during the process. The Mechanism is a free-standing body inside the CSCE which can be adapted to the needs of the disputing parties. If the parties are unable to agree on the composition of the mechanism, the proceedings, or the decisions, they can be assisted by the Committee of Senior Officials.

The Conference, attended by representatives from 35 European and North American countries, was assembled for the first time in Helsinki on November 22, 1972. The second phase of the Conference took place in Geneva in 1973, and the final phase was held in Helsinki, where the Final Act (containing the Ten Principles) was signed by all the participating countries on August 1, 1975. Follow-up meetings of a general nature are held regularly to ensure that the intentions of the Helsinki Final Act are carried through. Special meetings also take place on a regular basis, and are designed to address questions on a more specific level.

The issues treated in the CSCE process are divided into four major categories:
- Questions relating to security in Europe
- Co-operation in the field of economics, science, technology and the environment
- Co-operation in humanitarian and other fields
- Follow-up to the Conference

Institutional arrangements of the Conference include the Council, consisting of Ministers of Foreign Affairs of the participating States; and the Committee of Senior Officials. The Council provides the central forum for regular political consultations within the CSCE process, and the Committee prepares the work of the Council, carries out its decisions, reviews current issues and considers the future work of the CSCE, including its relations with other international fora.

The *Conflict Prevention Centre* in Vienna, Austria, assists the Council in reducing the risk of conflict, particularly in the areas of military conflict and emergency situations. [35] All decisions in the CSCE process are reached by consensus. Implementation of agreements reached by the CSCE process, especially from the second category (economics, science, technology and the environment), is to be carried out by ECE. In addition, ECE has been requested to prepare a draft convention on the Protection and Use of Transboundary Watercourses and International Lakes, and another on the Transboundary Impact of Industrial Accidents. Future areas of work could include preparing environmental profiles on each member state.

The close interaction between the CSCE process, the ECE and the EEC is an interesting model for other regions. [36] The effective division of labour increases the legitimacy of both organizations as well as avoiding institutional rivalry and duplication.

example, infrastructural changes, such as dams.[37])) It may be most effective in situations where the affected groups lack effective channels for communication with central governments where they are located in border landscapes.

The Red Cross

The International Red Cross and Red Crescent Movement traditionally has not been directly involved in the prevention and resolution of IECs. The Red Cross consists of three elements: the National Red Cross and Red Crescent Societies; the International Committee of the Red Cross (ICRC); and the International Federation of Red Cross and Red Crescent Societies (IFRC—see Box 6).

2.6 Organizational success in prevention and resolution of IECs

This chapter has presented some of the background for the role of the UN and other organizations in the prevention and resolution of IECs. It is clear from an historical perspective that the UN system has many important institutional resources that could be called upon to prevent and resolve IECs.

Some international organizations are suited to preventing and avoiding IECs, while others are better equipped to assist with settlement and resolution (see stages I and IV in the Escalation Model, respectively). For example, small specialized organizations are generally successful in the first two stages, but may lack the authority and resources to carry out implementation. Larger, established organizations with broad mandates and substantial resources for implementation may lack the expertise needed to work out sustainable solutions.[39]

If the four stages are examined, certain criteria for evaluating organizational success seem to emerge. While some of the following criteria play a key role at just one particular stage, others are important for every stage of the process:

Legitimacy is an important criterion for success at all stages. Not only must the organization be considered legitimate by its member nations, but the membership should also reflect legitimate interests.

Credibility, which is closely related to legitimacy, has to be perceived. This can be achieved by having multiple sponsors and by maintaining a neutral forum for discussing matters within the organization's jurisdiction. Credibility is more often attributed to established organizations than to newly created ones.[40]

A clear specific mandate which explicitly stresses the environment can assist IEC problem solving. Organizations with broad mandates (particularly if security-oriented) often function as vehicles for political expression rather than as effective mechanisms for conflict resolution (e.g. NATO).

> The Church has been playing an active role as facilitator of reconciliatory processes. There may be opportunities where the Church can play an active role as convenor

Box 6

The International Committee of the Red Cross (ICRC)

The ICRC is an independent humanitarian institution, whose neutrality is based on the Swiss model (only Swiss citizens can participate in the policy-making body). The ICRC is the founding body of the Red Cross. As a neutral intermediary in the event of armed conflict or unrest, it endeavours, on its own initiative, or on the basis of the Geneva Conventions, to protect and assist victims of international and civil wars, internal troubles, and tensions, thereby contributing to international peace. The ICRC is the one body within the Red Cross Movement which can and does play an active part in conflict resolution.

The Federation (IFRC)

The IFRC's function is to contribute to the development of the humanitarian activities of National Societies, to co-ordinate their relief operations for victims of natural disasters, to care for refugees outside areas of conflict, and, in so doing, to promote peace. The Federation provides leadership to national societies (150 member organizations).

ICRC's role in conflict resolution

The ICRC's actions and interventions are based on humanitarian rights. The ICRC's guiding principle is prevention (which also may be applied to IECs). The ICRC has adopted a policy to protect the natural environment in times of armed conflict, which may help prevent the escalation of IECs triggered by the environmental damage inevitably caused by war. International humanitarian law acknowledges the environment by requesting the parties to "limit environmental damage to a level deemed tolerable." [37]

For example, the ICRC intervened in the Gulf Crisis before the war broke out. Among other issues, the ICRC reminded the parties of the environmental aspects of the Geneva Convention and the obligations of the signatories to the Convention.

The ICRC intervenes in the humanitarian field, but does not solve political problems. It may indirectly contribute to the resolution of conflicts by various actions—for instance by caring for the wounded and visiting prisoners, and by liaising between the parties.

ICRC and the UN

There is no official co-operation between ICRC and the UN. The ICRC works in a 'quiet' way—that is, it acts on behalf of the people (on both sides of the conflict). The Red Cross Movement is not a governmental organization; the IFRC, on the other hand, acts as an auxiliary to governments. Despite these differences, the ICRC 'co-operates' at an informal level, since it shares many objectives. The ICRC has a potential role to play in the resolution or settlement of IECs, particularly at national or local levels.

Membership commitment is important, especially in smaller organizations. Member nations must realize that they have the most to gain when the organizations function effectively and agreements are reached and implemented.[41] A good example is ASEAN, compared to similar organizations in the South.

Access to appropriate scientific information and expertise is crucial for prevention of IECs as well as the pre-negotiation stage. With environmental conflicts in particular, accurate, up-to-date information is necessary for determining both the scope of the problem and the direction of the solution (the World Bank enjoys access to significant resources in this respect).

Standard setting/co-ordinating is important for long-lasting solutions. At a time when global frameworks are in their infancy, national and regional organizations frequently devise their own standards, which may conflict with other regional and national standards (as in the case of those set by the UN Economic Commission of Europe).

A specific mechanism for conflict resolution, perceived as appropriate and impartial by the parties involved, will help to keep the conflict resolution procedures moving in the right direction,[42] as for example in the case of CSCE's conflict Prevention Centre (see Box 5 on CSCE). Separating issues and breaking them down into manageable components, and creating alternative arrangements which involve working on more than one environmental issue simultaneously may be helpful (see, for example, the UN Economic Commission of Europe's work on the Convention on Transboundary Air Pollution, Chapter Five). This facilitates the creation of multiple options which offer parties various possible alternative courses of action and bases for agreement.[43]

Compliance is crucial to the implementation of an agreement and to the lasting resolution of a conflict (see discussion in Chapter Three). Smaller organizations may reach solutions based on scientific evidence and negotiation processes, but often lack the authority to implement them. Larger organizations may be able to encourage compliance through economic sanctions, penalties, or expulsion (for example GATT). The ability to generate funding may also be a determining factor for the ultimate outcome of the implementation of an agreement (as in the case of UNEP's Mediterranean Programme (see Chapter Six)).

On a global level, new ways of co-operating require mobilization of the institutional potential available through working with the Bretton Woods institutions in particular. Some independent organizations also have the potential to play a constructive role, especially in preventing IECs.[44]

The *Regional Economic Organizations* of the UN, independent and yet under the auspices of the UN, are developing a growing potential for conflict resolution. These organizations tend to have the legitimacy, credibility and scope (including economic capacities) required to implement solutions. As yet, however, few have prioritized the environment, or have specific mechanisms for conflict resolution. The UN Economic Commission of Europe is a notable exception and provides an example in this respect.

Regional Programmes Co-ordinated by UNEP, such as the Regional Seas Programme, are often successful in identifying the scope of the conflict as well as potential solutions. Much of their success in the resolution of IECs lies in the fact that the organizations themselves are centred on the environmental system in question. However, since these programmes tend to be policy- rather than operationally-oriented, lack of access to funds generally hampers implementation (compared, for example to the multinational development banks). Observations suggest that regional approaches are most effective working in co-operation with the UN (which provides a global framework) and with such funding agencies as development banks. Environmentally-oriented regional organizations are unequalled in their ability to define the scope and root causes of IECs in a given region. However, without a corresponding ability to implement agreements, they cannot achieve their full potential.

Chapter Three

Ways of managing international environmental conflicts

3

THIS CHAPTER assesses the suitability of some legal and non-legal approaches for several organizations involved in IEC prevention, avoidance, settlement and resolution. The chapter focuses mainly on the mechanisms themselves (as opposed to organizational capacities, which were the focus of Chapter Two); and on the prevention and resolution of IECs of a legal character. The chapter concludes by looking at central aspects of IEC prevention and resolution.

3.1 Non-legal management of IECs

Since 1970, there has been a significant increase in efforts to devise international obligations to protect the environment and manage shared resources through formal legal arrangements. Approximately two-thirds of all international environmental agreements have been negotiated since then, and the number continues to grow on both a regional and global basis. Although more difficult to quantify, most preventive measures taken to date are comprised of more informal and voluntary initiatives of a non-treaty character.

The World Commission on Environment and Development (WCED) and the report 'Environment Perspective to the Year 2000 and Beyond' both emphasized the need for a prompt supply of information before the onset of activities which are likely to have significant, adverse, transboundary effects on the environment.[1] Such information would enable countries which might be affected by these activities to participate in the prior evaluation of likely

Demonstrators at the Stockholm conference

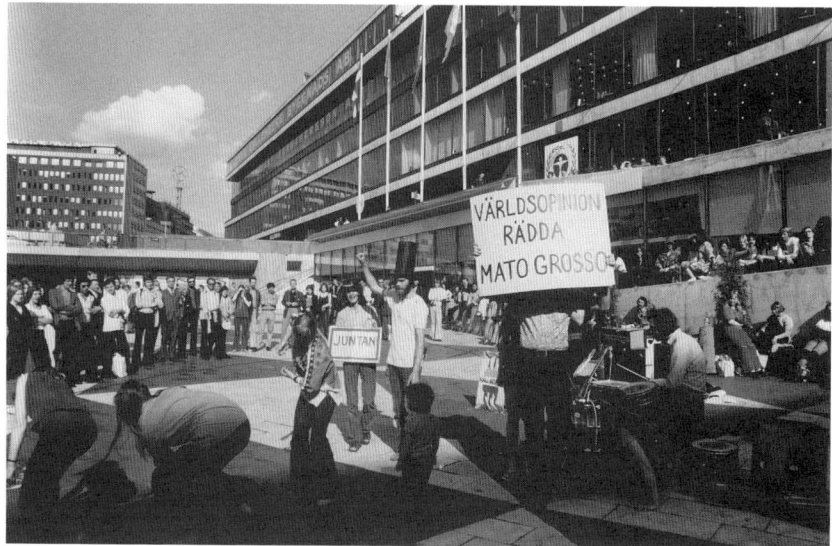

environmental consequences. The exchange of such information (sometimes referred to as a *Principle of Transparency*) ought to be routine for activities that may have significant adverse effects on the environment. Furthermore, the development of contingency plans between countries may increase the likelihood of remedial co-operation in case of accidents or damage resulting from environmentally hazardous activities.

As the case studies in Part Two suggest, access to authoritative and neutral information is essential to IEC resolution. The UN system, including the World Bank, and various independent organizations can improve co-operative efforts for the collection and prompt dissemination of such information.

WCED's 1987 report (Our Common Future) stressed the need for appropriate international organizations to pool resources and employ the most sophisticated monitoring technology available, in order to establish a reliable early warning system for environmental conflicts and risks. Such a system could be used to monitor such indicators as soil erosion, growth in regional migration and use of shared resources. The Commission recommended the establishment of a *Global Risk Assessment Programme* that would include: [2]

- identification of threats
- assessment of causes
- provision of reports and advice

Although the concept of an international environmental early warning system has a certain appeal, the Commission did not elaborate on the details required to implement such a programme. For example, the Commission argued that the programme would not require the establishment of any new institutions, but provided no further explanation of how the programme could be carried out.

Efforts to identify the causes of potential environmental conflicts for a given country should begin by evaluating the country's natural resources in terms of type, distribution and availability, and then develop scenarios that would be likely to occur in the event of major environmental deterioration or ecological change. This process may also assist efforts to determine the effects of various technologies on ecological stability.

UNEP plays an important role in environmental risk assessment and monitoring, and has a considerable advantage because of its legitimacy and credibility in this field.[3] UNEP's resources need to be strengthened in order to improve the systems so that it can also anticipate, monitor and assess changes in the state of the environment and natural resources. Although environmental emergencies are not necessarily international conflicts, they may lead to IECs.[4] For example, a failure in a nuclear power plant can pollute shared resources such as the atmosphere, land and water.[5]

Development of 'soft laws'

In recent years, a variety of resolutions, guidelines, recommendations and standards (often referred to as 'soft laws') have been established. Typically non-binding, the term 'soft laws' is used to distinguish such arrangements from more formal legal arrangements. UNEP has contributed greatly to the development of international environmental guidelines, norms and recommendations approved by UNEP's Executive Director and the UN General Assembly. Although the proposals are non-binding and states have the freedom to accept or reject them, they have achieved a respected status since they are often followed. Such proposals also may constitute a first step towards establishing formal, legally-binding instruments and may assist their eventual application. Easier to adopt than conventions, soft laws are immediately applicable and work well as long as the participating countries believe the benefits outweigh the costs.[6] Another important role they may be able to play is that of setting initial guidelines for the management of shared natural resources in order to harmonize different environmental standards (for example by establishing quota agreements for fishing, or by harmonizing emission standards).

National institution building

Many IECs are caused by the escalation of local conflicts arising out of unsustainable use of the environment, which highlights the fact that institutions operating at a national level have a crucial role to play in IEC prevention. National institutions are also important for monitoring, assessing and reporting on the state of the environment.

Some development assistance programmes are beginning to focus on expanding the natural resource management capacity of national institutions. In developing countries, it seems likely that UNEP, other specialized agencies,

UNEP plays an important role in environmental risk assessment and monitoring, and has a considerable advantage because of its legitimacy and credibility in this field

Soft laws

Non-binding, non-formal resolutions, guidelines, recommendations and standards

and the World Bank could maintain or extend their functions. While UNEP has initiated a number of such programmes, it has not achieved great success in the implementation process (often due to inadequate financial resources).

Licensing and authorization

Licensing and authorization practices have been in place for a number of years, and are an effective way of preventing conflicts related to the trade of commodities. The Convention on Import and Trade of Endangered Species (CITES)[7] provides permits to designated authorities in member countries for the import and export of plants and animals listed in the convention. The same system for notification and authorization is used for the Basel Convention on Control of Transboundary Movements of Hazardous Waste and Their Disposal.[8]

Compensation

Financial compensation is a mechanism that is applicable in both prevention and resolution of IECs. A number of IECs arise out of compensation claims due to negative side effects resulting from natural resource use ('externalities'—see Chapter One). Legal instruments whose scope is limited to technical standards and theories of liability are inadequate in this context because of the complexity of the issues. The broader North-South issues related to the availability of financial resources; transfer of technology and access to natural resources and markets, need to be addressed to help states to comply with

Figure 3.
Global Environment Facility (GEF)

GEF may eventually function as an important preventive tool and perhaps become a mechanism for conflict resolution.

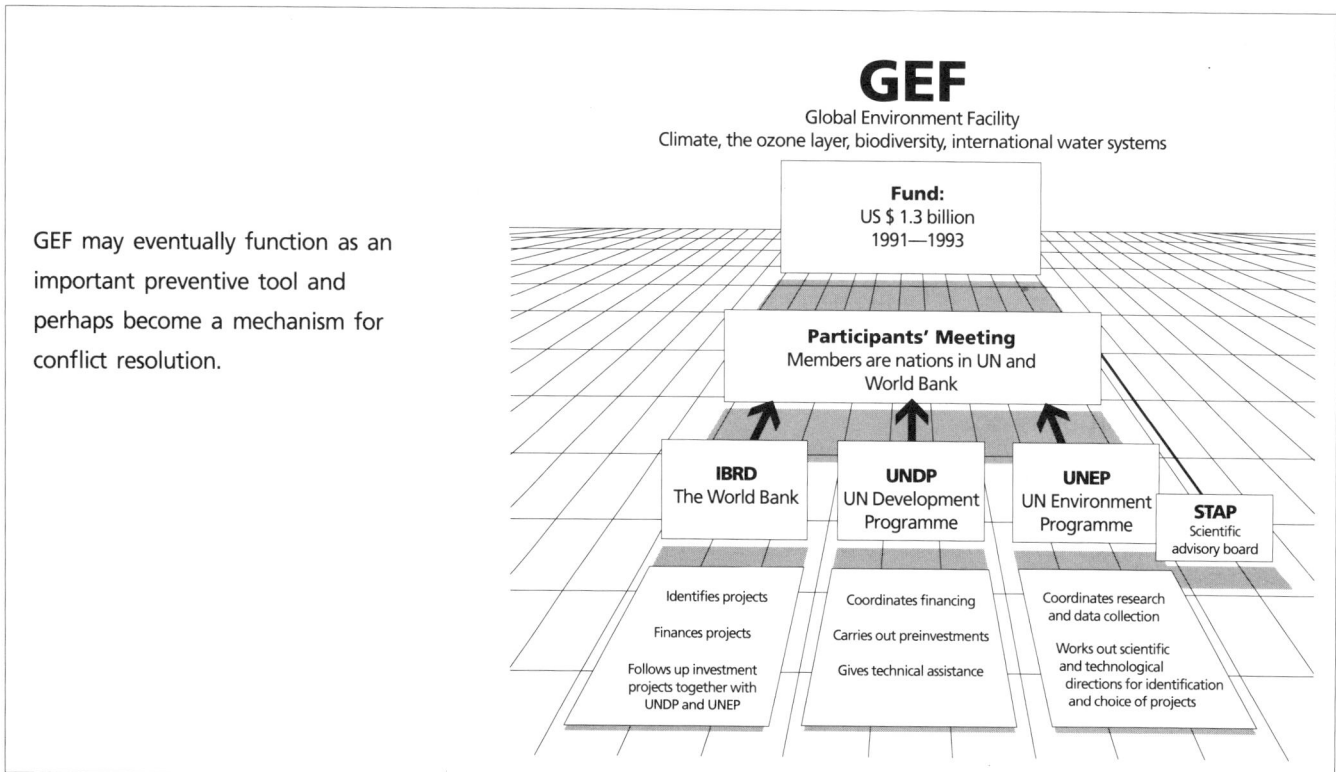

GEF
Global Environment Facility
Climate, the ozone layer, biodiversity, international water systems

Fund:
US $ 1.3 billion
1991—1993

Participants' Meeting
Members are nations in UN and World Bank

IBRD
The World Bank

UNDP
UN Development Programme

UNEP
UN Environment Programme

STAP
Scientific advisory board

Identifies projects

Finances projects

Follows up investment projects together with UNDP and UNEP

Coordinates financing

Carries out preinvestments

Gives technical assistance

Coordinates research and data collection

Works out scientific and technological directions for identification and choice of projects

international obligations that aim to protect shared resources. It is significant that these broader structural issues were part of the negotiations for the Montreal Protocol, the Basel Convention, the UN Economic Commission of Europe (ECE) Convention on Transboundary and Long-Range Air Pollution, and in the negotiations for the Global Climate Convention and Biodiversity Convention (all of which recognized the importance the transfer of financial resources and technology has to less developed countries as an appropriate form of compensation).[9] They are also good examples of the real-world pragmatism with which environmental and natural resource issues must be addressed.

The **Global Environment Facility (GEF)**—see Figure 3—which consists of a tripartite agreement between UNDP, UNEP, and the World Bank (IBRD), may eventually function as an important preventive tool and perhaps become a mechanism for conflict resolution (see a more specific discussion in Chapter Seven, Enclosure 1). Development banks have an important role to play in conflict prevention and also, potentially, in settlement.

A number of IECs arise out of compensation claims due to negative side effects resulting from natural resource use

The Global Environment Facility (GEF)

A tripartite agreement between UNDP, UNEP, and the World Bank (IBRD)

Uruguay and the United Nations Environment Programme signing an agreement

3.2 Legal management of IECs

There has been a gradual shift in the way legal management of IECs is perceived, from a situation where there were *polluting* and *polluted* countries to a situation where most countries are 'villains' and all are 'victims'. The traditional view was that conflict management was used to gain access and control over political and economic resources, but this is changing to a scenario where the following question is posed: who is most *responsible* and should pay the most, and who is most *affected* and should be most compensated? The issues of liability and compensation are quite evident in the continuing negotiations for global conventions on climate and biological diversity.

This changing perception has had a tremendous impact on the opposition between the rights and interests of individual states and the growing awareness of the international obligations concerning the environment. In contrast to centuries of custom and practice guided by the principles of national sovereignty, the past 20 years bear witness to a growing willingness among states to come together and to explore new ways of fostering international environmental co-operation. Such willingness reflects the growing acceptance and understanding that obligations over shared international environmental interests need to exist alongside traditional sovereign rights.

This has led to significant and rapid development in environmental law, especially treaty law. Although international legal regimes for the protection and management of natural resources are not new, the widespread enactment of such agreements is a relatively recent development (but they still lag behind the development of many national environmental laws).[10] The great increase in international environmental awareness is partly a result of the important contribution made by the scientific community. Science has helped considerably to advance understanding of environmental, developmental and security issues.

But in spite of the progress that has been made, the international legal system still has limited authority to legislate, adjudicate, or enforce legal rights and obligations, and there is no single body that deals with international environmental law. Similarly, because the development of effective conflict resolution regimes is hindered by the lack of an international judicatory and enforcement authority, the effectiveness of international environmental law should not be overrated.

Treaty law

Treaty laws are the principal source of legally recognized rights and obligations existing between states. However, multilateral agreements have two significant limitations: (1) international agreements are binding only on the signatories, and (2) international agreements are effective only to the extent that they are implemented by each of the signatories. Because international agreements are binding only on countries which are parties, the effectiveness of such agreements is largely dependent on who the signatories are and their willingness to comply. Also, since the international legal system lacks independent enforcement authority, the world community is largely dependent on voluntary compliance to secure the terms of international agreements.

There is increasing evidence of such compliance, more and more nations start to adopt legislation designed to implement their own obligations under international environmental agreements. The most significant recent example of widespread enactment of national legislation is the commitment undertaken by the parties to the Montreal Protocol to phase out the production and use of ozone-depleting chemicals.[11] The concurrent enactment of

---

The international legal system still has limited authority to legislate, adjudicate, or enforce legal rights and obligations, and there is no single body that deals with international environmental law

Limitations of multilateral agreements

■ International agreements are binding only on the signatories
■ International agreements are effective only to the extent that they are implemented by each of the signatories

national implementing legislation on such a widespread basis is unprecedented in the history of international environmental law.

Although conventional international legal instruments have several drawbacks (principally the slow process of negotiation and ratification, and the fact that they normally attain only the lowest common denominator necessary to reach agreement), they are indispensable for creating binding rules and regulations in situations where there are conflicts of interest.

Customary law

Customary practice is the second principal source of legally recognized international rights and obligations. However, the fact that different states frequently have different interpretations of the nature of the rights and obligations that are established by custom significantly hinders the process of obtaining international consensus on courses of action or codes of conduct. This is especially true when the issues are as complex as they are in the case of the environment.

The Stockholm Declaration

Adoption of the Stockholm Declaration in 1972 confirmed the need for common action to be taken to protect the environment. The Stockholm Conference was a landmark in the development of the international community's growing awareness of many global environmental problems. Principle 24 of the Stockholm Declaration stresses the duty of governments to cooperate through multilateral or bilateral arrangements, or other appropriate means in order to control, minimize or eliminate adverse environmental effects. Principle 21 of the same document, which is frequently referred to, states explicitly that: "States have, in accordance with the Charter of the UN and the principles of international law, the sovereign right to exploit their own resources pursuant to their own environmental policies, and the responsibility to ensure that activities within their jurisdiction or control do not cause damage to the environment of other states or of areas beyond the limits of national jurisdiction".[12]

Even though this Principle is part of a non-binding text, there are many indications that it has become a rule of customary law. Principle 21 has been referred to and reaffirmed in several declarations and international conventions which have been negotiated since the adoption of the Stockholm Declaration. For example, the 1979 Geneva Convention on Long Range Transboundary Air Pollution (LRTAP) referred to Principle 21 as "expressing the common conviction of States".

Principle 21 did not represent revolutionary new thinking in terms of states' obligations to refrain from actions within their territories that could cause environmental harm to other states; indeed, similar obligations have been recognized in 1941 in the Trail Smelter arbitration[13], in the 1957 Lake

Lanoux arbitration between France and Spain,[14] and in the 1968 Gut Dam arbitration between Canada and the United States[15]. These cases applied the principle of 'good neighbourliness', which recognizes an obligation of states to ensure that activities under their jurisdiction do not cause damage to the territory of neighbouring states.

State responsibility and liability

State responsibility and liability are complex issues, and they highlight the present inadequacy of international environmental law when addressing environmental problems, particularly global ones.[16] Although the principles of responsibility and liability are generally accepted, the practice is varying especially when dealing with common resources.[17] No agreement was reached at the Stockholm Conference over liability in international environmental conflict resolution.[18] In fact, the subject received only minor reference in Principle 22, which concerns state co-operation in the development of international law concerning environmental obligations and liabilities. In the past, states have resisted regimes that could imply 'state liability' for environmental damage. This can be explained in part because the parties responsible in cases of environmental damage ('polluters') are usually private entities (individual or corporate) rather than governmental. Not surprisingly, liability avoidance is as important to sovereign states as it is to private individuals and companies.

A major difficulty with establishing liability is that it is almost impossible to quantify the harm caused to the victims accurately—especially in the case of pollution emissions.[19] Even when the source of pollution or degradation can be easily traced—as in the case of the Chernobyl nuclear accident, for example—liability claims may still not arise. Experts in international law now consider it unlikely that Russia will compensate other nations for damage caused by the accident, or even that the victim states will file for compensation.[20]

International environmental law concerned with liability submits to politics for many reasons. The lack of an international legislative authority limits the development of binding international legal rules. This leads to uncertainty over international rules of responsibility and liability for transboundary environmental degradation. And the lack of judicatory and enforcement power also can limit the effectiveness of IEC resolution mechanisms.

International environmental law has progressively expanded its scope to encompass new areas and resources. At first the complementary principles prohibiting pollution and assigning responsibility were limited to protection of the territory and resources of other states. They were later extended to cover protection of the marine environment in general—including the high seas. Most recently, they have been extended to cover the protection of

---

Responsibility and liability

A major difficulty with establishing liability is that it is almost impossible to accurately quantify the harm caused to the victims

International environmental law concerned with liability submits to politics for many reasons

The questions of responsibility and liability become even more complex when addressing common resources where causal links may be difficult to establish

common areas, resources, and the environment as a whole.

The questions of responsibility and liability become even more complex when addressing common resources where causal links may be difficult to establish—such as the effects of long range pollution which may only be discovered at a great distance. For example, desertification, deforestation, acid rain, global climatic changes with potential sea level rise, and depletion of the stratospheric ozone layer all have causal links which are very difficult to establish directly.

There are several international conventions establishing responsibility or liability concerning protection of common resources (for example, the Convention for the Protection of the Ozone Layer, supported by the Montreal Protocol on Substances that Deplete the Ozone Layer).

In contrast to the area of international responsibility, which involves unlawful acts, the theory of international liability encompasses both lawful and unlawful activities. Recently, the international liability theory has focused particularly on lawful acts. For almost 20 years the UN International Law Commission has tried to codify rules of liability for such acts.

There are three ways in which responsibility and liability may be imposed upon a state which is violating the prohibition of pollution against another state or global commons:

■ Responsibility based on fault or lack of due diligence.

■ Objective or strict responsibility.

■ Liability irrespective of fault or of the lawfulness of the activity in question.

It is important to distinguish between *treaty law* and *customary law* when defining general rules for responsibility. In **treaty law**, the various agreements range from instruments that lack regulations on responsibility entirely, to agreements establishing responsibility based on fault, to agreements which stress an objective responsibility. In **customary international law**, primary obligations exist for states to supervise activities within their own territories in order to prevent transboundary pollution to other states, common spaces or common resources.

A concerned public may well apply political pressure to force states to meet their primary obligation to pay compensation in cases where environmental damage occurs in spite of attempts to comply with 'due diligence'. This would amount to a general acceptance of the 'polluter pays' principle.

The question of liability also leads to the issue of compensation for negative externalities. The polluter pays principle implies that the state where the source of pollution is located will be obliged to pay compensation for international negative externalities, even when the polluting activity is lawful and the state has taken all possible preventive measures.

The principles relating to liability for damage caused seem to be developing significantly, and the damage does not need to be of an economic nature in order to attribute responsibility. A general requirement of harmonization of liability and insurance seems to be emerging so as to ensure adequate compensation for the victims. This has been applied particularly to the field of marine pollution and transportation of hazardous goods; the 1989 Convention on Civil Liability for Oil Pollution,[21] and the Convention on Civil Liability for Damage Caused During Carriage of Dangerous Goods by Road, Rail and Inland Navigation Vessels[22] both apply such regimes. A similar system is being considered in the development of a liability regime under the Basel Convention, where areas under investigation include the establishment of special funds, and a system of supplementing intervention by the contracting state (subsidiary state liability). These elements are considered supplementary to civil liability regimes, and serve to provide maximum protection and compensation to the victims of environmental damage.

3.3 Preventive measures

The most effective way of developing a strategy to counter further degradation of the environment is to establish appropriate preventive measures and to make sure that there is flexibility to amend and modify these measures if they prove to be inadequate. For example, in 1941, when the Trail Smelter arbitration ordered the smelter to refrain from causing further damage, and to establish a regime for the control of emissions, including technical improvements, the court addressed preventive measures to avoid future harm to the environment.[23] Principle 21 of the Stockholm Declaration, which prohibits the inflicting of environmental damage on other states, states that precautionary measures must be taken to minimize negative externalities. 'Due diligence' is the key concept. The Bergen Ministerial Declaration on Sustainable Development in the ECE Region also stressed that "In order to achieve sustainable development, policies must be based on the 'precautionary principle': environmental measures must anticipate, prevent and attack the causes of environmental degradation." [24]

Awareness-raising and public participation are important for the development of preventive measures. In treaty law, conventions exist whose primary objective is to ensure the rapid exchange of information when accidents occur. The most important instrument of this type is the 1986 Vienna Convention on Early Notification of Nuclear Accidents.[25] The Bergen Ministerial Declaration emphasized the need "to reaffirm and build on the Conference on Security and Co-operation in Europe (CSCE) conclusions regarding rights of individuals, groups and organizations concerned with environmental issues, and, in addition, to safeguard the rights of individuals and concerned groups to have access to all relevant information, to be consulted and to participate in the planning and decision-making concerning activities which may affect health and environment with reasonable access to appropriate legal or administrative remedies and redress" (see Chapter Two for further discussion of CSCE). In 1974, the Nordic Environmental Protection

The most effective way of countering further degradation of the environment is to establish appropriate preventive measures and to make sure they can be amended and modified if inadequate

Convention established the principle of mutual responsibility for granting equal standards of access and treatment in judicial and administrative procedures to foreign individuals and foreign administrative entities.[26]

Environmental impact assessments and monitoring procedures are increasingly considered important elements when defining preventive measures in environmental treaties. The ECE Convention on Environmental Impact Assessment in a Transboundary Context, adopted in Esbo, Finland in 1991, aims at harmonizing procedures and planning activities to provide the best possible basis for rational decisions on a national level which might have an environmental impact.[27] When the eight Arctic countries were developing a comprehensive environmental protection strategy for the Arctic, they considered an environmental assessment and monitoring programme to be the driving force of the protection strategy. In the same way, when the Protocol on the Environmental Protection to the Antarctic Treaty was being developed, the consulting parties emphasized the environmental impact assessment programme.[28]

Development of adequate preventive measures is clearly related to the obligation for states to adhere to the Precautionary Principle when exercising national jurisdiction and sovereignty. Similar ideas are reflected in the Geneva Convention of 1979 on Long-Range Transboundary Air Pollution.[29]

Exchange of data, prior notification and fact finding procedures, which represent another set of preventive measures, are vital elements in prevention and avoidance of conflicts. The Hague Declaration has stressed the usefulness of fact-finding procedures in the clarification of cases where non-compliance is alleged.[30]

UNEP's role as provider of environmental information and consultancy services has given some precedent for other proposals related to conflict prevention. Increased use of environmental audits (similar to ILO's labour dispute audits) can also enable responses to environmental conflicts before they arise.

3.4   Settlement and resolution of conflicts

Most legal instruments relating to the environment lack formal compulsory dispute resolution or settlement mechanisms. Where there *is* provision for dispute resolution procedures, recourse to such procedures is generally dependent on the parties' mutual consent or common agreement. The absence of effective dispute resolution and enforcement mechanisms suggests the need for careful structuring of incentives to encourage and facilitate international compliance (for example, transfer of additional financial resources and transfer of technology).

3.5   Implementation of legal arrangements

While the technical material provisions in many existing environmental

Environmental impact assessments and monitoring procedures are increasingly considered important elements when defining preventive measures in environmental treaties

Exchange of data, prior notification and fact finding procedures, which represent another set of preventive measures, are vital elements in prevention and avoidance of conflicts

instruments are spelled out in great detail, provisions regarding preventive measures and guidelines on dispute settlements seem to be less stringent and sometimes lacking altogether. The effectiveness of environmental treaties is closely linked to how these provisions are formulated. This also applies to the provisions on verification and control, which are new in an international environmental context.[31] The lack of effective enforcement or dispute resolution mechanisms that characterizes most international environmental agreements demands a critical evaluation of the success of such agreements on a case-by-case basis.[32]

A lack of effective enforcement or dispute resolution mechanisms characterizes most international environmental agreements

Of crucial importance, of course, is whether or not agreements actually are implemented. In a 1985 study of 161 environmental conflicts (both site-specific and generic), it was found that agreement was reached on approximately 90 percent of the issues in dispute.[33] The bottleneck however, has been to work out provisions in the agreements that increase the chances for implementation. Clearly, then, the challenge lies in the task of devising effective compliance mechanisms for carrying out the terms of environmental agreements.

The Montreal Protocol is one example of the way the implementation phase can be managed, with the establishment of an Implementation Committee of 10 representatives of the Member States with a mandate to monitor the parties' compliance with the Protocol's provisions.[34] This action was taken in recognition of the weak compliance record that accompanies most international environmental agreements. The non-compliance regime focuses on mandatory reporting and environmental auditing for the purpose of public review, supported by a collective compliance control by the Implementation Committee. The system represents an interesting and promising new approach which may create an important precedent for future agreements. If this model for the verification of parties' compliance with, and implementation of, environmental instruments proves workable, it will be a more effective system of control with compliance than traditional judicial means.[35]

3.6   The realm of no agreed rules

No legally-agreed overriding principles exist to guide nations in international management of natural resources. Most countries would hesitate to neglect or violate 'soft agreements' (for example the 'Rio Declaration' from UNCED, 1992)[36] if this meant facing domestic or international criticism. Certain types of environmental behaviour may be censured by the world at large and may result in political and economic sanctions.[37]

Clearly, avoidance of such conflicts would benefit all states, and several proposals have been made to set up institutions for that purpose (see the Hexagonal Proposal, Box 7).[38]

3.7 Summary and conclusions

The issues of IEC prevention and resolution are as undeveloped as they are complex. Nevertheless, the potential is great for the UN to play an active role in both prevention and resolution, particularly in co-operation with development banks and regional organizations.

■ In *prevention of IECs*, the following issues are critical:

1. Improved procedures for authoritative and legitimized environmental monitoring, assessment, and reporting through public participation is necessary for improving the sharing of information between countries. Development of such global and regional procedures could be carried out by UNEP in close co-operation with other UN agencies, development banks and regional organizations.

2. Financial institutions, such as development banks, will play an increasingly important role in the prevention and settlement of IECs. In this respect, the Global Environment Facility (GEF) is a promising mechanism for prevention and settlement. Introduction of positive incentives in new treaties (such as transfer of financial resources and technology) could both avoid conflicts and encourage compliance. Traditional development assistance programmes (through UNDP, UNEP and the World Bank in particular) should address more explicitly improvements in national institution building related to natural resource management as a conflict prevention measure.

■ In the *resolution and settlement of IECs*, the following issues are critical:

1. Most legal instruments relating to the environment lack formal compulsory conflict settlement or resolution mechanisms. Where there *is* provision for conflict resolution procedures, recourse to such procedures is generally dependent on the parties' mutual consent or common agreement. The absence of compulsory conflict resolution mechanisms suggests the need for careful structuring of incentives to encourage and facilitate international compliance.

2. Issues of liability also remain problematic. Because IECs often relate to negative externalities generated by private rather than governmental activity, effective resolution or settlement may depend on a variety of factors, including satisfactory local institutional remedies, insurance arrangements or established claims settlement procedures. Use of such local procedures (where available and effective) can prevent a dispute from rising to supra-national levels.

3. Although there have been proposals to establish a Special Chamber for Environmental Law at the International Court of Justice, states' avoidance of adversarial state-liability approaches do not indicate a rapidly expanding World Court role for resolution and settlement of IECs.

Box 7

The Hexagonal Proposal

(The Hexagonal countries are Austria, Czechoslovakia, Hungary, Romania, the former Yugoslavia, and Poland)

In January 1991, the Hexagonal countries presented a draft proposal which laid out a possible institutionalized process for preventing environmental conflicts:

■ Sufficient information about situations with potential transboundary effects should be provided.

■ An Inquiry Commission to clarify and establish factual issues could be created at the request of any of the parties.

■ A Secretariat under UNEP should be established to assist the Commission, and would consist of one representative from each party and from UNEP.

The Inquiry Commission should not be expected to rule on any situation, but to scrutinize it carefully, and after obtaining all pertinent information, it should submit a report to the parties and to the Executive Director of UNEP.

■ Additionally, in *verification and compliance* of legal arrangements, the following issues are critical:

1. Provision for the exchange of information is an important mechanism for encouraging compliance that would otherwise be voluntary.

2. Where agreements do provide for the exchange of information, the effectiveness of verification procedures varies widely.

3. Imposition and enforcement of non-compliance sanctions remain problematic. The use of compliance-based incentives (rather than non-compliance sanctions and penalties) requires careful monitoring and evaluation. Although there is increasing use of commissions and other neutral fact-finders, states continue to avoid recourse to third party judicatory and enforcement regimes. As the above-listed critical issues imply, a set of political, legal, and other institutional changes should be implemented in relation to one another for the purpose of managing conflicts.

The following proposals are offered for consideration:

A. The UN could establish an institutional setting (e.g., at UNEP) which could provide a service for authoritative and neutral information and conflict assessment. At the same time, such a setting would assist national governments in finding legitimate third party representatives, for facilitating economic compensation for environmental damage (in the latter case through cooperation with the World Bank and regional development banks).

B. In order to achieve this, the UN could establish a roster of highly respected members and institutions, appointed by the institution (as described above), by the Secretary General, or by the Executive Director of UNEP on a representative basis.

C. The UN could develop authoritative opinions on such central issues as economic compensation for environmental damage experienced by affected and concerned states, by using GEF as a model (i.e., inter-agency co-operation).

D. Institutionalized workshops and diplomatic-scholar co-operation could be encouraged by the UN (for example, through United Nations Institute for Training and Research (UNITAR) and United Nations Development Programme (UNDP).

Part Two

International environmental conflicts and how they generate

Aims and approach of Part Two

The overall aims of Part Two are:

■ To develop analytical tools for the cases studies in the following chapters
■ To apply this approach to the various case studies
■ To draw some lessons of experience for ways of preventing and
resolving international environmental conflicts.

■ In recognition of real world complexity, each of the case studies in the
following chapters adopt a systems approach.

Chapter Four

4 Methodology
and analysis

THIS CHAPTER outlines the analytical framework for analysing international environmental conflicts, and looks into the use of a Systems Approach as a way of linking traditional conflict analysis methods with environmental analysis.[1]

4.1   A systems approach to IECs

A systems approach is valuable because it helps to explain the dynamics and interaction of resources, and economic and social systems at different geographic levels. It is very important to consider this interaction when forming policy for environmental management.[2] Although it is widely recognized that in order to understand the interaction fully it is necessary to provide a detailed description of the links between human behavioural systems and resource systems, there have been few—if any—attempts to build these links into a general model.

Foreign policy decision-making, conflict management, and international environmental systems have usually been viewed as separate disciplines.[3] No doubt this is partly because the models used for international political relations tend to have few links with the physical environment. In addition greater integration between the disciplines is hampered by the lack of a conceptual framework as well as divisions between social and economic theory and physical and biological theory.[4]

The systems approach is one attempt to bridge this gap by applying concepts, theories, and methods from environmental analysis and conflict analysis. Similar integrative approaches are increasingly being carried out in areas where the focus is on international natural resource management.[5]

There is a growing awareness of the divide between the competing methods of analysis. Most research on global systems uses modified stimulus-response models to study the behaviour of a system's key actors. In this cognitively-based approach, systemic processes typically pass through cognition and emerge as decisions. The cognitive processes themselves are usually described in such terms as 'image', 'operational code', 'belief system', and 'cognitive mapping.'[6] In contrast to this approach, there is the bureaucratic approach, which is now receiving more attention. It looks at how irregularities in the systems—such as the organizational and institutional milieu, vested interests, and the general public—affect or constrain the discretion of decision makers.

Most real world situations are complex and difficult to analyse. The modelling process super-imposes an abstract structure on the real situation, simplifying it and making the situation more accessible to analysis. The danger is that the model may over-simplify; accordingly, in practice, it is often preferable to develop a range of models to describe a situation (see further discussion on page 52— 'Applying the systems approach'). That means breaking large systems into sub-systems. If necessary, more complex models can be constructed based upon information gained from the simpler models.

A well-designed model can be useful for both analyst and decision maker. The best test of a model's accuracy is whether it produces reasonable answers when presented with actual problems. This relates to its effectiveness as a *predictive* tool, as well as an *explanatory* one. If the model falls short, it should be reformulated and the process repeated.

The systems approach can provide a solid base for the design of a suitable model. Of special interest are the long-term changes (past, present, and future) in the system's structure, function, input and output. Macro-scale theories may be formalized by constructing models where statistical techniques are the most important tools.[7] However, this study takes a global systemic resource-behavioural approach rather than a quantitative approach. That does not exclude the use of quantitative tools in examining causalities, but the approach taken here is a combination of quantitative and qualitative tools.

There is a considerable gap between formal theories of conflict management and real-world situations. For example, present formal models often fail to provide any significant explanations and predictions of multi-party negotiations, or guidance to practitioners. Nevertheless, they do provide some conceptual and analytical insights into the generation and escalation of IECs as well as the dynamics of conflict prevention and resolution processes.

The systems approach is an attempt to bridge the disciplines by applying concepts, theories and methods from environmental analysis and conflict analysis

A well-designed model can be useful for both analyst and decision-maker

There is a considerable gap between formal theories of conflict management and real-world situations

The existing formal models (for example, models in Game Theory) have mostly been devised by political scientists, lawyers, mathematicians and economists. The traditional negotiation models can be classified into three groups: Game-theoretic, Economic and Manipulative.[8]

Apart from in political science and related disciplines, little attention has been paid to the behavioural aspects of negotiation processes. Behavioural literature is rich in material which could be drawn upon to improve formal conflict management models. One of the greatest advantages of a behavioural approach is that it provides tools to analyse parties' underlying needs through their positions, interests, relationships, and options in a way that at least acknowledges the influence of non-rational decision-making.[9] The variables are outlined later in this chapter.

Applying the Systems Approach

The integrated approach provides a conceptual framework within which man-made and natural environment processes can be evaluated. Within this framework one can study the whole—'move from the whole to the parts, and move back again to the whole'.[10] In systems study, it is common to outline two general methods. In the first method, the systems analyst examines the various systems that occur in the world (for example, biological and political) and then draws up statements about the regular features of the different systems examined.[11] This method is essentially empirical. The second method involves starting by studying one system first, then a second, and so on, until we take the set of all possible systems and then reduce the set to a more reasonable size.[12]

This study applies both approaches—in a way that combines empirical, intuitive and deductive procedures. Taking a combined approach in this way acknowledges that there are limitations with a pure Systems Approach. A fundamental problem concerns the vague use of the word 'system' itself, as each discipline has its own interpretation of the term.[13] Problems of validity also arise when one tries to simplify the various interactions and sub-systems, (due to the complexity and the interdisciplinary nature of the issues). In an attempt to avoid these pitfalls, this study adopted the following approaches.

First, because of the desire to design analytical units with a wider application, and so as to avoid having to design *ad hoc* systems, the analytical units are founded on generally-accepted inter-relationships between human needs, production and resources. In recognition of the validity problems experienced with interactions, variables and systems—especially when models are to be quantified—this study also puts forward a conceptual, dynamic, and explanatory model rather than a quantitative one.

Apart from in political science, little attention has been paid to the behavioural aspects of negotiation processes

Systems approach: 'Move from the whole to the parts, and move back again to the whole.'

This study puts forward a conceptual, dynamic, and explanatory model, rather than a quantitative one

A Systemic Environmental Conflict Model (SEC-Model)

To understand the complex ways in which IECs are generated and escalate, it is useful to combine environmental analysis, behavioural analysis, and conflict analysis.[14] A Systemic Environmental Conflict Model (the SEC-model, figure 6) has been designed with this in mind.

The model is based on the assumption that there is competition for natural resources, and that tensions arise between the different users because of incompatible goals. It also assumes that there are at least two adversaries in any given IEC, which are represented either by states or groups of states. Each of the adversaries, or actors, has certain political, military, social, and cultural requirements which determine their use of resources. Economic and production needs affect resource utilization, and in the model they are classified as separate systems, because it is assumed that economic goals (attained through production) are the prime causes of IECs. Recognition of this may assist in the prevention and resolution of such conflicts.

The model also indicates that there are conflicts between the adversaries over the externalities, or side-effects, of the resource use, as well as over the resources themselves. Externalities cause changes in resource systems which are becoming increasingly unacceptable; later on, we will consider some examples. The production system may create such externalities (for example, transboundary air and water pollution), when economic systems fail to take the cost of environmental degradation and pollution into account.[15]

The demand created by human consumption impinges on natural resources. The scale of the demand is a result of *per capita* consumption levels and the number of people, which in turn are determined by value systems and other socio-cultural factors (for example, income levels and other eco-

To understand the complex ways in which IECs generate and escalate, we need to combine environmental analysis, behavioural analysis, and conflict analysis

The model indicates that there are conflicts between the adversaries over the externalities, or side-effects, of the resource use, as well as over the resources themselves

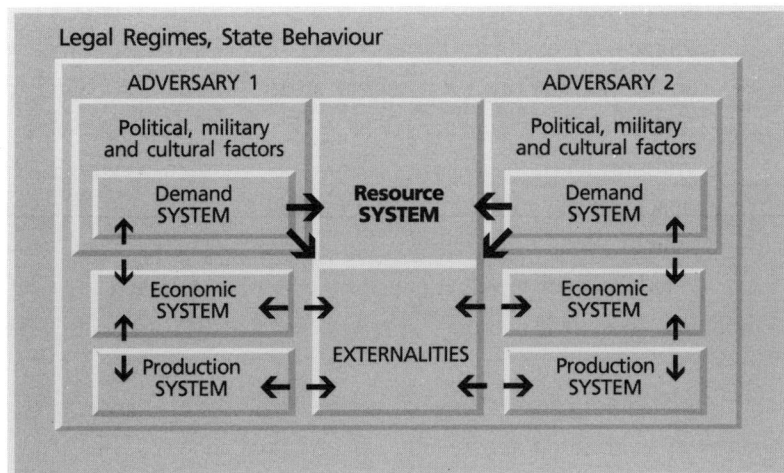

Fig. 4. The Systemic Environmental Conflict Model (SEC model)

nomic factors). Modelling this relationship could start by establishing that a system has at least three basic components: **elements, relations**, and **states**.

The **elements** (or components) in a system are often concepts or variables; the **relations** reflect the interaction between variables or systems; and the **states** describe values of interactions at different levels (for example, ordinal, nominal, or even geographical levels). (Note: the use of the word 'states' in this context should not be confused with political entities).

The Escalation and SEC Models are complementary. Whereas the Escalation Model (see Chapter One, Figure 1) describes the dynamics of the system, the SEC Model handles the interactions within the system, and depicts a system where environmental, behavioural, economic, and socio-political aspects are integrated.

Demand is the essential driving force behind IECs. To represent demand in a model, we need to account for resource supply, production and usage; three aspects, which for purposes of the model are referred to as the *natural resource system*, the *demand* or *behavioural system* and the *production system*.

The **natural resource system** consists of a hierarchy of geo- and bio-ecological systems and the interactions that take place between them. (They are examined more closely in the case studies). Changes in the resource system and the externalities that result from them (especially those imposed on other states) are significant factors in IECs.

The concept of 'carrying capacity' is a useful analytical tool for assessing the levels of acceptability of environmental changes, since the carrying capacity of a resource system is the level of resource utilization that a geo- and bio-ecological environment can withstand without being degraded.[16] Often, conflicts develop between nations because of differing perceptions as to what constitutes an acceptable level of resource utilization or carrying capacity. For example, in the Mediterranean there have been disputes between neighbouring states over the level of pollution from land-based sources in the Mediterranean Sea, and over what is an acceptable level of degradation of the resource—for example, bacteria levels. Similar disagreements have arisen over the negotiations for reduction of long-range transboundary air pollution and atmospheric emissions of NO_x, SO_x, and CO_2 in Europe. In this case, the emission levels are determined by what the parties agree to be the carrying capacity of the atmosphere (that is, the accepted degree of alteration of the resource). While earlier air pollution protocols aimed at a flat-rate percentage reduction of specified pollutants, the new approach involves determining an acceptable carrying capacity (see further discussion in Chapter Eight).

It is difficult to determine what 'acceptable levels' of changes in natural resources are in an international, national and local context. The acceptability level will vary even within a limited geographical location because peo-

Often, conflicts develop between nations because of differing perceptions as to what constitutes an acceptable level of resource utilization or carrying capacity

ple's attitudes are determined by economic, social, political and environmental factors. For example, in Northern Europe, heavily-polluting industry is located on the Russian Kola peninsula close to the Norwegian border. Norway has been willing to partly subsidize modernization of the Russian plants to install cleaner technology, so as to benefit from a reduction in the sulphur emission 'exports'. The level of pollution the local populations are willing to accept differs widely. On the Russian side of the border, acidification of lakes, soil and forests has lead to great loss of productivity, but has until now been accepted by the Russian decision-makers as a necessary cost of the benefits derived from the economic gains. However, on the Norwegian side of the border, as in the town of Kirkenes, the public has declared such environmental degradation to be totally unacceptable.

Over-use of resources

Many resource systems are under great pressure. They may absorb stress, conceal responses, and then generate 'environmental surprises.' For example, such surprises can include the sudden death of fish in rivers and lakes due to acidification shock from air pollution.

Much scientific effort has focused on the carrying capacity of various resource systems. There are two main points to be noted from this work. First, the carrying capacity depends upon the existing natural resource system, and geo- and bio-ecological conditions that may restrict social and economic development.[17] Second, the carrying capacity depends upon the society, its organization, management, capital and knowledge of the system itself.[18] Carrying capacity may even be increased in some cases with improved management practices.

> Resource systems may absorb stress, conceal responses, and then generate 'environmental surprises'

Rising demand caused by population growth and altered consumption patterns are the major factors in increasing resource utilization. It is not only the number of people that is significant, but also the population structure, mobility characteristics and scale of consumption.[19] The combination of institutional and technological aspects have a major effect on the utilization of natural resources.[20] It is therefore necessary to study the nature of human needs and factors which determine the utilization of the resources.

In the model, the **demand** or **behavioural system** represents the various kinds of needs the actors have, and their responses to cover those needs. There are two categories of needs: the need for access to and control over natural resources; and strategic, political, social and economic needs.[21]

These different needs are demonstrated by the incompatible goals that arise, and the positions taken by the parties in the conflict. To maintain position as a conflict escalates, parties often develop a behaviour which is a mixture of attempts to manœuvre strategically, provide partial or incomplete information, or manipulate fact—as well as attempts to truly understand the adversary's interests and motives. For practical purposes this text expresses the parties' behaviour through the parameters *parties, relationships, positions, interests,* and *options.*

The behavioural system includes sub-systems which are manifestations of the behaviour of local, national or international actors and deal more directly with management of resources. One of these systems can be described through an **economic sub-system,** since a state's demands drive economic policy and economic incentives in resource management.

The first of two main interactions in this system deals with national and international economic structures, such as the interactions between different economic systems (for example, market versus planned economies, which is significant in the Mediterranean case (Chapter Six)).

The second interaction includes financial mechanisms available for the international community in resource management. Unequal economic strength between states (as for example, measured by per capita income or GNP) increases the chances of generating and raising the potential for escalation of conflicts (for example, in North / South conflicts relating to resource conservation). Application of financial instruments such as the Global Environment Facility (a joint mechanism under the auspices of the World Bank, UNEP, and UNDP) is one example of a compensation mechanism for international environmental externalities.[22]

A common assumption is that the three means of production (resources, labour, and capital) prevail in all types of societies.[23] In this study, however, the economic sub-system is seen as a reflection of resources, management, labour and technology. Management, labour and technology can be described as another distinct sub-system.

The **production system** determines alterations of the resource base, and can create externalities.[24] The production system ranges from simple agricultural systems to complex energy systems. It is important to understand changes in the production systems both for analysis of the driving forces behind IECs and for assessment of conflict management tools. As illustrated in many of the IECs outlined in Part Two, the negative environmental effects of production systems vary widely. Some new production systems may reduce such effects, and one of the most important conflict management tools available in curbing pollution and environmental degradation is transfer of environmentally sound technology both in a North—South and West—East perspective.[25]

GEF: The Global Environment Facility

—A joint mechanism under the auspices of the World Bank, UNEP and UNDP.

It is one example of a compensation mechanism for international environmental externalities.

(See also: Chapter Three, Figure 3, and Chapter Seven)

Production systems causing externalities

4.2 The ABC Model

The analysis of the case studies is divided into various steps to assist understanding of the driving forces behind IECs, to improve the knowledge of applied conflict management tools, and to draw lessons of experience in successful conflict management relevant for the UN system.

Before starting this analysis, it is important to describe and briefly analyse the resources in question (international river systems, coastal areas, forestry and biodiversity, and land resources, respectively). This is intended to clarify the distinction between the multitude of resources utilized in various production systems worldwide, and the environmental effects. Close examination of the case studies has revealed that the causes of IECs often have similar patterns. This has led to the establishment of the three-step analytical approach described below. Each of the steps deals with conflicts in any situation where utilization of natural resources in one country has negative impacts for another country or group of countries. The negative environmental effects are perceived as the driving forces behind generation of IECs. Different types of such environmental effects constitute the core of the analytical model—*ABC-model*—which are evaluated in the context of the case studies presented in Part Two. Each of the three boxes A, B, and C represents one separate step in the analytical process:

A–type: Conflicts caused by unsustainable use of, control over and access to resources

A–type conflicts are generated by unsustainable use of natural resources, resulting in incompatible goals between the resource users. The **A**–type con-

Figure 5. ABC-Model

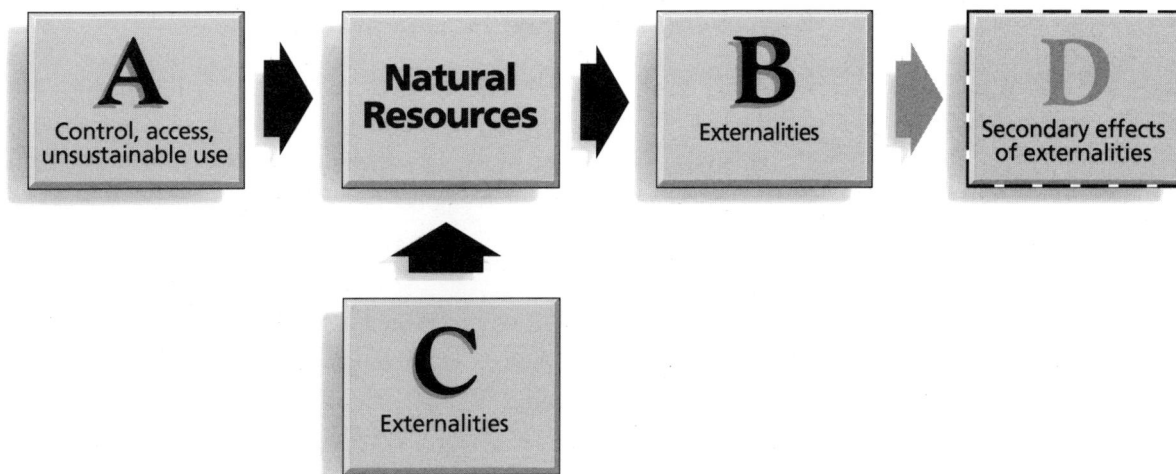

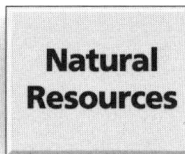

Unsustainable resource usage leading to incompatible goals between resource users

Negative side-effects (externalities) of resource use affecting two or more states

flict is actually more of a resource conflict than an environmental conflict. Examples of international resource conflicts include the overt conflict between Iraq and Kuwait over oil resources; and the incipient conflict between Norway and Russia in the Barentz Sea, concerning control over and access to oil and gas resources. Other examples, such as the conflict between Ethiopia and Germany concerning access to genetic resources, represent only the beginning of a series of conflicts over ownership of genetic resources (see Chapter Seven).

Other **A**–type conflicts occur in situations where another country perceives resource usage to be unsustainable. A typical example of this is the dispute between tropical timber-exporting countries (such as Malaysia or Indonesia) and European countries calling for a ban on the imports of tropical timber products made from unsustainable logging activities (see Chapter Seven).

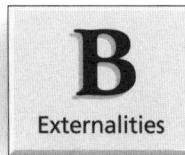

B–Type: Conflicts caused by externalities

B–type conflicts arise when externalities (negative environmental side-effects) affect two or more states. The states then have incompatible goals over the environmental effects of use of either their own, or a shared resource. Typical **B**–type conflicts involve pollution of a shared resource (for example the atmosphere, seas, or international rivers, where pollution is transferred to downstream countries).

Quite often, **B**–type conflicts are triggered because a country believes that it has more to gain than to lose from taking its preferred course of action over utilization of a resource. Examples include reduced discharge of international waterways through diversion through dam and reservoir projects that

result in reduced water flow to downstream countries. Another example of a **B**–conflict is the incompatible goals that have arisen between the US and Mexico over the negative environmental consequences of Mexico's commercial fishing. Dolphins are being trapped and killed by purse-seine nets, and the US has taken unilateral action, outside the limits of its jurisdiction, to protect this endangered species by prohibiting imports of tuna caught with these nets.

C–Type: Externalities from one resource affect another

C-type conflicts occur when the utilization of one resource has negative environmental effects on *other* resource systems, such as cross-boundary air pollution that has negative effects on land resources (acidification), forests and biodiversity (see Chapters Seven and Eight respectively). **C**-conflicts also typically involve coastal areas, when air- or river-transported pollution enters the sea.

A potential **C**-type IEC relates to climatic changes which may lead to sea level rise. At the moment, this is an incipient IEC, since the conflict is over how to prevent the sea level rise from occurring (by curbing emissions of greenhouse gases), rather than how to cope with actual sea level rise.

Utilization of one resource has negative environmental effects on **other** resource systems

D-type: Secondary effects of externalities

In one case study, a **D**-type conflict is identified. A **D**-type conflict can be described as an IEC resulting from the negative effects of resource use, which create circumstances which cause another conflict. Take a **B**-conflict—for example, over land degradation). People may be displaced internally or externally—so-called 'environmental refugees'—and this in turn may trigger international conflicts (see Chapter Nine).

This approach to the structure of IEC causes (A, B, C—and in some cases D) is reflected throughout Part Two. These categories are applied to the case studies in all chapters, and to specific conflicts in: Chapter Five—IECs related to utilization of the water from the Zambezi River System; Chapter Six— pollution of the Mediterranean Sea; Chapter Seven—utilization of the rain forest in Central Africa; and Chapter Eight—long range transboundary air pollution in Europe.

The cases presented in the following chapters represent only a small selection of IECs related to the water and coastal resources, as well as land resources, forestry and biodiversity resources, but they should represent a cross-section of the many IECs worldwide.

The step-wise analytical approach outlined above is adjusted to the particular requirements of the various cases.

CASE STUDIES

International river systems 5

5.1   Introduction

This chapter assesses the driving forces behind IECs related to international rivers, and illustrates some of their main components through brief case studies. A more indepth case study examines how IECs have been managed in relation to the Zambezi River System in Southern Africa.

Demand for water, and the services it can provide, is increasing worldwide, particularly in arid and semi-arid lands. Under pressure from rising demand, national water resources will become increasingly exploited. Some may even face depletion. Population growth, agricultural expansion, and the ever-rising expectations for improved standard of living worldwide, have all contributed to the realization that water is not an unlimited resource.

Competition for both quality and quantity of shared water at a local level often leads to international water conflicts. Many

IECs have been triggered because of the numerous shared water resources worldwide. Today, there are approximately 200 large river systems which are each shared by two or more nations. The need for basin-wide management is becoming more acute as the number of IECs increases.[1]

A river basin (also known as a catchment area, or a drainage basin) is an area which receives rain and which supplies water to a stream. River basins, drainage basins and catchment areas have both overland flow and groundwater. An international river system is a main river and all its tributaries, which run through, or separate, two or more states. As a result, co-operation at an international level is essential in order to manage the resource properly and avoid IECs.

While the potential for using river water in development plans is enormous, it cannot satisfy all possible uses. What happens upstream will inevitably have consequences for downstream uses. If countries continue to consider only national priorities while developing and using international river systems, conflicts will undoubtedly arise. Some are shown in Table 1.

5.2 The water resource system

Most international river systems, while large in terms of their physical proportions, are in fact sensitive natural resources. The watershed from which a river originates determines the quality and quantity of its water. Rivers can be seen not only as natural drains through which surplus water reaches the sea, but also as a means of redistributing water from areas with high precipitation to other, possibly drier, regions. Water as a natural resource is not only used for drinking, but also for household, industrial, agricultural and transportation purposes. Forests, vegetation, fish and wildlife also depend on water. However, the volume of fresh water which is readily accessible for users is only a tiny fraction of the total

amount which is transported globally by the hydrological cycle. This accessible water is mainly found in rivers, reservoirs and lakes, or a short distance below the ground. It typically has a brief residence time, and because of the spatial and temporal vagaries of the hydrological cycle, its distribution varies greatly from one part of the world to another. These variations cause serious problems for the assessment of water resources both globally and nationally, and even for a single river basin. Yet without such assessments there is no rational basis for planning how water resources should best be utilized and managed in order to reach prescribed goals.[2] Any particular use of water has consequences for other uses. Water extraction, water discharge and flow-regulation can all have basin-wide consequences, seriously affecting the nature and extent of benefits realizable throughout the basin.

Table 1. IECs over River Systems

River System	Countries involved with incompatible goals	Main subject of conflict
Nile	Egypt, Ethiopia, Sudan	Water flow
Euphrates, Tigris	Iraq, Syria, Turkey	Dams, water flow
Jordan, Litany	Israel, Lebanon	Water flow
Yarmouk	Jordan, Syria	Water flow
Indus, Sutlei	India, Pakistan	Irrigation
Ganges	Bangladesh, India	Siltation, flooding
Mekong	Kampuchea, Laos, Thailand, Vietnam	Water flow
Parana	Argentina, Brazil	Dam, flooding
Lauca	Bolivia, Chile	Dam, salination
Rio Grande, Colorado	Mexico, United States	Salination, water flow, agro-chemical pollution
Great Lakes	Canada, United States	Water diversion
Rhine	France, Germany, Netherlands, Switzerland	Industrial pollution
Elbe	Czechoslovakia, Germany	Industrial pollution
Szamos	Hungary, Romania	Industrial pollution
Danube	Czechoslovakia, Germany, Hungary	Dam / Water flow

5.3   Conflicting demands

Every international river system is unique, and the demands, priorities and suitability of a river system to different types of use will vary from place to place and from time to time. The location of a river system, together with such factors as climate, population, agriculture and degree of industrialization, determine which types of use are given priority and which create problems and conflicts.

Unless such conflicts are resolved and agreements reached on a co-operative basis, users decide individually how, and to what extent, they may utilize shared resources. The users' objectives are usually centred on claims and goals aimed at maximizing their own needs and values.

In order to analyse IECs related to international river systems, reference must first be made to the participants involved in different levels of conflicts. First, on a local level, competing groups may be national governments versus non-governmental claimants (e.g., individuals such as farmers and pastoralists, or private groups, organizations and associations). Water resource conflicts may also arise between such sectors as agriculture and industry (e.g., hydroelectric power generation).

Second, IECs may arise at, or escalate to, a regional level where two or more countries perceive that they possess mutually incompatible goals in utilizing the shared river system. Local conflicts, escalating from claims made by private individuals or groups, usually form the underlying element in claims advanced by national governments and presented at regional or international arenas.

Third, reference can be made to the independent sector level, a cross-level involving IECs between transnational corporations and local or regional user groups like farmers or environmental NGOs, where the contentious issues are the consumptive use and/or industrial pollution of the river system. (See Chapter Four). The global level is not relevant in this context, except where debt repayment issues or global climatic changes are linked to international river systems.

5.4   Driving forces behind IECs

The analysis of driving forces behind IECs often has to be based on conflicts arising at a local level. Conflict issues and their motivation are still the same at an international level, but man-made national borders, and additional difficulties, such as national sovereignty claiming power over its 'own' river resources complicate the conflict management process at this level. The three-part model described in Figure 1 illustrates the basic types of conflict that may arise:

A—incompatible goals related to access to, control over, and unsustainable use of international river systems (for example, through water diversion, dams and reservoirs);

B—externalities created by utilizing the international river systems (for example, salination as a result of irrigation; changed water flow as a result of regulation; pollution from industry using water in the production process; sewage from cities and communities); and

C—IECs arising as a result of externalities from other activities affecting the river systems (for example, eutrophication, pollution from industries which do not use the water resource in the production process, soil erosion and siltation of water courses following deforestation or over-grazing).

Figure 6. The ABC model and international river systems

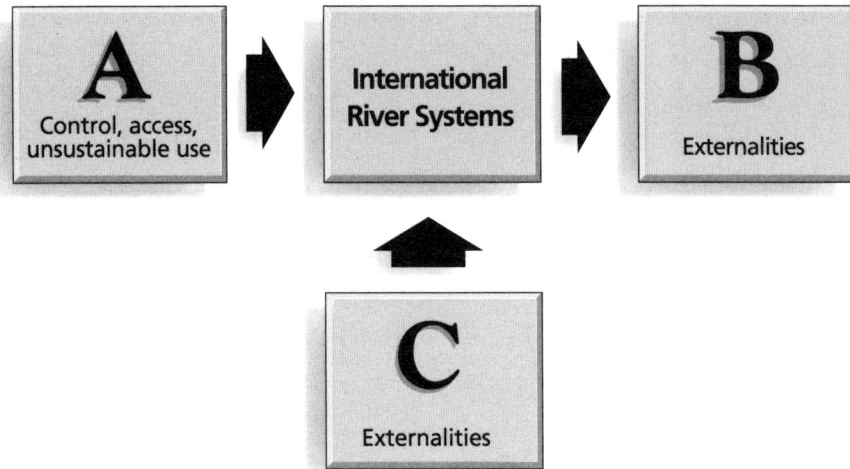

5.5 (A) Access to, control over, and unsustainable use of international river systems

Access to water resources is determined by the location of a country in relation to a river system. Climate has considerable influence on a country's access to water resources. The amount of inflow from upstream countries depends on the nature of water-consuming activities in these countries; and downstream countries depend on their upstream neighbours for their own water-consuming activities.

Control of water in international river systems is mainly determined by the location of the riparian states in relation to the watershed, as well as the division of power between the countries—be it economical, political or military.[3]

Domestic and municipal uses of river water rank highest on the priority list, since no community can survive without an adequate drinking water supply. Cities, with their expanding populations, face higher demands for water for drinking and sanitation purposes; and in cases where there may not be enough water to satisfy all demands, a question of priority arises.

In arid and semi-arid countries, diversion of water for agricultural irrigation is a high priority, while in countries which are well-supplied with water, generation of hydroelectric power and industrial use may be given greater priority.

Water use may be consumptive or non-consumptive. Non-consumptive use, such as navigation of international river systems, has led to international conflicts in the past. Today, however, because of well-established rules and existing international administrative regimes, navigational use of international river systems does not give rise to serious conflict (which is why navigation is excluded from this study). Other forms of non-consumptive water use, however, such as recreation and non-commercial fishing still cause serious national conflicts in several industrialized countries. And as more developing countries are turning to tourism as a source of national income, recreational use of international river systems will be given higher priority, which may lead to new IECs. Consumptive use covers various interests:

Domestic and municipal use

Increased demand for water is resulting in excessive pumping of groundwater aquifers, and a deterioration in quality of both surface and groundwater supplies.

The demand for water and its different uses depends on the numbers of individuals to be supplied. The larger the population, the less water is available on a per capita basis, making population growth a real dilemma in countries where the supply of water is scarce. (A modern urban household may use 400 to 800 litres of water daily.) A common characteristic of almost all semi-arid lands in the world is a relatively high rate of population growth, whether in Sub-Saharan Africa, India or southern California. It is estimated that by the end of the century, the world will gain an additional 1.1 billion people, with 20% of this population growth in arid and semi-arid regions.

The quality of available drinking water is also an issue of importance, as illustrated by events such as cholera epidemics. A satisfactory domestic water supply must be free from harmful bacteria, and chemicals that give it an unpleasant taste (whether or not they are actually harmful). As populations increase, and as manufacturing industries grow, it becomes increasingly difficult to find and maintain supplies of good quality water.[4]

Perhaps the most pertinent international effort seeking to improve standards in the provision of water supply and waste disposal was initiated with the launch of the United Nations International Drinking and Sanitation Decade in 1980. The Decade called for safe water and adequate sanitation facilities to be made available to all rural and urban areas by 1990.[5]

On a global scale, approximately 71% of the urban population (excluding China) has access to drinking water supplies. The availability of most services is greater in urban areas than in rural areas, and the supply of drinking water is no exception. At present, only 41% of the world's rural population has convenient access to adequate drinking water supplies.[6]

Irrigation in industrialized and developing countries

Industrialized countries

Although municipal and industrial water needs are growing, water use in industrialized countries continues to be dominated by irrigated agriculture, which globally accounts for about 73% of water used in arid and semi-arid regions.[7] Irrigation is normally water-intensive, with a higher consumption-to-withdrawal ratio than other water uses, which means that proportionately more of the water diverted from streams or aquifers evaporates from the soil or transpires from crops instead of returning to the sources for re-use. This ratio averages about 60%, compared to 25% in municipal use

and between 0% and 25% in industrial use.[8] There are some exceptions, however, as in the case of Israel with quite a low ratio average.[9]

In industrialized countries, much of the water supplied for agriculture originates in national water projects subsidized by taxpayers, as in the Columbia River Basin, or as in Scandinavia through district equalization policy. Water is therefore cheap for farmers and the subsidies offer no incentive to conserve surface water. Rising water costs have, however, generally triggered shifts to higher-valued crops and crops needing less water to grow.

Crops currently use only about half of the water applied with most irrigation methods. Efficiency varies, however, according to the type of technology employed and the capital investment in the land and physical structures, and may reach 75% of supplied water.

Developing countries

Irrigation in developing countries ranges from capital-extensive and labour intensive recessional systems, (water variations from lakes and rivers, as in the Gambia and Senegal river), to highly sophisticated capital-intensive systems (for example, in India and Pakistan).

Increasing populations and standards of living in developing countries require substantial growth in agricultural output (at least 3% per annum), which is unlikely to occur without an intensification of agriculture.

In many river basin countries, development of agriculture has the highest priority, because of its importance to the national economies. This implies that more and more land with arable potential will be cultivated, large-scale irrigation schemes will be promoted when funds are available,

Table 2. The Indus River System.
A manifest IEC related to water-flow / irrigation

Actors	Interests	Strategies
India	India contended it had proprietary rights over the water and was thus entitled to exclusive use of the waters of the eastern rivers of the Indus system.	The Sutlej waters feeding certain canals leading into Pakistan are considered to be closed.
Pakistan	Pakistan advocates the principle of territorial integrity.	The view of the West Punjab Government is that water cannot be stopped on any account whatsoever. Pakistan wanted to secure sufficient and regular supplies of usable quantities of water for agricultural irrigation.

and increasing amounts of pesticides and fertilizers will be used.

Extension of agriculture into marginal land areas could help a little, but limited land resources and declining yields on marginal land restrict this. Intensification of rain-fed agriculture should be a major element, especially in areas of better rainfall. Progress in dry zones, however, will probably continue to be slow. Irrigated agriculture, with a shift towards perennial irrigation, will therefore play a more proportionate role. To ensure an overall growth in agricultural output by 3% per year, output from irrigated agriculture will have to increase much faster. Intensification of cultivation and higher yields on existing cropped areas under irrigation may account for part of this output, but most of it will have to come from an increase in double cropping and expansion of the irrigated area.

This suggests that a substantial growth in the irrigation-cropped areas and in the demand for irrigation water will be necessary over the next few decades. Because there are already local water shortages in arid and semi-arid areas, this also implies a need for improved efficiency in water usage.[10] The scope for improvements in overall irrigation efficiency may, however, be fairly limited. Conservation efforts are likely to cause a large increase in the need for additional irrigation water. (See Table 2– The Indus River System).[11]

Industrial purposes

There are few forms of manufacturing which do not require water at some stage. For example, the pulp and paper industry, the metallurgy industry, and brewing, chemical, and mining industries, are all heavy water users. Expanding industry, such as water cooling of fossil-fuelled power-stations, claims a substantial share of available water resources. Industrial water uses are mainly non-consumptive, and the water is often recirculated in order to save expense and conserve resources. The control of water discharge for this purpose is a frequent cause of IECs (such as in the Rhine or Danube in Europe).

Hydroelectric power (HEP) generation

Another important use of water in connection with urban and industrial life is for energy, with a great potential for further development of hydroelectric power (HEP) in almost all international rivers in developing countries. HEP can most conveniently be integrated in multi-purpose water resource projects intended also for irrigation and flood control. Even though HEP does not directly consume water in the produc-

Box 8

The Jordan River System
A manifest IEC over waterflow diversion

The Jordan River System is shared by Jordan, Syria, Israel and Lebanon. Competition for water in this area is greater than anywhere else in the world, because of the region's aridity, population pressure and geopolitical situation. Israel diverts water from the Sea of Galilee, through which the Jordan River passes, to its Kinnert-Negev conduit. Jordan diverts water from the Yarmuk River, a tributary to the Jordan River which forms the border between Syria and Jordan, to the East Ghor Canal, its national water artery. (Charnock, 1983)

Controversy over water issues, although until recently largely undocumented, is one of the reasons why no peace agreement has been achieved in the area since 1947. According to many scholars (e.g., Cooley 1984) the constant competition over the waters of the Jordan, Litany, Orontes, Yarmuk, and other life-giving Middle East rivers was a principal cause of the 1967 Arab-Israeli War, and could help spark new conflict again. It is also a major aspect of the Palestinian question and the struggle over the future of the West Bank.

In the case of the Jordan River Basin, it is evident that both Israel and Jordan already face serious problems, which can only worsen in years ahead. Israel uses more than the entire amount of its water allocation. After several winters with below average precipitation, the Sea of Galilee's water level is at its lowest in 60 years: just 50 cm over the red line where all pumping should stop. In the heat of summer, evaporation alone can lower the water level at least 1 metre in just a few months.

Jordan has not been using all of its water allocation, and its per capita use has been extremely low. The situation is precarious since Jordan produces an extremely small amount of staple food and at the same time has a yearly population growth rate of 3.8% (one of the world's highest). Consequently, to meet its growing water needs, Jordan is relying on incremental solutions, including deeper drilling for groundwater sources and such expensive technologies as drip irrigation.

Compared with its neighbours, Lebanon has plentiful water resources which could potentially be shared. Its numerous rivers and underground systems are reliably replenished from ample precipitation. However, because of lack of orchestrated water management at the national level, Lebanon has serious water problems: severe water shortages in Beirut, seawater intrusion in the coastal aquifer, lack of irrigation water, and pipelines as well as aquifers that have been severely damaged by civil war.

tion process, it usually demands a man-made reservoir, which implies resettlement of people; changes in the local environment; loss of discharge; and (at least in arid and semi-arid areas) more significant seepage and evaporation. This also means that HEP cannot be classified as non-consumptive use, as was generally done a few years ago. The dam entails control over the discharge which may cause severe implications politically as well as physically for downstream countries (for example, the Ataturk dam in Turkey with Iraq, Jordan, Israel and Lebanon downstream).

Recreation and tourism

International river systems and rivers in general are very attractive for recreational use. Rising real incomes and shorter working weeks have encouraged such river uses as swimming, boating, canoeing, rafting, fishing, hunting at the waterfront and sightseeing. The recreational capacity and value of rivers may sometimes be increased by the building of dams and creation of reservoirs. Incompatible values and interests may, however, develop between conservation of the environment and recreational user groups and other water resource users, such

Table 3. Actors, interests, and strategies in the Jordan River System

Actors:	Interests:	Strategy:
Syria	To secure sufficient quantities and regular supplies of usable qualities of water for the future. Protect the waters of the Orontes River for irrigation of farmland in western Syria.	To link the lower reaches of the Hasbani River with the Banias River. To link the headwaters of the Yarmurk River. To obtain guarantees that the headwaters of the Orontes River would never be controlled by Israel.
Lebanon	To secure sufficient quantities and regular supplies of usable qualities of water for the future.	To link the headwaters of the Hasbani River with the waters of the Litany River. Military defence and diplomatic negotiations.
Israel	To gain access to the lower reaches of the Litany River and the Orontes River. Israel perceived that the Arab diversion plans presented a serious threat to its security. Israel fears that the Wahda Dam on the upper Yarmuk River could seriously affect its ability to meet its growing water requirements, and it wants a fair share of the Yarmuk waters.	Israel has launched a pre-emptive strike on Syrian construction sites, damaging equipment. Israel has withheld its approval of the Yarmuk project, implying that the World Bank will not proceed with the financial support.
Jordan	To secure sufficient and regular supplies of usable qualities of water for the future.	To withdraw water from the sea of Galilee (depending on Israel's approval). To supply water from the Maqarin project on the Yarmuk River (depending on Syria's approval). To transfer water from the Euphrates River which could create a dependence on Iraq.

as manufacturing industries or water regulation projects for hydroelectric power generation. Many of these conflicts are national rather than international.

Water diversion, dams and reservoirs

Diversion and damming must be considered to be the most important sources of IECs, as they serve as means of increasing access to, and control of, water in order to satisfy the water uses described above.

The majority of IECs related to *diversion of water* fall into the category of consump-

tive uses. Since all water diversion projects directly affect downstream water quantity, these projects are an immense source of conflicts, particularly when the diversion of river systems goes beyond the area of national jurisdiction. (See box on the Jordan River System).

Dams and reservoirs aim to store water resources for more efficient water distribution. Water demands vary according to the season; and the time of peak demand may not correspond to that of peak supply. Therefore, water supply can be increased during certain periods of the year, or stabi-

Box 9

The Ganges River System

The Ganges River System, the basin of which is shared primarily by India and Bangladesh, passes through one of the poorest regions of the world. Its waters have traditionally been regarded as an inexhaustible gift of nature. The regional population explosion and the rapid development of agriculture and industry in both India and Bangladesh are, however, putting increasing strain on this water resource through greater consumption, and deterioration of water quality. (Choudhury & Khan, 1983)

An ongoing 30-year dispute over the sharing of the waters of the Ganges River System is focused mainly on water diversion by India at the Farakka Dam just upstream from the Bangladeshi border. The aim of the project is to flush more water through the Hoogly River and port of Calcutta in order to reduce siltation. Bangladesh is threatened by the decrease in the dry season flow that can be caused by this withdrawal. After some 20 years of fruitless negotiations on joint use of the river water, a temporary agreement on a six-week trial at Farakka Dam was finally reached in 1975. India, however, prolonged this diversion for more than two years, which created problems in Bangladesh, because the extremely dry seasons which followed produced a series of adverse effects. The extent of seawater intrusion was exacerbated by the extremely low water level in the river; the upstream penetration extending some 160 km further than usual. Groundwater salination occurred over vast areas. (Zaman, 1983)

Bangladesh brought the issue to the United Nations, and in 1976 the General Assembly urged the parties to meet in order to negotiate a fair and expeditious settlement. (UNGA, 1976; 31/404) In November 1977, a five-year Ganges Water Agreement was reached. This treaty among other things seeks a long-term solution for augmentation of the dry season flow. Unfortunately, Bangladesh and India have divergent points of view as to how to increase the dry season flow of the Ganges River: (see table below)

Table 4.	Actors, interests and strategies in the Ganges River	
Actors	**Interests**	**Strategies**
India	To solve the low flow problems in Bangladesh without water withdrawals from the Ganges River. To secure sufficient quantities of water to reduce siltation in the Hooghly River.	To transfer waters from the Brahmaputra River in Assam through Bangladesh.
Bangladesh	To secure sufficient water flow in the dry season in Bangladesh.	Bangladesh rejects the canal scheme (see India's strategy) as ecologically ruinous and technically and economically unfeasible. To build storage dams in the upper reaches of the river in Nepal and India that would store wet season flow for release during the low flow period.

lized by damming rivers, to help reduce local periodical water shortages.

However, significantly reduced discharge of an international river causes IECs, as for example in the case of the planned dam near Gao in Mali (triggering conflicts with Niger over the loss of essential water for irrigation) and in Senegal (adversely affecting the Gambia and Mauritania, who will experience salt intrusion moving inland from the coast, which will subsequently ruin recession agricultural systems).[12]

Large-scale dams are usually multi-purpose projects (for example HEP, irrigation flood control, and navigation). One objective is the regulation of flow by storage so that water is available when needed. Another is flood control, preventing danger by withholding flood waters until the flood peak has passed. Thirdly, flow regulation may keep stream erosion under control.

IECs related directly to access to, and control and use of, water often arise as a result of large scale dam projects since these projects reduce the flow of water to downstream countries (as, for example the highly contentious Ataturk dam in Turkey).

5.6 (B) Externalities from utilizing river systems as causes of IECs

Water quality is particularly important when water is to be used for domestic and industrial purposes. If quality at the source is poor, the cost of treatment is greatly increased. Often some adverse qualities, such as unpalatable taste, cannot be entirely removed by treatment (and in some circumstances the treatment process itself creates a taste problem because of high residual chlorine, as in the case of the Rhine in central Europe). For irrigation, the main quality problem relates to salt. Some reservoirs can raise the salt content of the water, particularly in arid zones where the reservoir holding time is long and evaporation rates are high. Also for industrial and domestic water, high salt content greatly increases treatment costs.

Eutrophication (when the increase in mineral and organic nutrients in the stored water is sufficient to reduce the dissolved oxygen) is also a major water quality problem.

Monitoring of water quality is an essential long-term activity for all rivers and reservoirs, and is usually focused on biological quality and on the associated oxygen content; and (in the longer term) on chemical quality.

The domestic and municipal sector

Large concentrations of people have always resulted in waste disposal problems. Historically, the most common method has been to throw waste into the nearest waterway (regardless of whether or not the waterway is also used to supply drinking water). As long as settlements are small, and waste disposal is low in relation to the absorption capacity, waste disposal is generally not a serious problem; river flow or the tide will eventually take refuse away from its source. As cities grow in size, however, more elaborate methods of waste disposal must be developed, as now urgently required by the Danube in the intersection between Austria, Czechoslovakia, and Hungary. Nevertheless many towns and cities still return raw sewage to rivers which may provide part of the water supply for other centres or countries, or to the estuaries and beaches where large numbers of people may go for recreation (see Chapter Six for further discussion).

Irrigation

The common decision to postpone implementation of expensive drainage systems to a later stage of an irrigation project means that short-term financial constraints get transformed into long-term, and even more expensive, degradation problems.

The major water quality problem in arid and semi-arid agricultural areas is salinity, which affects many river basins. River waters become increasingly saline from the headwaters to the river mouths as seepage and return flows from irrigated lands empty into the rivers. This is an obvious cause of IECs, where the quality of the water for downstream users is severely affected.

In many areas, groundwater is severely polluted by deep percolation of irrigation water and seepage from irrigation-conveyance systems. The groundwater system can act as a conduit for saline waste water to enter rivers or international aquifers.

Salinity is not just a problem of in-stream water quality. Soil salinity also poses a major threat to agriculture and can worsen as saline water is used for irrigation, or as waterlogging of poorly drained land oc-

curs. The lack of drainage in many agricultural areas causes the water table to rise, subjecting the productive soil layer to severe salination, and reducing crop yields (waterlogging).

Each year, salinity and waterlogging cause millions of dollars of damage to agriculture, as well as to industrial and municipal water users, and these costs are increasing.

Industrial sector

Most industries do not include the negative environmental side effects of their activities in the price of their products. They therefore use water as free goods to dispose of wastes that accumulate in processing. Detergents have come into wide use, both domestically and industrially, and the production of synthetic materials and complex pesticides and chemicals has resulted in problems of a far greater order than those of a few decades ago. Many of these pollutants cannot be broken down and rendered harmless by natural self-purification.

Thermal pollution stems from water discharged from power stations and factory cooling plants. The water may be chemically and bacteriologically unexceptionable, and may have a much higher temperature than when it was pumped out. The animal and plant population of a river may therefore be adjusted to a temperature range which is exceeded by the artificially warmed water. They may be killed, leaving a barren stretch of water, or they may be replaced by other, perhaps less desirable, species.

Another externality of industrialization is water pollution by the accumulation of heavy metals, nutrients and toxic chemicals in the river bed mud in deltas and estuaries. Sediments that are dredged up normally cannot be used for such projects as landfills in populated or agricultural areas. IECs in arid zone developing countries relate to the water quality as well as quantity. The problem is exacerbated when industrialization based largely on industrial techniques imported from developed countries are adopted. Techniques that have been developed in countries with plentiful water resources often depend upon volumes of water that are unrealistic by arid zone standards. Among the consequences of adoption of such techniques is that the water coming to a downstream country during the dry season may be highly polluted.[13]

Water diversion and dam and reservoir projects

Dam and reservoir projects improve water supply for irrigation and households; they provide power, and control floods, which in turn reduces fossil fuel depletion and the negative environmental effects of fossil fuel burning. However, as with many other projects, particularly in the tropics, there may be adverse environmental impacts. Dam and reservoir projects normally affect a very large area, and can flood thousands of hectares of prime agricultural land, precious rainforests, highly productive cotton-lands as well as timber and wildlife habitats. Construction of dams may also create easy access to tropical forests and wildlife that can be lost to indiscriminate harvesting.

Designing water projects, in the context of overall river basin and regional development plans, normally reduces the potential for unanticipated cumulative adverse environmental effects and intersectorial and regional international problems. Many critics, however, recognize that there is too much variation in the designs of large dam and reservoir projects to generalize about

their socio-economic and environmental impacts.[14] Highly polarized IECs related to water diversion and dam and reservoir project, such as in the case of the Gabcikovo projects (affecting Czechoslovakia, Hungary, and Austria), reveal the need to pay attention not only to comprehensive environmental and socio-economic impact assessments, but also to the decision-making process itself through the participation of the parties involved.

Erosion and siltation

Erosion upstream in the catchment area leads to sedimentation or land slips which can impair storage (as in the case of the Aswan dam on the Nile river in Egypt). There may also be increased erosion of the river bed and structures below the dam, including deltaic and coastal changes (as might happen on the coast of the Gambia if Senegal built a dam upstream). Changes in stream flow and water releases from a large dam can cause increased river bed erosion, undermine downstream water structures, deplete nutrients which would otherwise be carried by fine sediments, and

also radically reduce groundwater levels, thus having negative effects on existing agriculture. The erosion rate along the coast of the delta also accelerates as a result of deprivation of silt nourishment after dam construction.

Wetland destruction

Reservoirs regulate downstream flow by increasing river flow during the dry season, or low water period, and by virtually eliminating annual flooding. As a result, riverine habitats, especially wetlands, below dams and often in another country, have been drastically reduced, as has the productivity of riverine communities (as in the Diama Delta in Senegal).

Resettlement

Land flooded by a dam is typically more productive than neighbouring uplands, and is therefore more densely populated by people and livestock. Displacement of the lowland population to the uplands often endangers the environment, as more people and livestock must survive on a reduced resource base. Demand for arable land, fuel, fodder, potable water, building materials and other resources may increase dramatically.[15] At the same time, the sustainability of upland areas may be quickly exceeded unless development assistance increases the productivity of the remaining resource base. Neither involuntary resettlement nor migration caused by a depleting resource base respect international borders, and there are many examples of conflicts, particularly national ones, as a result of this.[16]

Unfortunately, no way exists for avoiding disruption to the lives of people displaced by a dam or reservoir project. The flooding of land causes major economic losses and socio-cultural disruption, for instance to farming systems, and it leads to loss of arable lands and forests, and to the disappearance of land improvement. As a result, many small- and medium-scale farmers and other traders become impoverished.[17]

The contrast between technically elaborate dam design technology and the sociological inadequacies of resettlement components calls for improved policies, and a guarantee that resettlement standards meet the same exacting criteria required for other technical aspects of dam construction. (See further discussion on Environmental Refugees in Chapter Nine).

Health

Construction of dams and reservoirs, especially in warm climates, may increase water-related diseases (e.g., schistosomiasis and malaria) unless precautions or mitigatory measures are implemented. Reservoirs in tropical areas create favourable habitats for the breeding and survival of snails, mosquitoes and black flies which transmit these diseases. The typical development-induced disease is schistosomiasis. Wherever the snail vector is found, it is always in connection with projects such as reservoirs and irrigation (e.g., lower Aswan dam, Akosombo dam, Gezira irrigation).[18] Malaria is more often associated with irrigation systems, particularly for rice cultivation, than with the reservoirs and dams that serve them.

Proliferation of floating weeds (e.g., water hyacinth and water lettuce) can impair water quality and increase disease vectors. The control of these diseases is necessary in all reservoir areas, and imposes a large financial burden on the affected countries.

5.7 (C) Externalities from other activities affecting river systems as causes of IECs

The many factors described under this section underline the increased danger for IECs as water quality diminishes, particularly for shared waters and watersheds.

Eutrophication

A serious source of pollution of natural waters comes from fertilizers applied to agricultural land. Aerial top dressing with phosphates and other fertilizers is a common and accepted agricultural practice, at least in developed countries. The result is increased fertility, increased yields of crops and animals, and good vegetative cover which is vital in order to combat erosion. It is, however, almost impossible to prevent some of the fertilizers from finding their way into rivers and lakes. This results in an increase in the nutrient level of water, perhaps most noticeable in lakes where phosphates tend to be stored. One of the changes observed may be an increase in the growth of algae resulting in surface algal blooms, which can be toxic to animals. While consuming the nutrients, algae also use oxygen and may seriously reduce the oxygen content of the water. This may result in depletion of the fish population and other forms of animal life, and may increase certain kinds of lake weeds, causing clear water to be spoiled by vegetation masses.

Pesticides

In many developing countries, major ecological problems exist due to usage of such persistent pesticides as DDT. The downstream effects are often severe and a source of many IECs as in the case of pesticide pollution of the Rhine River Basin in Europe (triggering conflicts between Germany and the downstream countries).

Soil erosion and siltation of water sources following deforestation or over-grazing

Forests and vegetation are very effective in combating run-off and erosion, since they induce considerable storage of water in the ground, increase the natural permeability of the soil, and increase the evaporation rate. There is clear evidence that unless forestation and vegetation are integrated into water management plans, soil erosion, deforestation and over-grazing may contribute to large silt loads in the rivers and lakes and thus become a cause of IECs. (See, e.g., textbox 'Siltation of Sudanese Irrigation Schemes' in Chapter Eight.)

Wildlife

In general, wildlife is adversely affected by artificial variations in water discharge as well as water pollution. Hydroelectric power projects, agricultural and industrial development, and the sharp increase in population, have an adverse effect on wildlife in many river basin countries. Destruction of wetlands also eliminates valuable habitat (which in turn endangers many wildlife populations). All of these lead to loss of wilderness and subsequently wildlife. With dam projects, however this may be mitigated by including a wild-land management area equivalent to the flooded area.

Wildlife along international rivers is the object of significant, and increasing, tourist activity in many developing countries, bringing in much needed hard foreign currency.

In many countries, governmental actions have been taken to protect wildlife from the adverse effects of water projects, but problems and conflicts still arise when these different national views and actions necessarily have to be joined in common action plans for entire international river systems (as, for example, in the Nile River Basin). These problems are further complicated by national differences in the use and management of wildlife (see further discussion in Chapter Seven on forestry and biodiversity).

Social implications and economic aspects

Proper identification and analysis of the impact of a water project on socio-economic conditions must be carried out in conjunction with an effective monitoring and evaluation system. However, some environmental impacts are very hard to quantify.[19] For example, it is difficult in dam projects to evaluate in quantitative terms the flooding of archaeological sites, the elimination of rare species, or changes in landscapes. It is even more difficult to express these losses in economic terms.

While river basin development projects often favour hydroelectric power (HEP) generation for commercial, industrial and residential sectors to the benefit of some nations' economies many river basin development projects have actually degraded riverine habitats and worsened the plight of riverine populations. To date, the developmental potential of riverine habitats and production systems has been seriously diminished by river basin development strategies. Throughout tropical Africa, these strategies have damaged flood water agriculture, high and dry season grasslands for livestock, and fisheries.[20]

While the economies and lifestyles of riverside populations depend on annual flooding, too much flooding sweeps away crops, while too little leads to inadequate harvests and increased migration to cities. The elimination of downstream flooding has devastated many local production systems. Riverine habitats for flood water farming and livestock management are adversely affected, and fisheries' productivity and fish landings for consumption and commercial purposes are greatly reduced.

Negative effects of water projects, including dams or reservoirs, can be minimized by, for example, linking hydroelectric power and irrigation to dam-controlled downstream flooding and regular reservoir drawdowns. [21]

Debt repayment

Most developing countries use a great deal of their hard currency for debt repayment. Mexico, Peru and Brazil, for example, are in such oppressive debt crises that they are forced to exploit their natural resources on a short-term basis in order to pay foreign and international lending institutions, making long-term sustainable development and conservation almost impossible. The front-loading of any kind of investment in large dams puts a heavy burden on countries in the first years. Long-term objectives involving neighbouring state relations, as well as social and environmental conditions at a local level tend to be minimized.

5.8   Conflict management

International conflict management related to international river systems focuses on both water quality and water quantity. Both of these related aspects have environmental and socio-economic implications on an international level.

In view of the fundamental importance of water for different sectors of the economy, it is evident that protection from water-related natural hazards (flood and drought), from health hazards (waterborne diseases), and from hazards to aquatic ecosystems (pollutants) should form the cornerstones of national and international water management policy if IECs are to be effectively avoided and resolved.

Conflict management doctrines on international river systems

The outflow from upstream countries depends on the nature of water-consuming activities in these countries. Water-consuming activities, such as irrigation or water transfer out of the basin, reduce the inflow to the downstream country and often degrade its quality as well. In many river basins, downstream countries are at the mercy of their upstream neighbours. Measures taken by upstream countries which in some way threaten the water supply of downstream countries will create uneasiness among the latter. As a result, the location of a country along a river can have a considerable influence on its international relations. For example, diplomatic activities of such downstream countries as Jordan, Bangladesh and Egypt seem to reflect a concern that their future is being endangered in this way. The interdependence between riparian countries' environmental policies (i.e., the extent to which decisions taken by actors in one part of the river system affect (intentionally or unintentionally) other actors' policy decisions elsewhere in the river system) illustrates some of the potential risks involved in unilateral policy-making. (See boxes for discussion of different policy doctrines).

It is useful to relate different policies to different situations. In general, it can be said that the more polarized a conflict, the more extreme the policy adopted by the parties.

Box 10

Measures to minimize negative social and economic implications

Developing local involvement, and incorporating social impacts analysis in the planning process, is of vital importance but not widely recognized as such. In order for river basin development to be sustainable, current accounting of costs and benefits at the national level must be complemented by regional, international, and local environmental accounting. The short-sightedness of national economies accounting only for the benefits of the projects leads to the costs to riverine populations being discounted and ignored. Appraisals often place too little emphasis on the total resource base, on indigenous knowledge of it, and local systems for resource utilization. Too much emphasis is often placed on economic rates of return on a national level, while the redistribution of wealth and indirect effects are ignored. Least-cost solutions for electricity generation are especially inadequate, since they tend to compare dams with thermal stations and other power sources as if energy production were the only issue involved. Complexities and difficulties concerning water projects notwithstanding, the conflict between various departments and countries, and the disputes between environmentalists and water project designers, must be analysed thoroughly. In most cases, compromise consensus approaches need to be exploited. In the long run, developing countries; in urgent need of exploiting their water resources for social and economic development, will suffer most. (See also Cernea, 1985).

The most extreme policy models (see (a) and (b)) are said to be more or less abandoned today; nevertheless one may well imagine that states involved in a river conflict could still adopt these doctrines and positions. This is especially true in areas where some form of water scarcity is an underlying cause of a conflict between co-riparian states. That is, parties in a conflict tend to adopt extreme positions when for some reason the conflict becomes more polarized. This corresponds to the 'manifest conflict levels' in the Escalation Model (Chapter Four). The increased polarization may result from a mutual perception among the parties that there is greater competition for the amount of water available in the river system; either because of drought, increased population pressure, high levels of water pollution, too much diversion of water from the river system, or a combination of these causes.

Antagonism between co-riparian states, often rooted in regional historical events, may, in addition to increased competition for water, also contribute to such polarization.

The more moderate policy models ((see (c), (d) and (e)) reflect a balanced approach that may assume a surplus of water in the region—so that harsh competition for water is avoided. These situations correspond with the 'Potential Conflict Levels' in the Escalation Model. Third party intervention in the conflict may also enhance the chances that the parties to the conflict will adopt moderate rather than extreme policies (see Chapter One).

Most riparian states have, either implicitly or explicitly, expressed a list of priorities as to how they want to manage their water resources. In some situations, these official priorities prove incompatible with the needs and interests of the local population.

The positions, and thereby the policies adopted by the conflicting states, are to a large extent a reflection of these states' relative location in the river system. Whether the relationships between co-riparian parties to a river conflict are antagonistic or co-operative determines to a certain degree the positions taken by the parties.

New challenges in international river management

As socio-economic development proceeds, and supply and demand in the context of limited river resources become more difficult to balance, the need for more sophisticated water management mechanisms and policies arises.

As demand for water increases, water management changes from supply-oriented to demand-oriented.[22] In the early stages, measures are taken to satisfy the demands as they develop. As demands increase, water storage and redistribution projects regulate the supply. Finally, as river systems are developed and considered acceptable and there is no more water to allocate, further development must be supported by reallocation and control of demand; that is, by accepting water availability often as a *regional constraint*. Control of demand may lead to changes in crops, increases in the efficiency of irrigation (e.g., by changing from furrow irrigation to drip irrigation), recirculation and re-use of water.

Since the turn of the century, the exploitation of international rivers for economic purposes has required a radical solution, namely the internationalization of the entire basin of the river so that no single basin state may solely utilize any single branch or tributary situated in its territory, without regard for the other basin states.

Box 11

Conflict management doctrines on international rivers

(a) Absolute Territorial Sovereignty: Harmon Doctrine

According to the reasonings behind this doctrine, a state may adopt all measures deemed suitable to its national interest in regard to water courses within its territory, irrespective of their effects beyond its borders. Accordingly, it may freely dispose of waters flowing in its territory, but cannot demand the continued free and uninterrupted flow of water from upper-basin states.

Proponents of this doctrine argue that an international water course in the territory of a state constitutes part of the public domain of that state; and that since a state has dominion over its own territory, another state acquires rights only with the agreement of the first state. This doctrine clearly favours upper-basin states.

Today, 'absolute territorial sovereignty' is quite often abandoned because it neglects interdependence and co-operation between states. The principles are equally contradictory to the principle of territorial integrity of states provided in Article 2 (4) of the UN Charter.

(b) Absolute Territorial Integrity

This policy model is the direct opposite of the theory of absolute territorial sovereignty, and states a policy of water rights whereby a lower riparian state claims the right to the continued, uninterrupted (or natural) flow of the water from the territory of the upper riparian (basin) state. The doctrine is favourable to the lower-basin state.

The theory is sometimes criticized because it allocates rights without imposing corresponding duties. It has been invoked in situations where the continued flow of waters was critical to the survival of the state concerned (as in the case of Iraq and the River Euphat).

(c) Limited Territorial Sovereignty and Limited Territorial Integrity

Theories of limited territorial sovereignty and limited territorial integrity are in practice complementary; even identical. They state that every state is free to use the waters flowing in its territory, on the condition that such utilization does not prejudice the territory or interests of other states. In short, they state that states have reciprocal rights and obligations in the utilization of the waters of their international drainage basins.

(d) Community of Interests in the waters

Some authorities argue for a 'community' approach (i.e., state boundaries should be ignored and a drainage basin be regarded as an economic and physical unit). There would be a collective right of action by all basin states in such a manner that no state could dispose of the waters without consultation with and co-operation with the other states (as in the case of many rivers, such as the Senegal river). The doctrine claims that the water system ought to be managed as an integrated whole. This consideration leads to the implementation of basin-wide development programmes designed by all the riparian states in the river basin.

(e) The Doctrine of Equitable Utilization

This policy model has evolved gradually in the framework of the long-standing conflict among the competing theories discussed above (a, b, c and d), and proposes that each basin state has a right to utilize the waters of the basin, and is entitled to a reasonable and equitable share of the basin water.

The principle of equitable utilization reflects three fundamental concerns. First, it takes into account the socio-economic needs of the basin states through an objective consideration of various factors and conflicting elements relevant to the use of the waters; second, it aims at distributing the waters among the basin states in such a manner as to satisfy their needs to the greatest possible extent; and third, it seeks to distribute the waters so as to achieve the maximum benefit for each co-basin state with the minimum detriment.

One may argue that many of UNEP's international river basin initiations are based on a combination of (c), (d) and (e), depending on site-specific conditions and progress in accepting international law.

Source: Revised after Godana, 1985

Traditionally, every state exercised exclusive sovereignty over natural resources, including water. In effect, the implicit legal doctrine was absolute territorial sovereignty. These traditional concepts of national sovereignty are, however, no longer sufficient for a world altered by ever-increasing interdependence between nations on economic, ecological and security fronts (Chapter One).

In view of the peculiar characteristics of drainage basins, and particularly the fact that water generally does not respect political boundaries, the claim of absolute sovereignty over a portion of an international drainage basin meets with strikingly different problems from those generally associated with sovereignty over land territory. This inherent difference between the nature of land and water has led, in the latter case, to the emergence of conflicts of interests between co-basin states.

An interesting path to explore would be to assess the replicability of lessons of experience in water management at national levels where strong competitive interests exist. The Columbia River Basin, which is shared by several different states in the United States, provides one example.[23] Underlying political and administration infrastructures should not be overlooked (namely, the existence of a unified legal system with effective enforcement authority to ensure compliance and a developed economy which entails use of economic incentives for compensation and improved compliance).

Another example from the developing world is provided in the case of the Lake Chad Basin.[24]

Co-operation in the development and sound environmental management of these fresh-water resources can provide opportunities for political and diplomatic co-operation (as in the case of UNEP's Mediterranean Programme, described in Chapter Six). A general principle illustrated by international legal development in drainage basins is the emergence of a more dynamic concept of joint development. Integrated development presupposes co-ordinated or joint action for the development of water resources considering the basin as a unit; an approach which includes concerted action in data collection, investigation, planning, operation and management. The recent increase in the development of international river systems along such co-operative lines is practical and illustrates how states have realized both their mutual interdependence and the wide possibilities for development through co-operation (e.g., in the Rhine and the Danube River Basins in Europe).

Recent agreements concluded in the cases of the Niger,[25] Senegal,[26] Lake Chad Basin[27] and Zambezi River Basin[28] all testify to this trend and exemplify the increasingly important principle of mutual co-operation and joint development of international river systems.

International river systems are likely to form an important component in the future political relationships between the countries within these river systems. Co-operation or confrontation in the utilization of freshwater resources will characterize this relationship.

The existence of accepted regional legal regimes applicable for the conflicts enhances the potential for successful conflict management.[29] As the case from the Zambezi River Basin demonstrates it is important to strengthen existing national institutions and to have a national body or authority to co-ordinate national activities to become a focal point and represent national interests at the international level.

5.9   Case Study:
The Zambezi River System
Introduction

The Zambezi River System represents a unique opportunity to study IECs related to utilization of a common water resource by eight countries. Together with its tributaries, the system forms the fourth largest river system in Africa, and drains almost the entire south central region of the continent. The basin stretches over territories in Namibia, Angola, Botswana, Zimbabwe, Zambia, Tanzania, Malawi and Mozambique. It flows eastwards for approximately 3000 km, draining an area of about 1,300,000 km^2.[30] The population living in this area is about 26 million, and is expected to double in 20 years.[31]

Available water resources in most parts of the basin greatly exceed demand. However, this situation will certainly not last for ever: the region's anticipated population growth, increased food demands, and improved standard of living imply a higher utilization level of the water resources, and increase the risk of environmental conflicts. The importance of the Zambezi River System is mainly related to rural activities. More than 70% of the population in the basin is involved in agriculture. Today there is only limited use of water for irrigation, but as a result of the increasing demand for food, new irrigation projects are being planned and some are being implemented. Recent droughts in the region have exacerbated this trend, and large-scale water projects for irrigation purposes are under development in several of the riparian countries.

The Zambezi River System is an immense source of HEP, and this is and will continue to be, at least in parts of the river system, the most important sectorial use of the Zambezi water. Ongoing and planned large-scale HEP projects are sources of local

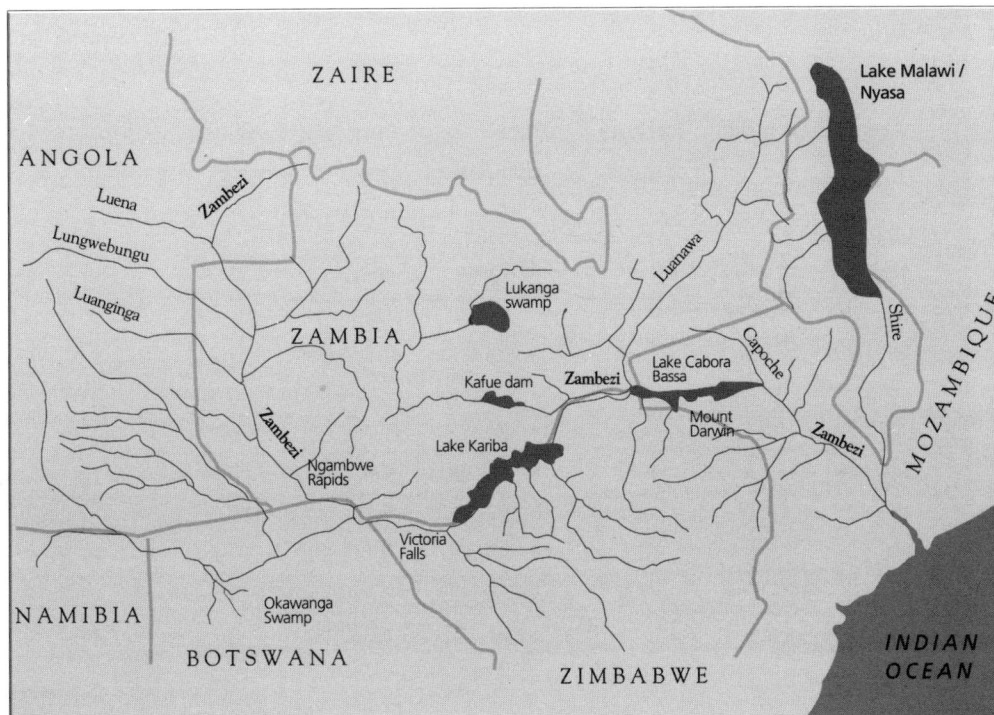

Figure 7.

The Zambezi River Basin

and regional water resource conflicts.

At present, there are actual and potential conflicts over water use and the maintenance of water quality in the Zambezi River System.

The Zambezi River System provides a rich example of IECs for a number of reasons. First, the Zambezi River System Action Plan (ZACPLAN) is the first project under UNEP's programme on Environmentally Sound Management of Inland Waters (EMINWA). Second, the ZACPLAN was initiated before serious water resource conflicts in the region occurred, which makes it interesting to see if, and how, such a plan can prevent conflicts and be used as a resolution mechanism. Third, the region is situated in arid and semi-arid climatic zones, which is typical for regions with serious water conflicts. The Zambezi River System is the main life-giving artery in the region, and the creation of a legal management regime to administer this artery is crucial to the development of the whole region.

A more general understanding of water management issues, discussed in earlier sections of this chapter, is not sufficient to understand the specific regional development and management of the Zambezi River System. A more integrated analysis may reveal important links between the resource system, the economic system, the demand system and the production system in the region. Examples will also be given of on-going and planned large-scale water projects with environmental, economical and social impacts outside the executing country.

Along its longitudinal profile, the Zambezi River System can naturally be divided into three sections[32]: **upper**—from its sources to the Victoria Falls; **middle**—from Victoria Falls to the Cabora Bassa Rapids; and **lower**—from Cabora Bassa to the Indian Ocean. The Zambezi River System's sub-

Table 5. Share of the Zambezi drainage basin and population distribution by country

Country	Total Area	Area inside basin		Territory of basin %	Total population	Population inside basin in persons and in %		Basin population
	km²	persons	%	%	persons	persons	%	%
Angola	1,246,700	145,000	11.6	10.9	9,215,000	340,000	3.7	1.3
Botswana	582,000	84,000	14.4	6.3	1,320,000	11,000	0.8	0.04
Namibia	824,300	24,000	2.9	1.8	1,520,500	56,000	3.7	0.2
Zambia	752,600	540,000	71.8	40.6	8,398,700	5,900,000	70.2	22.1
Zimbabwe	390,800	251,400	64.3	18.9	10,752,700	7,750,000	72.1	29,0
Mozambique	799,400	140,000	17.5	10.5	16,343,800	3,140,000	19.2	11.8
Malawi	118,500	118,500	100	8.9	8,450,200	8,450,200	100	31.6
Tanzania	945,100	27,100	2.9	2.1	26,827,100	1,070,000	4.2	4.0

catchment areas correspond to the drainage basins of the Zambezi's main tributaries (see map).

Natural resource system

The Zambezi River System is situated south of the equator between 12° and 20° latitude. The cool dry season is between May and September. The tributaries coming from north of the Zambezi belong to the tropical summer rainfall zone, and as one moves southward, the tropical summer becomes progressively more arid due to a prolongation of the dry season. Thus, the upper and the middle sections of the Zambezi are defined as warm temperate regions with dry winters, the warmest month reaching 22°C [33]; while the Okavango basin and the southern part of middle Zambezi belong to the arid steppe zone with a mean annual temperature of more than 18°C. The lower Zambezi moves from the arid climatic zone in the west to an equatorial climate with dry winters in the east.

The average rainfall is 990 mm, but the runoff is only 120 mm in the outlet at the coast. Thus, under average conditions 88% of the water evaporates and only 12% of the precipitation reaches the Indian Ocean. The flow variations are exceptional, and as the figures in Table 6 indicate, the hydrology of the Zambezi is unusually vulnerable.

Swamps and lakes

Swamps and lakes play an important role in the water balance of drainage basins, especially in tropical regions, where the evapotranspiration process is intensified. The Zambezi River System contains several water storage systems such as lakes and swamps. Lake Malawi / Nyasa is the only natural lake, which is shared by Tanzania and Malawi. The Shire river is the outlet river of the lake, and joins the Zambezi in its lower reach.

In the middle section of the Zambezi, two man-made lakes (Kariba and Cabora Bassa) regulate almost 570 km, or 65% of this part of the river. There are also other man-made lakes in the Zambezi tributaries, such as Itezhitezhi in the Kafue River in Zambia and Lake Darwendale in the Hunyani River in Zimbabwe. There are also several swamps in the catchment area of the Zambezi River System. The Barotse swamps lie in the upper source of the Zambezi in the Central African Plateau in Western Zambia.

Hydroelectric power (HEP)

The Zambezi River System is an immense potential source of HEP, with an estimated HEP potential of 20,000 MW. Today's installed HEP capacity is about 4,500 MW, but there are ongoing and planned large-

Table 6. Hydrology. Flow pattern at different stations in the Zambezi River (m³/s)

	Victoria Falls	Tete (1959–1988)	Marromell (1962–1988)
HQ	12,000	17,140	11,600
MQ	1,550	2,500	3,358
LQ	300	18	374

Source: Nordic Mission, Draft Main Report, May 1989

scale HEP projects which will increase the capacity in the near future. Some examples are: the Katombore reservoir above the Victoria Falls, Batoka Gorge above Kariba, and Mupata Gorge above Cabora Bassa. Based on recent HEP plans, as well as regulations that already exist in middle and lower Zambezi, the Zambezi River System is likely to be tied more to HEP development in the foreseeable future than to other uses such as irrigation and industrial development directly.

Demand system

Because the countries are situated in arid and semi-arid zones, the demand for water is increasing as industrialization, domestic and municipal use, and agricultural irrigation progress. The demands and priorities of different types of water use will vary from country to country, and from time to time, as discussed earlier. Some of the riparian countries in the Zambezi River System (e.g., Zambia and Zimbabwe) have large settlements along the river system, and use water directly, while other countries need to divert Zambezi water to large population settlements outside the river system (e.g., Botswana). In other situations, such as in Mozambique, civil strife has forced the population to move away from the Zambezi watershed area, which means losing access to water and fertile land.

Even though there are believed to be no serious conflicts at the moment over water use between the riparian countries in the Zambezi River System, recent years of drought have accelerated the national water plans in the various riparian countries.

Another factor accelerating water resource competition is South Africa's plans for utilization of Zambezi water. South Africa enjoys military, economical and tech-

nological superiority over its Southern African Development Co-ordination Conference (SADCC) neighbours. Unless the SADCC countries can find counter-measures in close regional water management co-operation, they could lose control of and access to significant quantities of Zambezi water.

Conflicting demands for water resources in the Zambezi River System (ZRS)

The following cases from the ZRS reveal potential and manifest IECs as a reflection of conflicting demands for the available water.

The Chobe-Vaal Water Project attempts to divert water from one of the main tributaries (the Chobe) for the benefit of Botswana and South Africa. The project is considered to have serious environmental impacts on the downstream countries (Zimbabwe, Zambia, and Mozambique—see Box 12).

Another case, the Southern Okavanga Integrated Water Development Project, aims to supply water for irrigation, households, and to a diamond mine in Botswana. The core of the conflict is related to a series of planned dams on the Boro River in Botswana's unique Okavango delta ecosystem. The project has triggered great international attention, and can be described as a 'third level conflict' (see Box 13).

The Batoka Gorge hydro-electric project with part of the Zambezi river is shared by Zambia and Zimbabwe. The downstream effects for Mozambique are uncertain, but will probably have effects on its water quantity and quality. This case also reveals conflicts of interest between institutions which deal with shared water management (ZRA vs. SADCC —see Box 14).

Box 12

The Chobe-Vaal Water Project

One of the main tributaries of the Zambezi, the Chobe, flows through the northern part of Botswana, and marks the border of the Caprivi Strip. South Africa has detailed knowledge of its own resources through national studies, and has a thorough appreciation of the future limitations of its own resources. Therefore, it has designed plans for diverting water from the Zambezi at its confluence with the Chobe, just upstream of the Victoria Falls. The water would flow in an artificial canal to southern Botswana and Rand, and then be lifted by a pumping station across the escarpments to the Vaal river system in South Africa, a total distance of approximately 1300 km. The project would give access to an additional amount of about 2,400 million m^3 of water per year, approximately 130% more than currently available in the Vaal district.

Because the Chobe area is a sparsely populated region of Botswana, and the eastern and southern parts of the country where the population density is highest often suffer from droughts, this project would also benefit the national interests of Botswana. Botswana would have a stable and safe water supply for the most populated and driest region of the country, and would have economic advantages from selling surplus water to South Africa. This is one reason why Botswana, despite traditional opposition to the South African regime, has now taken a positive position related to this water diversion project.

The project is considered to have serious environmental, economic and social consequences for the downstream countries of Zimbabwe, Zambia and Mozambique. Zimbabwe has explicitly objected to the project plans, and has warned Botswana not to attempt to carry out the project. This means that if Botswana and South Africa decide to execute the project, conflicts at a regional level, between Botswana and the downstream countries, may quickly escalate.

The project will also go against one of the fundamental rules of SADCC—to ensure that all SADCC countries share in the benefits from development, and work towards disengaging themselves from dependence on South Africa. There are also indications that South Africa will continue to apply its manpower and technology to acquire additional water resources from the SADCC area.

Bulawzyo is a water diversion project, which generates IECs of a different nature. The conflict is manifest at a national level (i.e., local people vs. central government), but with clear linkages to both Zambia and Mozambique (see Box 15).

The Okavango delta

The two river systems, Cubango and Cuito, which flow south from Angola, merge to form the Okavango River before entering and forming the Okavango delta system.

The Okavango River fans out to drain its waters into the Kalahari desert in northwest Botswana. The inflow of the Okavango is about 11 million m^3/year, and usually the whole amount evapotranspires in the delta. The resulting delta system of channels and pools is Africa's largest oasis, and one of the world's most famous wetlands and diverse habitats for wildlife. There is one small game reserve inside the delta, but Okavango has (at present) no protected status.

Box 13

Southern Okavango Integrated Water Development Project (SOIWD)

The purpose of the Southern Okavango Integrated Water Development Project (SOIWD) is threefold: (1) to supply water for the irrigation of 10,000 km² of land; (2) to provide drinking water for the cities of Maun, Mopipi, Orapa, Toteng and other communities; and (3) to increase the water supply to the Orapa diamond mine, which, as one of the world's richest, currently uses about 5 million m³ of water a year and the demand is expected to double by the year 2000. In order to meet the demand for water, construction of a series of dams along the delta's southern fringe is being planned, in addition to dredging about 40 km of the Boro River in order to increase the outflow of the delta.

The area under direct influence from this project will be only about 250 km², or 1% of the Okavango Delta, but the indirect ecological implications may be much wider. These indirect environmental effects are difficult to foresee in the highly vulnerable ecosystem which supports a delicately balanced network of human, plant and animal populations.

The core of the conflict is centred on these planned dam projects in the Boro River in Botswana's unique Okavango Delta. The conflicts initially occurred at a local level, where the indigenous people have repeatedly expressed opposition to the project. Based on experience from previously failed drainage projects, they are concerned that their own water supply, livelihood, and wildlife will be affected. Nonetheless, the government of Botswana and outside project consultants are the most enthusiastic proponents of the project. The Orapa diamond mine, which is a joint venture of the government and a South African mining company, accounts for an important share of Botswana's foreign exchange earnings. Botswana's powerful cattle ranchers have also helped the project to continue, because draining of the Okavango Delta would release great areas of land for cattle ranching. This interest is also shared by the government, as export of beef to Europe is the second greatest export earner for Botswana.

The SOIWD project does not seem to have severe downstream effects like most other water projects on the Zambezi River System. The participants in the international arena are therefore not the various riparian countries, but rather tourism interest groups, conservationists, and environmental and wildlife groups worldwide. For example, Greenpeace (which campaigned against the project) has recommended that the delta be nominated as a protected site in the World Heritage and Ramsar Conventions.

Conflict management:

Development and implementation of the ZACPLAN

In 1983, the Governing Council of UNEP voted to establish a new programme entitled 'Environmentally Sound Management of Inland Waters' (EMINWA), a project to be analogous to UNEP's highly successful Regional Seas Programme. One of the sub-programmes of EMINWA is the African Inland Waters Programme (AIWP), which lends high priority to water management and the reduction of the effects of droughts in Africa. The Zambezi Action Plan, or ZACPLAN, was initiated by the riparian states and further developed by UNEP as its

---

Box 14

The Batoka Gorge HEP Project

The Zambezi River Authority (ZRA), is an administrative body established in 1987 to manage water resource issues and oversee developments in the part of the Zambezi River shared by Zambia and Zimbabwe.

The Zambezi River Authority has done site investigations for further HEP developments in this part of the Zambezi River, and has found the Batoka scheme above Kariba economically more viable as compared to the other options: the Mupata Gorge, Devil's Gorge, and Katombore. A study is continuing to provide the ZRA with a firm basis upon which to recommend the implementation of the project to the Zambian and Zimbabwe council of ministers. The Batoka project is to be funded by the African Development Bank.

The provisional design of the dam plans a structure 196 m high and 695 m long, which would make the Batoka dam the highest dam of its kind in Africa. The reservoir will have a small surface area (approximately 27 km²) and therefore low surface evaporation. The proposed power generation capacity is 1600 MW and is likely to be fed into the regional grid.

Potential regional conflicts related to this project are predictable. Uncertain about the project's influence on downstream water quantity and quality, Mozambique (as the downstream country) will certainly voice opposition to possible negative effects from the project. Another potential conflict is between ZRA and SADCC, for when the time comes that SADCC /SWCLU manage to actively integrate all ongoing and planned water projects in the Zambezi River System into the ZACPLAN, the ZRA will not be able to continue managing its own projects outside, or parallel to, the ZACPLAN. Both the projects and the ZRA must be incorporated, or at least closely co-ordinated with the ZACPLAN and SWCLU, which will require considerable organized flexibility.

---

first sub-programme under the EMINWA and the AIWP. The framework of the ZACPLAN was also included in the Cairo Programme for African Co-operation in 1985.[34]

In 1985, the first step was to establish a working group of experts from all the riparian countries (with the exception of Angola) as well as representatives from SADCC and UN organizations. The first meeting of the Working Group was held in Nairobi in April 1985 and was followed by two other meetings (in Lusaka, Zambia, in March 1986, and in Gaborone, Botswana, in January 1987).

A diagnostic study prepared by the Working Group during 1985–87 summarized the present state of the ecology and the environmental management of the Zambezi River System. This was used as a background document for the Action Plan.

A draft agreement drawn up by the Working Group was adopted in May 1987 by the Conference of Plenipotentiaries on the Environmental Management of the Common Zambezi River System, in Harare.

During the Conference of Plenipotentiaries, it was decided that the ZACPLAN should be implemented within the framework of SADCC. Later in 1987, the SADCC Council of Ministers adopted the ZACPLAN as a SADCC programme.

Box 15

The Bulawayo Water Diversion Project

This project includes water diversion from the Zambezi River down to Bulawayo City in Zambezi, a distance of about 500 km. After more than ten years of drought, Bulawayo and the surrounding district face a critical situation for more than 3 million people. In August 1991 it was reported that Bulawayo's four water magazines were storing less than 30% of their capacity, and that this water will not last for more than ten months. Each Bulawayo citizen's water quota has already been reduced by 75%.

The water scheme for supplying Bulawayo with Zambezi water was first made in 1932, but the government of Zimbabwe has not found it economically viable to execute the project.

The conflict is highly manifest at the local level, with clearly incompatible goals between the people from the Matabeleland district, those from Bulawayo city and the government of Zimbabwe. The conflict has been continuing for years, and is fuelled by ethnic dimensions between the Ndebele people in southern Zimbabwe and the Shona people in the North. The government in Harare is dominated by Shona people, and Matabeleland is mainly populated by Ndebele people.

The drought of the last decades has contributed to the conflict and thus to the increased governmental pressure. (A government spokesman has indicated that a decision about the water project will be taken in 1992).

Another reason why the government has not given priority to this project up to now, is undoubtedly the reluctance of the neighbouring states (Zambia and Mozambique) to support the project. The IECs can be described as latent, but when the time comes for Zimbabwe to execute the water diversion project, the conflict may easily escalate into a high tension manifest phase.

Overall implementation was entrusted to the Sector Co-ordinator for Soil and Water Conservation and Land Utilization (SWC-LU) in Lesotho, one of a number of sectorial co-ordinating bodies created by SAD-CC.

Member countries of SADCC are: Angola, Namibia, Botswana, Zambia, Zimbabwe, Malawi, Mozambique, Tanzania, Lesotho and Swaziland. With the exception of Lesotho and Swaziland, all the other SADCC countries belong at least partly to the catchment area of the Zambezi.

In 1988, the SWCLU unit approached the Nordic governments for assistance in further development of the ZACPLAN. A team of experts[35] evaluated the situation and made recommendations on how the Nordic countries should participate in the implementation of the ZACPLAN.[36]

When UNEP initiated the ZACPLAN project it appeared that several important criteria for a successful project were fulfilled:

■ There were few manifest IECs related to water resources.

■ Compared with other African regions, a political dialogue existed between the riparian countries.

Box 16

The ZACPLAN

The ZACPLAN or Action Plan for the Environmentally Sound Management of the Common Zambezi River System, has the following main elements:

1) Environmental Assessment: the collection and development of comparable data and information for the continuing and systematic assessment of the main factors influencing water management and water-related environmental quality.

2) Environmental Management: to ensure sustainable, environmentally-sound development of the resource base, taking into account the assimilative capacity of the environment, national development goals and the economic feasibility of their implementation.

3) Environmental Legislation: development, review, and, where necessary, expansion, updating or strengthening of national legislation; and development and adoption of regional instruments.

4) Supporting measures: such as intensive training programmes, promotion of public awareness, development of education and information programmes, and development of the water supply and sanitation sector.

■ Few strong ethnic conflicts occurred in the region.

■ The riparian countries had a joint interest in limiting the dominance of South Africa (which provided a sense of solidarity).

■ There appeared to be no funding problems because of the interest expressed by several donors.

The regional water management co-operation and efforts to implement the ZACPLAN have nevertheless been fraught with difficulty and are currently at a standstill. The reasons for this standstill are complex and include not only water management issues, but also the region's historical and cultural background, the different levels of economic development of the riparian countries, current democratization processes with unstable political structures, the region's relations with the existing global economic and political system, and South Africa's economic and political role in the

region. As an in-depth analysis of all these factors would be beyond the scope of this study, a few key factors are highlighted.

Because almost all of the riparian countries have worked out large-scale national water projects, the competition over water resources will soon become more visible. In addition, the co-operative process is further hampered by the perception that national sovereignty is being threatened, and by some nations seizing the opportunity to maximize their own needs and profit at the expense of regional interests. Both of these factors serve to obscure the mutual gain which could be earned by co-operation. Therefore, one of the central challenges of the ZACPLAN co-ordination unit is to convince all riparian countries of the advantages to be gained from participating in ZACPLAN.

Experience has shown that international environmental conflicts become more complex and more difficult to avoid, solve

or settle when they have been allowed to escalate; which suggests that developing a sense of mutual interest in problem-solving should take place at all levels and even before complete background information has been obtained.

The Role of SADCC in Conflict Management of the ZRS

SADCC was established by countries with disparate socio-economic policies ranging from planned economies, to capitalism, to some behavioural ideologies, such as Zambia's 'humanism' and Tanzania's 'ujumaa'. Despite this, SADCC has experienced 11 years of regional co-operation. Unlike many regional organizations, which often lack a clear and specific mandate, SADCC has confined itself to co-ordinating the development effects of the member states. Setting realistic goals and programmes, rather than creating large bureaucracies, SADCC delegated sectorial responsibilities to each of the member states and maintains only a small secretariat in Gaborone, the Botswana capital.

SADCC has acted as a catalyst in development programmes and has made great improvements, mainly in the transport and communication sectors. Since 1987, SADCC has turned its attention to the production sector as a base for trade co-operation between the SADCC countries.

SADCC has had to make numerous adjustments to cope with shifting political, economic and social conditions. The political climate is markedly different since SADCC was first formed in 1980. Previously it seemed that South Africa might close its frontline borders, but with the lifting of international sanctions, the political situation is altering and it is unlikely that South Africa will close its borders on its neighbours. This creates a new and real challenge for SADCC; to strengthen the economic entity of the 10 member countries to meet South Africa on an equitable basis. This will be quite a leap forward, since intra-regional trade consists of only about 5–6%, and there are no common tariffs or travel barriers. Today the SADCC states seem to exert only marginal control over their water resources, with rudimentary initiatives at best. There is a growing awareness of the urgency for SADCC to look at their regional waters in a holistic context, and the implementation of the ZACPLAN is the first test case. So far the budgetary allocation to the water development sector has been minimal and the advanced professional manpower and technology in the field is limited. Therefore a matter of priority for the SADCC states is to develop and mobilize technology and advanced manpower to study the waters of the region as a whole.

SADCC is discussing advancing its mandate beyond the facilitation of investment projects by each country, to promote in-depth regional co-ordination, including legally-binding treaties and the creation of new legal and institutional frameworks to form an acceptable regional legal management regime.

Strengthening of high-level capability

in water resource management within the SADCC member states will contribute to the following critical functions: first, it will enable the states to deal with the critical task of water resource management, as water is the single most important item in development. Second, it will enable the states to deal with the most critical environmental stress brought about by poor distribution of water by location and season within the region. Third, it will enable the states to deal with a critical source of political conflict.

Establishment of specific conflict resolution mechanisms perceived as adequate and impartial by the member states may help keep conflict resolution procedures moving forward. SADCC may look at the Conference on Security and Co-operation in Europe (CSCE is discussed in Chapter Two) as a model with special emphasis on the ability to institutionalize issues.

5.10 Conclusions to be drawn from the Zambezi River System

It has been suggested that regional organizations deal most effectively with regional problems and conflicts. The various complex IECs related to management of the water resources in the Zambezi River System show that effective regional management is dependent upon each participating country's willingness to co-operate.

NGOs seem to play an increasingly important role in influencing the separate countries to join in such programmes.

Preventive regional water management co-operation is difficult to implement effectively (at least not before severe water scarcity or pollution are acknowledged).

UNEP's EMINWA programme, including preparation of action plans, provides a functioning framework for regional water management. UNEP's catalytic role does not cover project implementations. In the Zambezi case this has created a vacuum after the ZACPLAN was adopted as a SADCC programme. In this project implementation phase, substantial conflicts usually arise (see also Chapter Six, UNEP's Mediterranean Action Plan). Unless the regional organization is strong enough to handle these conflicts, alternative applications could be made for this transition phase. The proposal to expand UNEP's mandate to cover project implementation might result in improved assistance in the critical transition phase into project implementation. There seem, however, to be few strong arguments for a more active role for UNEP in implementations, except for a catalytic role in bringing financial institutions in at an early stage in the planning process.

Innovative solutions such as the use of problem-solving groups with substantial expertise could be established in order to follow up project implementation or serve as impartial resources to facilitate negotiations between the riparian countries at the organizational level.

Chapter Six

CASE STUDIES

6 Coastal areas

COASTAL AREAS, as transitional zones between land and sea, are increasingly affected by both aquatic and terrestrial human activities. The many national and international interests associated with the use of these areas make them particularly interesting to study in the light of international environmental conflicts (IECs). A case study from the Mediterranean Sea, which is shared by 18 nations, is carried out in the light of the origins and management of coastal IECs.

6.1 Introduction

Environmental changes in coastal areas may tilt the balance of local, national and international power, as well as producing social and political instability. By applying a systems approach, we shall attempt to capture some critical links between coastal environmental changes and conflicting user-needs in these areas. The Mediterra-

nean has been selected as an illustrative case study in conflict management related to coastal areas.

Coastal areas, which cover both aquatic and terrestrial areas, include the belt of terrestrial land and the adjacent ocean space in which land ecology and land use affect ocean-space ecology, and vice versa. The inland boundary of the coastal zone is somewhat unclear. The seaward boundary has been defined as the extent to which man's land-based activities have a measurable influence on the chemistry of the water or the ecology of marine life.[1] Coastal areas are transitional zones, affected by human activities both in marine and terrestrial environments.

The coastal area is a zone in which different interests which do not follow geopolitical and administrative boundaries can merge into conflicts. In many cases, increasing demands on coastal areas are met by a decreasing supply, which may eventually lead to overt competitive behaviour. The Preparatory Committee for UNCED (United Nations Conference on Environment and Development), Working Group II, pointed out the increased potential for environmental conflicts over marine resources: "Free use and open access when demand is low poses no problem. However, when demand nears or exceeds supply, policies of open access on the ocean environment create conflict among users and significant resource and environmental degradation".

Driving forces

One of the root causes of increased pressure on coastal areas lies in the distribution, size and growth rates of the human population in different regions. In a global context, there are trends towards:

Population growth: Africa has the greatest average annual population change in percentage terms, whereas Asia (including China) has the highest population growth. More than half of the total increase in population is taking place in Asia or near coastal areas.

Increasing urbanization: Urban areas are expected to increase in number and areal extent, replacing biologically-productive areas with infrastructure and the pollution that results from it. According to UN projections, urbanization is expected to increase significantly in the future.[2]

Increased economic activity and infrastructural expansion in coastal areas: A large share of urbanization is taking place in coastal areas, with approximately three billion people living on, or within 100 km, of a sea coast, comprising 60% of the global population.[3]

This distribution pattern is also expected to continue in the future. In 1980, eight out of the ten largest urban concentrations in the world were in coastal areas.

Population growth, increased urbanization, increased industrial activity (with the water as a receptor of wastes), infrastructure expansion, and fishing interests have generally fuelled the large number of conflicts in coastal zones. During the period 1950–1988, six violations of territorial waters were reported (four between 1980–1988); 17 territorial disputes (seven between 1980–88); seven disputes over freedom of navigation (three within 1980–1988); and 11 fishery disputes (all after 1972).[4] The term 'territorial dispute' includes skirmishes and wars over access to other resources, especially potential gas and oil fields. There also appears to be an increase in the number and extent of conflicts in coastal zones resulting from environmental degradation. During the Gulf War of 1990–1991, environmental degradation was used as an eco-weapon (oil was pumped out of wells to degrade the environment and deplete remaining oil resources). The introduction of eco-weapons as a means of warfare prompted an immediate reaction from the UN, not only through condemnation at the Security Council, but also through international agreements.[5]

6.2 Diversity of conflicts

Coastal areas exhibit several important resources: harbours; navigation (transportation); aqua- and agricultural activities; recreation; and siting of settlements and industry. Also, coastal areas are still major dumping grounds for a vast array of human and industrial wastes. Any assessment of IECs related to coastal resources should include all these resource uses. The analysis focuses on only a selection of these resources (and

Figure 8.
The ABC model and coastal resources

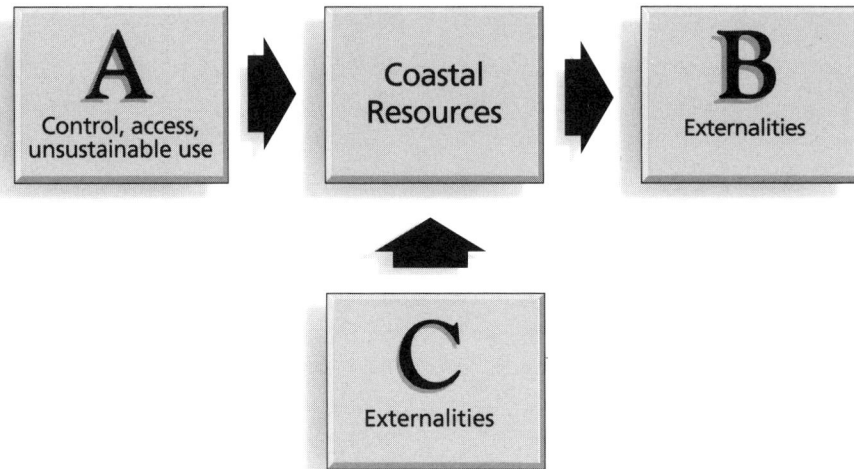

the associated IECs). The conflict analysis is divided into three aspects: conflicts related to access to, control over and unsustainable use of coastal resources (**A**) which are shown on the left-hand side of Figure 8.

The main focus, however, is on the right hand side of the Figure, which depicts conflicts emerging as a result of the externalities from using the coastal resources (**B**— for example, water as a receptor of wastes). Externalities from other activities which affect the coastal resources (**C**—for example, river-transported and airborne pollution) can trigger other conflicts and are depicted in the lower part of the Figure.

The different factors under each group (**A**, **B** and **C**) which may lead to IECs are outlined as follows:

6.3 (A) IECs generated by access to, control over, and unsustainable use of coastal resources

Territorial conflicts in coastal areas (land and sea) are often expressed through competition for access to resources, since they reflect different resource-strategic intentions for the adversarial states. Access to

energy resources such as fossil fuels will probably become a more significant source of conflict due to their uneven spatial distribution. The sovereignty issue is critical in this context, since territorial boundaries in many countries extend beyond the immediate shore into near-shore waters, which have previously been considered common property (see Box 17). Because of the general view that seas are a 'common heritage of mankind', and because of the increasing competition for resources, regulation of this territorial expansion has been considered necessary. Under UNCLOS III, 40% of the sea area has been claimed by, and become the responsibility of, one or more states.[6] When new land appears, for example as a result of volcanoes, or in river deltas, questions arise over who has the right to claim sovereignty over these new areas, including the new Exclusive Economic Zones (EEZs). UNCLOS defines several zones in order of increasing size: (1) Internal waters; (2) Territorial Sea extending 12 nautical miles from land (in which the coastal states have sovereignty but are obliged to allow innocent passage of foreign shipping); (3) Contiguous Zone extended to 24 nautical miles;

Box 17

Territorial conflicts

Conflicts over the extension of EEZs

There have been several disputes over the extension of EEZs of adjacent nations (common terrestrial borderline) and of nations facing a sea that is too narrow to give room for, for instance, a 200 nautical mile EEZ for both of them. Some examples are well-known: Norway—Russia: both claim EEZs within the same part of the Barrentz Sea; Greece—Turkey: (the Greek Islands being close to the Turkish coastline); and Libya—Malta.

Conflicts over access to harbours for landlocked states

This is mainly a question for African states, but there have been some conflicts elsewhere as well: Bolivia—Chile (where Bolivia previously had access to the sea through Chile); Zambia—Angola/Namibia; Zimbabwe—Mozambique; Israel—Jordan/Egypt: where all parties have been fighting for, and now protect, their access to the Red Sea.

Conflicts over sovereignty of territory to gain access to resources in the territory, or within EEZs in the territory

Examples are numerous and distributed all over the world, but apparently to a somewhat greater extent in the southwest Pacific than elsewhere. Islands are often the subject of such conflicts, often to gain access to potential oilfields, sea-bed minerals or fishery resources—for example: Argentina—Chile: the Beagle Channel islets (for access to oil / fish); China—Taiwan—Japan: the Senakaku group of islands (for oil); China—Taiwan—Vietnam—Malaysia—Philippines: the Spratly Islands (for oil); China—Vietnam: the Parcels (for oil). Conflicts over deltas are: India—Bangladesh: agriculturally productive areas and potential oilfields, but also a possibility for expansion of inhabited areas and potential oilfields, and in addition a possibility for expansion of inhabited areas. Conflicts over coastal territory: Civil war in Nigeria where Nigeria would not let go of the land of the rich oilfields in southeast Nigeria to form an independent state, Biafra.

(4) the Continental Shelf; (5) Exclusive Fishing Zone; and (6) Exclusive Economic Zones.

Coastal areas also provide access to resources in the oceans. In 1988, global fishery catches amounted to some 85 million tons (which is still 15 million tons below the FAO estimates of a global sustainable yield of 100 million tons). During recent decades, catches have increased substantially. Currently, output is quickly approaching FAO estimates of maximum global sustainable yields, which may well lead to an increase in disputes over existing fishery resources.[7]

In addition to conflicts over access to resources, coastal areas are arenas for multiple uses that are often in competition with each other. Coastal areas have been used for industrial waste and sewage disposal, fishing, aqua- and agricultural activities, recreation, location of industries and housing, transportation, conservation of nature, research, and military strategic pur-

Nuclear Wastes

Examples of radioactive pollutants from nuclear tests are Muroroa Atoll; Christmas Island Atoll; Eniwetok and Bikini Atoll in the Pacific and Monte Bello Island off North-West Australia). Examples of discharges of low-level nuclear waste from coastal nuclear plants are by Japan (1955–68), and South Korea (1968–72), in northern parts of the Pacific. Additional examples are Japan's dumping in the Marianas Trench up to 1981, and the former Soviet Union's dumping in the Barentz Sea close to Novaja Semlja. In the future, we may expect a large increase in industrial nuclear waste from nuclear power plants, which may quickly cause ocean contamination if deposited. Several nuclear power plants have been built in coastal areas and use ocean water for cooling (which creates a risk of releasing radioactive elements into the environment). Transuranics (nuclear fuels), fission products, and induced radioactive species have been detected in seawater and in the ocean biota in most areas, ranging from Baltic herrings to Pacific whales and Antarctic penguins.

poses. Some of the uses are mutually exclusive, but others may complement one another. For example, the protection of a marine reserve which attracts recreational activities and research may lead to sustainable use of resources, which will in turn increase yields, as well as attract the growing 'experience nature and wildlife' brand of tourism (as in the case of protected coral reefs in the Caribbean).

6.4 (B) IECs over incompatible goals over externalities from the use of coastal resources

The combination of increasing coastal industrialization and population growth signals an increase in resource usage, which may generate externalities. In this context, the focus of this study is put on: (1) waste disposal, (2) extractive activities, and (3) aqua- and agricultural activities.

Use of the resource system as a receptor of wastes

Externalities generated from using the ocean as a receptor of wastes will, by definition, be considered to be pollution. The Joint Group of Experts on the Scientific Aspects of Marine Pollution (GESAMP)[8] has given a very strict definition of pollution, which may be used for reference when looking at externalities as a source of IECs:

The introduction by man, directly or indirectly, of substances or energy into the environment resulting in such deleterious effects as harm to living resources, hazards to human health, hindrance to activities, impairing of quality for use of resources and reduction of amenities.[9]

Pollutants have a variety of origins, but in this section (B) only the following will be considered: (a) pollutants produced by industrial and nuclear activities and from sewage outlets within the area itself; and (b) pollutants from offshore activities, transported to the shores by currents, tides, and waves. Pollutants may be arranged into sub-groups: hazardous wastes, hydrocarbons, sewage, agricultural fertilizer nutrients, sediments and biological pollutants (see Box 18 on nuclear wastes).

Hazardous wastes in coastal waters comprise one of the most serious health threats resulting from externalities of resource usage. Hazardous substances include those which are carcinogenic (causing cancer), mutagenic (producing mutations), and teratogenic (causing birth defects). Several hazardous substances may have more than one of these properties, and are considered hazardous due to their persistence (in a physical, chemical and biological context), toxicity, accumulation in biological materials or in sediments, and biochemical transformation producing harmful compounds (see Table 7)[10]. Introduction of such substances, either through deliberate dumping or through untreated outlets, often generates externalities for other systems and degrades biotic resources.

Oil pollution in the marine environment originates mainly from oil tankers, and is mostly avoidable pollution such as

that caused by washing out ballast tanks, in contrast to accidental spills or blow-outs from offshore drilling. Several West African countries have experienced deteriorating coastal environments caused by oil slicks originating from passing tankers; this is an issue of liability conflict. Of particular significance are microslicks, sea surface hydrocarbon microlayers that cover the coastal waters. These microslick films can act as an accumulation layer for trace materials (for example, heavy metal ions, vitamins, amino acids, DDT residues, or PCBs).

In addition to sewage from direct outlets, sewage circulating back to shore after having been dumped from barges just a few

Table 7. Some pollution sources and their effects on coastal environments

Activity or substance	Major Human Source	Potential effects
Hazardous wastes	Industry, sewage, nuclear activity	Contamination
Hydrocarbons	Shipping; industry, urban runoff, sewage	Contamination, oiling of animals, seafood tainting
Nutrients	Sewage, industry, aquaculture and agriculture	Eutrophication
Sediments	Degraded hinterlands, dredging	Inhibits biotic regeneration, causes anoxic conditions
Biological pollutants	Aquaculture, shipping, artificial channels	Disturbed ecosystems, changed yields

Oil spill in the Atlantic Ocean

biota (particularly coral reefs) and may cause anoxic conditions due to lack of light for photosynthesis. These sediments have, however, not yet been found to cross international borders, and conflicts must basically be considered to be at a local or national level. Fishing is also putting strain on the environment, and if the sustainable threshold (i.e., the level at which the species can reproduce optimally) is exceeded, there is a risk of loss of yields in the long run. Blast fishing (that is, using dynamite to kill or stun fish) is still being used by local fishermen in North Africa, the Caribbean and southeast Asia, even though it is prohibited. It destroys entire ecosystems, such as coral reefs, and degrades the resource system to such an extent that future yields may become impossible. Decreasing stocks may increase international competition, as fish is considered to be a vital source of food in many regions.

Extractive activities that surpass sustainable yields lead to loss of biodiversity. Several entire coastal ecosystems and particular species are threatened with extinction (for example, the coral seagrass mangrove ecosystem in some tropical coastal areas, and marine mammals such as dugongs, etc.). In both the Barentz Sea and the Mediterranean, over-exploitation has caused a change in species composition, leading to an overall decline in production, or a shift towards use of economically less valuable species. Coral reef ecosystems are particularly vulnerable to this degradation, as a coral community needs hundreds of years to grow and develop. Corals are exploited commercially despite the proven relationship between coral communities, seagrass beds and mangrove ecosystems which provide nursing grounds for more than 50% of tropical species. Mangrove forests are also

miles off the coast represents a major problem. Phosphates and nitrates in sewage are vital nutrients, but in excessive amounts, fertilizers and organic matter cause an overproduction of algae, which leads to eutrophication. Over-production of a particular type of 'killer' alga gives rise to the so-called Red Tides. This leads to anoxic conditions where nothing can live, although a regeneration may be possible after some time. A special characteristic of sewage is its tendency, in tropical waters, to promote the growth of coral-smothering algae, which may lead to the loss of many pollution-intolerant species of coral.

Extractive activities
Extraction of gravel, sand, and other minerals in coastal areas has been increasing, partly due to relatively easy access. These activities may, however, cause increased beach erosion as bottom formations are changed. Sediments from dredging operations inhibit the regeneration of several

threatened with extinction in some areas. Deforestation due to agricultural activity in coastal areas has led both to increased soil salinity and to erosion. This possible loss of biodiversity must be considered a threat to the common heritage, and is therefore a global issue.

Aqua and agricultural activities

Biological pollution—that is, the introduction of non-native species—is rarely discussed, although it is a major contributor to the degradation of biotic resources, and is a potential source of IECs. The introduction of new species (which suddenly find themselves in altered living conditions, without predators, parasites or competitors) may severely affect food chains, stability, and biodiversity. After the opening of the Suez Canal in 1869, several changes in ecosystems were detected in the Red Sea and the Mediterranean Sea. Besides accidental, marine transportation-related sources of biological introduction (for example, through ballast waters, sea level canals, biofouling from vessels and mobile drilling rigs), non-native species may also be introduced deliberately, as in the case of clumps of transplanted oysters. The question of liability may arise in cases of proof of loss of biological productivity.

Aquacultural activities may pollute in other ways as well. Aquacultural farms have been the source of diseases spreading over larger areas and crossing borders. This, and the use of pharmaceutical products in these artificial environments, has in some cases changed the natural balance between species, thereby altering the ecosystem and affecting potential yields. Coastal plains are used for agricultural activities, due to their potential for high yields. Excessive use of artificial nutrients and pesticides causes

run-off into marine environments, acting in much the same way as sewage or other forms of hazardous waste.

6.5 (C) Externalities from the use of other resources

IECs related to externalities caused by use of other types of resources are exemplified by pollution (whether river-transported or airborne), and climatic changes (in particular sea-level rise).

Many manufacturing industries are located in coastal settings, but in many coastal regions, as in the Mediterranean, river-transported or airborne pollution from hinterland activities is the main source of pollution. Most hazardous wastes, such as heavy metals, originate from these sources, and can cause IECs. International environmental conflicts may also occur as a result of cross-boundary transfers of pollution from hinterlands causing local biotic degradation in estuaries and lagoons. For example, hydrocarbons emitted from refineries and motor vehicles have been found to be a major contributor to pollution in some regions. This is also the case with sewage and fertilizer nutrients which stem directly from the sewage systems of cities.

A commonly-discussed issue is the deforestation of hinterlands causing transport of sediments in rivers. Sediments reaching coastal areas have the positive effect of creating new land, but also have a strong negative effect on ecosystems, since large amounts of sediments crossing buffer zones along the coast have a detrimental effect on the potential biological yields of the area (as in the case of the Ganges River).[11]

In some cases (as in the River Nile), dam construction has stopped the natural inflow of nutrients to coastal waters, causing degradation of biotic resources. Dams also prevent the transport of sediments, disturbing the natural balance between sediments brought into the coastal areas, and thus leading to coastal erosion (as discussed in Chapter Five).

The case study described later in this chapter looks at IECs over pollution from land-based sources in the Mediterranean region, and provides an example of conflicts arising from externalities created by the use of resources outside the coastal area.

Potential climatic changes—Sea-level rise

One of the likely implications of potential climatic changes is sea-level rise. It is difficult, however, to identify IECs caused solely by sea level rise, since the changes may take place over several decades. Permanent global climatic change is considered to be the main cause of rising sea levels, excluding short-term meteorological changes. While geostatic events and tidal shifts are important when considering the local effects of sea level rise, they are not significant in a general sense.[12]

The Intergovernmental Panel on Climate Change (IPCC) recently issued a report which concludes that a one-metre rise in sea level over the next century could be likely, and the rate of rise implied in the business-as-usual scenario is three to six times faster than that experienced over the last 100 years.[13]

The prospect of such an increase in the rate of sea level rise has major significance for many low-lying coasts subject to permanent and temporary inundation, salt intrusion, cliff and beach erosion, and other deleterious effects.

By the year 2100, IPCC's worst case scenario predicts a sea level rise of 110 cm, whereas the best case scenario predicts a rise of 31 cm. Scenarios compiled by other sources vary to an even greater degree, ranging from Hoffmann's estimates of a 28 to 230 cm rise, to Oerlemans' estimate of a 56 cm rise by the year 2100.[14] As a mid-level point, a scenario of a 100 cm rise in sea level over the next century is generally

Figure 9. Potential global sea-level rise

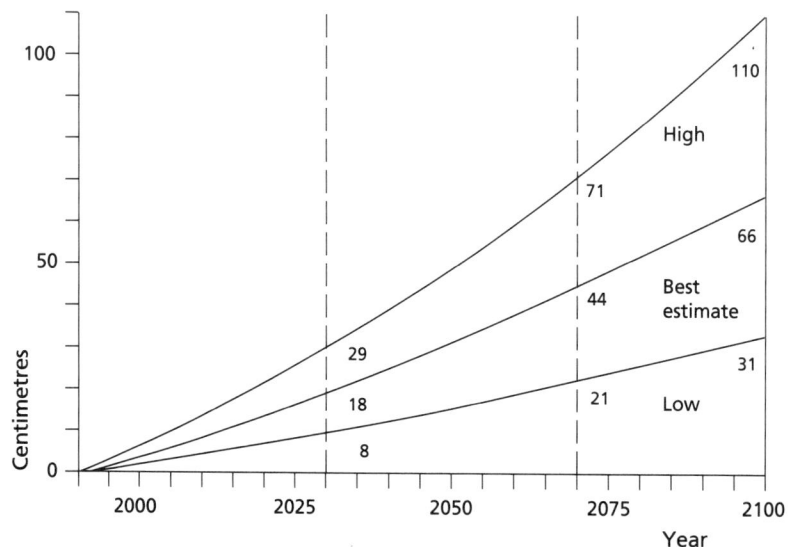

Potential global sea-level rise, 1990–2100, for policy scenario 'business as usual'
Redrawn from IPCC (WMO/UNEP), 1991

accepted, as reflected in the Second World Climate Conference,[15] although this may be too conservative as it does not take into account the impact of Antarctic ice shelf melting.

A rise in sea level of approximately one metre would potentially affect land up to the five-metre contour line, if storm surges and the effects of salt water intrusion along river mouths are taken into account. Under such circumstances, the area that would be affected is five million square kilometres (about three percent of the global land area, representing one third of the world's total crop-land). The map of the world would effectively have to be re-drawn, and many densely populated areas (with a total population of one billion) could be flooded.[16]

The implications of such a change would be most severe for delta areas, as they are generally densely populated. Erosion would be less severe in areas where a sufficient transfer of sediments from the hinterlands takes place.

Coastal plains would be affected in the same way as the deltas. Beaches could be moved and narrowed, and inlets, bays and estuaries could be enlarged and deepened. Coastal lagoons, too, could become larger and deeper, but the enclosing barriers might transgress landwards onto them. Many industrial plants and some nuclear installations are located in low-lying areas (for example on the East Coast of the United States and in England). Low-lying areas on coastal plains on arid coasts, such as *sebkhas*, would be flooded, forming permanent lagoons. In areas with gradients between 1:60 and 1:80, a one metre sea level rise could bring about a coastline regression of 60—80 metres. This could greatly affect the outermost areas of developing nations like

Sri Lanka, Maldives, Tuvalu, Kiribati, and other island states of the South Pacific. Even inundation from a moderate global sea level rise could have serious implications for the populous river deltas and coastal areas such as Egypt, Bangladesh, India, China, and Indonesia.[17] Coastal areas of such industrialized nations as the United States, Japan, Denmark and the Netherlands, would also be threatened, although these nations would be better-equipped to meet the challenges than developing countries. Of 40 selected nations worldwide, sea level rise was already found to be a major cause of coastal erosion for all, and it is expected to be the most significant natural cause of erosion in the future.

Deepening coastal waters would increase wave heights during storm surges, further eroding the beach profile. Changes in near shore beach profiles may cause a build-up of expanded wave action. The coral reefs in the southern hemisphere may not be able to provide the same buffer effect against waves as they do today. Coastal flora and fauna would be affected because it is doubtful that coral reefs could grow at the same pace as the rise in sea level, and it is more likely that the reefs will not receive enough sunlight and would therefore eventually die. The seagrass beds could face the same problems as the reefs, when the reefs no longer offer them protection.

Along karst limestone coastlines in particular, salt water intrusion would be experienced primarily in estuaries and aquifers. Fresh water in estuaries dilutes salt water, and is therefore important for fish, shrimp, oysters and other biota in the complex ecology. As fresh water continues to be withdrawn from rivers upstream, and as population tends to increase in coastal areas, the amount of accessible fresh water could decrease, causing further landward salination. Drinking water would be affected, particularly in those regions where there is already a shortage of clean drinking water.

Many urban areas could face increased problems with drainage systems. Agricultural areas in the coastal plains might have to find new drainage solutions to limit the possibility of increased salination.

It is likely that there would be large amounts of mud and sediments reaching productive waters due to the elevated sea level. As mentioned, this would affect the penetration of light which is needed for photosynthesis.

Economic and social implications of a potential rise in sea level

Physical changes caused by a potential sea-level rise would have clear social and economic impacts. Drinking water in many coastal plains could be contaminated, in which case there would be a need for new techniques to purify the water before consumption. This could also result in rising costs caused by the need to construct more desalination plants for drinking water. The rising saline water tables also could affect crop yields, both in terms of the amount and the type of crop that could adapt to the more saline conditions. The economic value of land would then change, leading to additional social changes. Due to the fact that marine and coastal resources may become more important economically, local and national economies would have to be reshaped. Some nations, with a potential for intensification of agricultural production encouraged by increased pay-off from investments, might become more influential, due to the more strategic position of food production. This might fuel a new set of

IECs, since the nations' relative power bases might be altered.

Migration from degraded areas and resettlement of communities could result in social changes. Many societies may lose younger and more active members, as they attempt to make a living in non-affected areas. This must, however, be seen in relation to the general trend of migration towards the coasts and not just to urban areas (see discussion on Environmental Refugees in Chapter Nine).

The economic costs of transforming former agricultural land into maricultural farms could go far beyond the capacity of many poor people who currently live in these areas, and who would have to move. A new structure of ownership might appear. The greatest economic costs would be connected to the protection of urban areas, and to the construction of dykes and dams in an attempt to minimize the effect of the rising sea. Only the larger and economically better-off cities would be able to afford larger constructions, putting increased economic strains on the surrounding regions to meet the costs. The loss of productive crop-land might affect the global food situation. The poor would suffer the most as they would be driven off productive land, and would experience difficulties in meeting increased costs. In the poor coastal regions of the South, migration might be the only solution—and might eventually become transboundary. This is particularly true in the South Pacific, where the very existence of nations could be threatened by inundation from the sea; the Maldives may actually disappear due to a combination of sea level rise and the increased erosion resulting from it. Some developing countries might be able to transform the lower parts of their coastal areas into productive aquacultural areas—for example, shrimp farms—even if affected by salination. Alternatively, they might be able to change the crops to more salt / brackish-water-resilient varieties, that biotechnology may be able to develop in the near future. This might require significant investment, but far less than that which would be needed to construct barriers against the sea (as for instance the dykes in the Netherlands), which would probably only be possible for the wealthiest nations.

6.6 Case study:
The Mediterranean Region

The Mediterranean region presents a unique opportunity to study IECs related to utilization of a common resource by many nations. The early start on regime formation designed by UNEP is an excellent example of the limitations and opportunities in conflict management and in the implementation of agreements. In this discussion, the Mediterranean region is analysed from the standpoint of the negotiations on management of pollutants from land-based sources (LBS). This case is an example where clearly discernable polarized positions and interests of the parties are visible during the negotiations for the management of the land-based sources of pollution.

The populations of the 18 nations situated on the coast of the Mediterranean are socio-culturally, politically, strategically, and economically divergent. They share fragile coastal environments of great morphological and biological diversity. This diversity may be a basis for conflicting interests in many areas, and undoubtedly affects the way the various nations look upon environmental issues. The economic and socio-cultural differences between the European and African continents bring in a North–South dimension which makes study of the pattern of interests compelling, and extremely complex. A third group of nations, the Middle East, increases the complexity of the factors leading to IECs. Efforts to harmonize economic growth with protection of the environment have proven to be an important additional factor in the political and social stability of the region.

Figure 10. The Mediterranean Region

Analytical approach

The analytical framework for this discussion is, as in the other thematic cases, based on putting the ABC-model into operation (Chapter Four). Analysis comprises a more in-depth identification of the individual demands through focusing on positions, interests and relationships. The demand system will be seen in relation to the natural resource system, which in this case refers to the coastal resources in the Mediterranean.

Other factors which could affect the relationship between the demand and natural resource systems (such as the economic system, production system, and political/sociocultural factors), will be brought in to clarify and explain the dynamics. Finally, an effort is made to draw conclusions which could indicate replicable features of the conflict management mechanisms undertaken by UNEP.

The formation of the Mediterranean Action Plan

As early as the 1970s, there was an increasing awareness of the environmental problems faced by the industrialized nations of the Mediterranean Region. In an attempt to address these problems through its Regional Seas Programme, UNEP created the Mediterranean Action Plan (MAP) as the first of ten successive regional seas action plans. MAP has subsequently been deemed a success story of prevention and resolution of IECs related to coastal management. For this reason, it has been used as a model in both negotiations and international agreements. But how successful has it actually been, and in which ways? MAP has been analysed and extensively discussed, but not from the perspective of conflicting interests and management efficiencies.

Part of the international legislative basis for MAP is The Protocol for the Protection of the Mediterranean Sea against Pollution from Land-Based Sources, which was established in 1980 (hereafter referred to as the LBS-Protocol) consisting of a legal text and technical annexes. Since land-based pollution is considered the main degrading factor in the region, the focus of the analysis will be on this initiative as a measure of MAP's achievements. The LBS-Protocol is currently in the process of implementation and has been characterized as a milestone in negotiations on the Mediterranean environment.

The history of the development of MAP clearly underlines the importance of actual problem definition in any conflict resolution process. As outlined below, the early perception of the problems does not correspond with the problems as defined today. UNEP's struggle to determine the cause of the problems must be seen in the light of historical events.

As early as the beginning of the 19th century, researchers observed extensive organic pollution near Trieste and Marseilles due to expanding industrial activity. It was not until the 1960s, with increasing tanker traffic at sea, that the Mediterranean states were facing hard evidence of pollution in the form of tar balls on their beaches. Except for these tar balls, there was little scientific evidence of environmental deterioration, although the popular scientific accounts were effective in increasing concern about pollution.[18] *The Economist* maintained that the Mediterranean's ecological balance was not seriously disturbed until the early 1960s. It argued that "over-population, the tourism boom, industrial development and maritime irresponsibility were combining to turn it into a dead sea". The oil industry had to take the blame for much

Box 19

Bombing of the Italian Consulate in 1973

The Italian chemical firm Montedison was regularly dumping titanium dioxide wastes from its plant in Scarlino into the sea outside territorial limits between Corsica and Tuscany.

Titanium dioxide, being dumped as a 'red mud', was easily detected by the fishermen, as it discolours the water. The fishermen feared that it would harm the fish, and rioted to protest against it. Then, in 1973, the Italian consulate (in France) was bombed. A French court awarded the fishermen US$ 13 million in compensation, and criminal charges were brought against Montedison executives, but overturned by a Leghorn court in 1976. In 1974 the Scarlino plant installed new waste-processing equipment, and now wastes are stored on land.

of the degradation, with the tar balls as the most visible pollutant. Soon, however, some of the external effects of other industrial activities received more attention as well. There were even some overt conflicts of interest over the use of the sea. (See Box.[19.])

The effects of pollution became increasingly obvious to the public. In 1973, Italy was the hardest hit; a cholera epidemic struck Naples and southern Italy with 325 reported cases and 25 deaths. The source of the epidemic was traced to mussels contaminated with raw sewage.[20] And in 1974, Genoa closed 34 of its beaches during the tourist season. The transnational problems of maritime pollution, loss of marine habitats, and over-harvesting of such migratory species as tuna and swordfish, were placed at the top of the political agenda.

At the same time, more scientific arguments and research were produced in 1970. The Mediterranean was acknowledged by the IOC's (Intergovernmental Oceanographic Commission) Group of Experts on Long-term Planning as potentially 'severely threatened' by pollution. IOC also tried to launch a joint research programme, Cooperative Investigations in the Mediterranean (CIM), but this effort was turned down by most of the nations of the region because it was seen as an excuse for carrying out research for the benefit of external interests. Some even argued that CIM was a front for the Soviet Union or the US to gain data for sea-bed exploitation and submarine activities, and that the whole affair was symptomatic of an attempt by outside powers to use marine scientific research as a cover for resource exploitation and intelligence gathering.[21]

In 1972, FAO's General Fisheries Council for the Mediterranean (GFCM) issued a report, State of the Marine Pollution in the Mediterranean, which stated that most pollution was largely caused by, and affected, the industrialized North.[22] These

findings led FAO to prepare its follow-up report, 'Guidelines which Could Serve as a Basis for the Drafting of a Framework Convention on the Protection of the Marine Environment Against Pollution in the Mediterranean', for regional discussions (in December 1973, February 1974, and May 1974). However, it was soon argued that the scope of problems was too broad for FAO. The LBS-Protocol was signed by the parties at the meeting of the plenipotentiaries in 1980, and enacted in 1983.[23]

In August 1974, after receiving a formal request from Spain, UNEP informed FAO that it would convene a meeting of governmental representatives to discuss a framework convention, based on FAO's consultations. By September, a joint workshop on pollution in the Mediterranean, with scientific representatives (from UNEP, IOC, GFCM, and ICSEM) was established. This workshop produced an extensive list of pollutants and sources of pollution, creating a platform for many of the discussions that were to take place in the negotiations. The workshop also identified several problems of pollution: lack of sewage treatment and its consequences; lack of industrial discharge treatment (primarily transported by rivers); pesticides transmitted by run-off and atmospheric fallout; oil pollution from ships; and pathogenic organisms.[24] Since 1972, these workshops on pollution in the Mediterranean have been scheduled twice a year. An action plan was established at the Intergovernmental Meeting on the Protection of the Mediterranean Sea against Pollution on January 28, 1975 in Barcelona. This Mediterranean Action Plan (MAP) was introduced by UNEP's Executive Director, and the Parties were asked to approve a framework convention to be adopted at the meeting of plenipotentiaries in Barcelona.

The Convention on Protection of the Mediterranean Sea against Pollution (hereafter referred to as the Convention) was ratified by 16 signatories in Barcelona in 1975 and was enacted in 1976. MAP and the Convention provided the framework and conditions for several protocols, including the LBS-Protocol. Offers by France and the EEC to draft such a protocol were rejected so as to avoid bias, or suspicion of bias. UNEP played the role of Third Party in the negotiations and prepared a draft protocol in co-operation with the World Health Organization (WHO)[25] based on monitoring, scientific findings, EEC-directives, and the Paris Convention on Protection of the Marine Environment against Land-Based Sources of Pollution.[26]

The legal framework was built upon well-accepted principles. First, two general principles of international law were applicable to pollution from land-based sources entering the marine environment:

1. The principle of prohibition of the injurious use of territory is supported in Principle 21 of the Stockholm Declaration (see extensive discussion in Chapter Three).[27]

2. The principle of good neighbourliness (as doctrines c and d discussed in Chapter Five) implies a more positive obligation for co-operation (although basically being used in the law of international river systems, this does not imply that it may not be applied in cases of land-based pollution at the coast).

Second, there are some international agreements and guiding principles that may be applied, such as the Convention of the High Seas requiring regulations to prevent pollution from pipes.[28] The 1972 Stockholm Declaration also states in Principle 6:

"The discharge of toxic substances or of other substances and the release of heat must be halted in order to ensure that serious or irreversible damage is not inflicted upon ecosystems..."[29]

Among post-Stockholm conventions, the United Nations Convention on the Law of the Sea (UNCLOS) forms a major global approach to controlling pollution of the marine environment, including pollution from land-based sources.[30] States have the obligation to protect and preserve the marine environment, and the contracting states are to take action to prevent, reduce and control pollution of the marine environment from any source.

Identification of conflicts

The Mediterranean region may be noted primarily for its political, social, economic, and environmental diversity. This leads to similarly divergent demands which sometimes cause conflicting interests regarding the use of the sea and its surrounding shores. The divergent interests have increasingly come into conflict with each other over the last 20 years as the pressure on the environment exceeded an important threshold at which not all interests could be fulfilled independently of each other. The need for managing a shared resource, the Mediterranean Sea, became clear. The first question to be raised deals with Europe versus North Africa over the Mediterranean, where the latter declared a fundamental right to economic growth through industrialization, free of extra costs due to environmental restrictions (such as using the Mediterranean as a recipient for wastes). The Europeans proclaimed an urgent need to improve the quality of the Mediterranean through international legislation. During the negotiations on the LBS-Protocol, some particular points illustrated these conflicting interests:

—How clean should the Mediterranean Sea be?
—What were acceptable environmental standards?
—What pollutants were to be regulated?
—What should the timetables be for implementing the agreed standards?

The element of technology transfer permeated discussion of the above questions, bringing in the additional question of which charges were reasonable and who was to pay.

Conflicting interests associated with the use of the Mediterranean were, at a practical level, manifested as: tourism and biotic resource quality and quantity, versus using the sea as a waste receptor for cutting the costs of the industrialization process. In broad terms, the North African states argued that the Mediterranean should be considered as a sink and a receptor of pollution for their industrialization process just as it had been for the Europeans for so long, whereas the Europeans argued for an international legal framework (using EC standards) for controlling pollution in the Mediterranean.

Conflict analysis

Natural resource system

The Mediterranean can be defined as an open system, influenced by a set of external geophysical factors.

The hot, dry summers and mild, moist winters affect both sea and land. The high degree of evaporation from the sea causes a higher than average sea water salinity. The evaporated water is replenished through several river systems pouring into the Mediterranean as well as through direct precipitation. 25% of incoming water enters through the Straits of Gibraltar. Due to the Mediterranean's enclosed nature, and the undersea ridge from Sicily to Tunisia, the circulation of potential nutrients from the deeper waters is minimal (due to restrictions of tidal movements and currents). The Mediterranean is a so-called 'nutrient starved' sea, and this is a controlling factor for the extent of sea life.[31]

The fisheries seem to have reached sustainable yields a long time ago. In 1973–75 the total fish catch was 1,268,000 tons, whereas the estimated sustainable yield was 1,090,000—1,410,00 tons, with 78.5% of these catches made by the Europeans.[32] Along the North African coast, the local fishermen are still using blast fishing in some places.[33] Such fishing practices as drift netting or trawling have proven just as harmful. Trawling destroys sparsely distributed sea-bed vegetation, and a seaweed of particular importance, the 'Ocean Posidonia', unique to Mediterranean ecosystems, is threatened with extinction.[34] This plant has fruit and flowers, it forms submarine grasslands, and it provides protection for hundreds of species of alga and several thousand marine species. In addition, each square metre of leaf provides 10 litres of oxygen per day, and the annual production of organic material is 2030 tonnes /ha/year.

Some migratory species, like tuna and swordfish, are threatened, and the sardine and anchovy fisheries outside Egypt were devastated when the High Aswan Dam reduced the water flow, cutting off the vital nutrients which the river transported.

The adjacent land may be characterized as barren; as much as 64% of the land of most nations in North Africa is wilderness.[35] The lack of water is the main reason for the low land biomass productivity. For instance, in Egypt, the main productive area for agriculture is the Nile Delta, now threatened with salt-water inundation and increased coastal erosion, mainly due to damming at High Aswan. Irrigation is used to varying degrees in the countries of the Mediterranean, but this affects the entire freshwater outlet situation. In Israel there has been a serious lowering of the water tables caused by groundwater being pumped out for irrigation. Increasing tourism, industrialization and urbanization significantly worsen this situation in the region, in spite of increased recycling of waste water.

Due to coastal development, the littoral areas have been facing degradation, since industrial development is basically located on the coast.[36] Wetlands, which are of great ecological importance (in particular for migratory birds), as well as the forests and the Mediterranean Maquis are being depleted.

There are some significant mineral sources, in the form of oil and gas fields, in Libya, Algeria, and Tunisia. Even though the sources are limited, there is still some mining activity.

Demands on the natural resource system

The relationship between the European and North African countries in the region is characterized by a history of colonialism and struggles for independence (with many North-South trade patterns). The long history of wars and disputes between the various nations are linked to conflicts over resource allocation; for example Libya vs. Malta; and Italy vs. Tunisia over the median line in the sea; Spain vs. Morocco; and Albania vs. Yugoslavia over fisheries; Turkey vs. Greece over access to marine-situated hydrocarbons; Libya vs. Tunisia over vast oil resources; and several political and ethnic disputes and military clashes along the Lebanon-Syria-Israel coast.

Box 20

The Actors

The opposing parties can generally be described as the North, that is, the industrialized nations of the region; and on the other side, the South, or the developing countries. There are, however, other organizations more indirectly involved, such as the EC. The parties can therefore be described as follows:

The European states include France, Italy, and Monaco which constitute 43.3% of the regional population, and 65.6% of the regional GNP.[37] Some 70% of the Mediterranean Sea Region's manufacturing industry is located in France, Italy and Spain.[38] The European position was most forcefully argued by France and Italy.

The North African states include Algeria, Egypt, Lebanon, Libya, Morocco, Syria, and Tunisia. These countries (plus Albania) make up 28.8% of the region's population and eight percent of the regional GNP. In the early phases, Algeria and Egypt were the strongest opponents of the MAP, including the LBS-Protocol.

The middle income nations of Cyprus, Greece, Israel, Malta, Spain, Turkey, and former Yugoslavia, comprise 35.2% of the regional population and 26.4% of the regional GNP. Yugoslavia, Turkey and Israel put themselves in a more intermediate, yet active position, whereas the others expressed little interest.

The EC played an important indirect role in the negotiations. Through its member states (France in particular), the EC was able to reach several of its goals. The EC already had a strong established legislation, and wished to take an equally strong line on environmental issues, but lacked a comprehensive environmental platform, which made direct involvement in negotiations difficult. The EC eventually adopted MAP's initiative, but since specific measures had yet to be agreed on and adopted, implementation has been slow. Part of the problem is that the EC and MAP use completely different parameters, (for instance monitoring systems), which makes comparisons difficult, although the EC standards are considered to be much less comprehensive. MAP staff members nevertheless see it as an important step that the need for standardization has been acknowledged.

Positions and interests

A variety of underlying demands are associated with the actors involved. The distinction has been made between North and South, but great variations exist among nations within these groups (see Box 20).

Formally, the Europeans demanded a regionally accepted and compatible environmental legislation to protect the Mediterranean's coastal and marine environment. The Europeans' primary interest was to make the international legislation of the region compatible with that of the EC, with which they already had to comply as member states. However, in recognition of the fact that they were the main polluters of the region, they wanted to keep their pollution control efforts to a minimum, due to the possible loss of competition as a result of increased costs of production. This is illustrated by France in 1976 blocking funding for research that might have weakened their position in the negotiations. They also expressed an interest in environmental upgrading, at the same time restricting information on environmental status. They feared that negative publicity might affect their tourist industry and their exports of aquatic biotic resources, e.g., fish and oysters.

They wanted the programme to be restricted to information exchange, but with limited distribution of data to the public (see box). There were certainly opportunities for the Europeans to export high technology monitoring equipment and expertise to North Africa (and others) when the Convention was in place.

The North African states demanded economic growth through industrialization without limitations, extra costs, and restrictions on exported goods resulting from environmental protection measures. The Algerian president expressed it simply: "If environmental protection means less bread for my people, then I'm against it." As an example of this viewpoint, Algeria slowed down discussions in 1978 by objecting to every paragraph and questioning previously made compromises.[39]

Even though most interests are connected to the negotiations concerning the environmental management of the sea, others are connected to the negotiation process itself. Algeria, France, Israel and the Arab States were able to sit around the same table to work on resolving common problems. The MAP negotiations were also used to establish more friendly diplomatic links. Other 'hidden' interests in the negotiations were displayed by some of the countries, who used environmental co-operation as leverage to assert an open foreign policy.

The main interest of the North Africans

was to attain economic growth through industrialization; but also, by developing tourism, to cover their needs for foreign currency. As the pollution problems of the Mediterranean were believed to be collective, the North Africans wanted to use this as leverage to push for 'environmentally sound technology' at a 'reasonable price', or they would pull out of the negotiations. It was, however, very important that any pollution control measures should not affect their industrialization policies or divert economic resources from industry.

It was also important to avoid stricter requirements on production, as this might exclude some North African products from the markets in Europe. Increased costs of industrialization in order to meet changed environmental standards would affect their competition in a negative way and were to be avoided. The complex picture of the adversarial positions, as well as factors which are presumed to contribute to resolution are shown in Table 8.

Conflict management

The negotiation process leading to regime formation (both the Convention and the associated protocols) managed to address several deep-rooted conflicting interests. Overall, five main areas of conflict were visible during the negotiations (Table 8):

1. Controversy over list of substances to be covered by LBS Protocol

The WHO draft had based its list of substances on the existing EC standards and the 1974 Paris Convention for the Prevention of Marine Pollution from Land-Based Sources, but chose only six out of the 20 that were listed by the EC.[40] Spain, Italy, and France insisted on the full EC list. At the request of the North Africans, an addi-

Table 8. Matrix of positions, interests and factors contributing to resolution

	North	South	Factors aiding resolution
Positions	Environmental protection of the sea through a legal framework on pollution from land-based sources	Economic growth through industrialization, free of extra costs due to environmental protection restrictions	
General interests	EC standards quickly implemented	Avoid affecting industrial policy. Avoid additional production costs. Avoid non-tariff barriers	UNEP acting as a third party
Special interests: List of substances	EC list of substances (avoid further limitations)	Avoid listing substances that affect their industry	Scientific knowledge in published UNEP report: IRPTC 1978
Scientific co-operation	Avoid information that would harm tourism and fish exports (having polluted beaches)	Information exchange, increase maritime scientific capabilities (having fairly clean beaches)	Avoid identifying particular nations (regions). Deal with the pollution and not the polluter
Transfer of technology	Sell technical equipment	Receive transfer of technology at lowest possible prices	UNCED negotiations
Channels of transmission	Only cover coastal outlets	River- and airborne pollutants	Scientific knowledge. Rivers fully included. Atmosphere to be implemented later
Installations covered	All installations	Exclude old installations to be replaced	Public pressure to reach agreement
Standards	Emissions standards (UES)	Emissions standards on black-list and ambient standards on grey-list	UES EQQ
Timetables	Deadlines for adoption	Separate timetables for each product considered	Different time schedules for North and South on some substances

111

tional list was made to include radio-nuclides (French nuclear reactors are the main sources of radio-nuclides in the Mediterranean), and some other substances. In disagreement with these points, France once again blocked funding for further research; being by far the largest financial contributor. Italy also objected to the inclusion of some substances not on the EC list. Some North African states were not fully aware of the effects of some of the industrial chemical wastes they produced. Tunisia, for example, first opposed the inclusion of phosphorous and fluorides on the list, as they believed they were a result of their phosphate mining on the coast. A comprehensive technical report on the harmfulness of the substances on the Black and Grey lists, published by UNEP in 1978, convinced the scientists of the need to control these substances and the lists were agreed upon at the June 1979 Geneva meeting.[41]

2. Controversy over which channels of pollution transmission to control

As the substances were more or less agreed upon, this became a contentious issue. At the 1977 Inter-governmental meeting in Athens, Italy and France were opposed to including river systems.[42] However, the convincing conclusions of the MED-X report put all discussions aside. The scientific data was convincing. At the same meeting, Italy and Spain also opposed the inclusion of airborne pollution because there was no scientific or technical evidence of the effect of this channel.[43] France blocked funding in 1979 for studies of airborne transmission of pollutants to avoid a technical basis for this annex. Tunisia and Yugoslavia were the main proactors for the inclusion, but had to concede to lack of scientific evidence. The

result was that river-transported pollutants were included, along with atmospheric channels as an area of control, but were to be defined some time in the future "...under conditions to be defined in an additional annex to this Protocol and accepted by the Parties in conformity with the provisions of Article 17 of the Convention." [44]

3. Controversy over covering both existing sources and new installations

The Europeans saw the distinction between new installations (Article 6) and existing sources (Article 3) as indispensable. The North Africans, having basically older installations that were about to be replaced by newer ones, argued that many should be excluded from regulation, or at least be subject to a more appropriate time schedule.

4. Controversy over standards for reduction of amounts of permitted release

One of the most disputed issues was how the substances should be controlled. The Europeans preferred emission controls (Uniform Emission Standards (UES)), whereas the North Africans wanted ambient standards (Environmental Quality Objectives (EQO)) to be decisive for regulation. The North Africans argued that their environment was able to sustain more pollution than that of Europe and that this should be taken into consideration when planning the industrialization of the Mediterranean coastal regions of North Africa.

5. Controversy over timetables for implementation

The Europeans wanted deadlines for adoption of measures; for implementation of both the blacklist of substances (to be totally abandoned) and the greylist (to be reduced), in accordance with the deadlines of the EC. The North Africans, on the other hand, argued for separate timetables for each substance. As they were both facing different environmental problems and were industrially at different stages in development, an agreement was made to give room for differentiated timetables among countries within the region. Even though the last four measures for implementation of the Black list were adopted at the 1991 Cairo meeting, there has been a low degree of action to implement agreed measures into national legislation. Only a few of the parties have implemented the measures.

Lessons of experience

While it is impossible to distinguish individual elements which made the conflict management process successful, some general factors seem clear.

1. Several parties maintain that the low degree of implementation is due to lack of financial means. Progress has been made because International Financial Institutions such as EIB, the World Bank and GEF have been involved. The lesson to be learned seems to indicate the unique role of UNEP up to a point where financial institutions can more effectively implement the convention.

2. Simply defining the geographical area to be covered by MAP was important in making negotiations progress at a reasonable rate. A more complex situation might have occurred if, for instance, the former Soviet Union had been a party. This complexity might have led to a higher escalation phase, creating a tendency towards less suitable solutions. Thus, in the geographical definition of the Mediterranean Sea by the LBS-Protocol, the Black Sea states are left out.[45] The definition also excludes non-littoral states with rivers that feed into the Mediterranean (including Portugal, Sudan, and Switzerland) which, although simplifying negotiations, fails to cover some sources of pollution, for instance the heavily polluted Gulf of Izmit and the Sea of Maramara.

3. MAP's programmatic structure (built on long-term research and monitoring, integrated planning, a legal component and institutional arrangements) has made up the framework for most of the negotiations. This structure reflects an effort not only to deal with short-term crisis situations but also to consider the causes of the conflicts and long-term resource management. The 'package deal' goes even further, in the sense that no state could be a party to the Convention without also being a party to at least one protocol, and no state could be a party to any protocol without being a party to the Convention. In this way, implementation of the Convention began, and it was hard not to become a party to the protocols. The negotiations took place on two separate but connected levels: workshops and meetings of experts (which is now the Joint Scientific and Technical Committee) as well as meetings at the diplomatic level (inter-governmental meetings every two years and an elected body called the 'Bureau'). UNEP operated at two levels: with international concern for sustainable development, but also through establishment of scientific relations between nations.

4. UNEP facilitated the negotiations, which enhanced the interest differentiation and led to increased pressure for agreement. UNEP pushed for solutions when progress was slowing down (and when conflicting interests escalated to Phases 3 and 4, i.e., acknowledged and overt behaviour, respectively) by pulling in outside evaluation (e.g., Group of Experts on Atmospheric Pollutants, GESAMP). UNEP was also able to keep the overt conflicts at a level of 'non-co-operation' rather than having any party leave the negotiations (e.g., as in the case of France and Algeria).

5. The negotiations were problem-oriented, minimizing finger-pointing at specific polluters and maximizing problem-solving by focusing on the sources of pollution.

6. The principle of neutrality was sought to be enacted at all levels; drafts for the LBS-Protocol by the EC and France were refused; monitoring equipment was bought from external companies.

7. Implementation seems to have been the most difficult step. In order to encourage the process, biennial inter-governmental meetings were to evaluate the process from the beginning, which may have created an incentive for implementation (no-one wanting to have achieved the least). The North Africans were given a longer time schedule for implementing the grey-list—that is, they could await domestic proof of degradation.

6.7 Conclusions

The LBS-Protocol was completed because the parties made mutual concessions. The North Africans were assured that river-transported and airborne pollution, radioactive wastes and technology transfer would be covered by the Protocol, and that some environmental ambient standards would be included. The Europeans were satisfied by the full EC list of toxic substances to be eliminated, even though France had to accept some ambient standards and some controls exceeding those of the EC directive.

Implementation of the MAP has been low, even though the Coastal Area Management Programme (CAMP) is being launched. CAMP is an effort to implement the entire action plan for the Mediterranean Sea Region at specific locations. The World Bank is currently taking part in these projects, seeing that progress is made. MAP/MEDU is however trying to restrict action to a manageable number of projects.

UNEP played a crucial role in providing a forum for negotiations, and functioned as a broker during the negotiations by assisting in:

i) Identifying the problems and incompatible goals between the various parties.

ii) Bringing the problem identification phase into a format in which the parties were able to address the concerns in a constructive way.

iii) Channelling the process into development of a legal framework.

iv) Successfully bringing in unbiased scientific groups as brokers for several of the most controversial issues.

v) Using financial mechanisms as important means to resolve IECs. The involvement of international financial institutions leads to faster implementation, for instance by financing the CAMP in the North African states. A somewhat low level of co-ordination seems to exist, however, between other UN programmes, financial institutions, and other regional organizations (e.g., the EC and the Arab League).

One of the main obstacles to implementation is the lack of national co-ordination. In addition, financial means have been critical, especially in the compensation of externalities and filling the gaps between 'polluting' and 'environmentally sound' technology (as seen by South and North, respectively).

One of the greatest challenges has been to mobilize the scientific knowledge at the appropriate time and in the correct format. Conflict resolution in the case of the LBS-Protocol is, however, a notable exception in many ways.

Chapter Seven

CASE STUDIES

7 Forestry and biodiversity

THIS CHAPTER examines some of the driving forces behind IECs relating to forestry and biodiversity, and assesses some of their main components through case studies. Case studies outlined include the conflict between Germany and Ethiopia over access to gene-resources; Guinea versus transnational corporations and international NGOs over mining in a 'World Heritage Site'; Djibouti versus Kenya over trading in endangered species; and a broader thematic North–South conflict accompanied by a national conflict (PLANO 2010, in the Brazilian rain forest). A more in-depth case study focuses on conflicts related to the tropical forest shared by Cameroun, the Congo, and the Central African Republic in Central and West Africa.

7.1 Introduction

Forests comprise an essential part of both the natural environment and the domain dominated by human life. The ability of forests to maintain sustainable levels of soil, water and genetic production is of direct relevance to human welfare. Forests provide food and fuel in the form of wood, as well as other resources essential for economic and social development.

The need to protect and maintain or even increase forest productivity in a way conducive to sustainable development is being increasingly recognized at local, national, and international levels. Such development requires production systems to take into account the needs of future generations. With ever-increasing demand on forest resources, attaining such a balance will present greater challenges to decision-makers at all levels.

Extensive degradation of forests is taking place worldwide, which increases the likelihood of conflict. Different societies and countries have divergent models of

Box 21

Biodiversity: Five Key Components

Biological diversity consists of:

Species Diversity: Species diversity has two aspects, usually referred to as 'species richness' and 'species evenness', and both are considered by many societies to be of importance, especially when it comes to endangered species.

Genetic Diversity refers to the variety of genes present within individuals and their propagules (seeds)—both within a single species and between species. Because the likelihood of species survival increases with genetic diversity, a small, isolated remnant of a species can be much more vulnerable to extinction than a genetically diverse population.

Habitat Diversity refers to the variety of biotic and abiotic elements that a species needs in order to survive within the environment of (for example) a river, a lake, a pool, a forest, a tree, or even in different parts of a tree.

Successional Diversity refers to the variety of forests regenerated through a pattern of development called ecological succession (for example, from the open, harsh conditions immediately following a clearing, towards the closed canopy of the mature forest). There may be a number of varieties of "maximum forest," and natural processes such as fires, storms, floods, and landslides may continually prevent a forest from reaching, or remaining at, these later stages. Nevertheless, the different stages (that is, early, middle, and late succession) are identifiable and must all be considered simultaneously in any protection plan.

Landscape Diversity refers to a land area containing many habitats and many different stages in the development of a forest, so that the landscape resembles a mosaic with great spatial and ecological diversity.

development, priorities, and plans for the management of resources—or none at all—which tends to aggravate existing conflicts or generate new ones.

The lack of clear international and national guidelines and effective local means of enforcement commonly results in non-co-ordinated activities by different groups, which often results in damage to forests and to their genetic diversity and productivity. This is particularly evident in developing countries where the logging industry sometimes exploits forests unsustainably on a large scale; landless small-scale farmers clear the land along newly opened forest roads; transnational corporations convert forests into grazing land for cattle ranchers or agricultural industries; and dams flood large areas leading to loss of forests and biodiversity. These processes may in turn trigger migration and resettlement of large sectors of the population.

Relationships between forestry and biodiversity

Population growth and economic activities increase pressure on practically all the ecosystems in the world. The consequences of rapid and large-scale reduction of biological diversity through loss of habitat and species extinction are far-reaching. When focusing on biodiversity as a conflict issue, one must relate this to the management of such varied resource systems as waterways, wetlands and forests, or to single species. However, the single most important factor contributing to loss of biodiversity is the destruction of equatorial and tropical rain forests. These ecosystems, which cover seven percent of the world's area, contain a large portion of the world's total terrestrial genetic biodiversity (see box on definitions of biodiversity).[1]

Critical issues related to forestry

Forests cover about a third of the world's land area, and most of the forests classified as tropical are located in developing countries.

During this century, the total area of forested land in most industrialized countries has stabilized (compared to the heavy deforestation of the last century) and in some cases it has actually increased—primarily due to economic development and subsequent development moves away from using wood as an energy resource.[2]

In contrast, the forested land area in developing countries is continuing to be encroached upon at an increasing rate in some areas. This is the cause of growing concern among the international community, which is seen by many developing countries as impinging on their national sovereignty. Many of these countries now favour rapid exploitation of their forests as a source of funds for promoting rapid eco-

nomic development, as many industrialized countries did a century ago.[3]

Considering this dilemma from a local, national, and global perspective, the critical issue is how to balance protection of the environment with sustainable production goals in a way that will advance social and economic development.

Many of the conflicting statements regarding the increasing rate of destruction of tropical forests have arisen because different definitions of tropical forests have been applied. The classification made by UNEP/FAO makes a distinction between two main types: *closed forests* and *open forests*.[4] A third major type is *shrubland*, with the remaining classification units referred to as *closed forest fallow, open forest fallow* and *plantations* (in other words, replacement vegetation).

The bulk of closed forests are found in Latin America, which has 57% of the world's total. Africa is the continent of savannas and shrubland, containing 66% of the world's open broad-leaved forests, and 71% of its shrublands. The world's tropical rain forests are divided into three large blocks: (1) the Latin American rain forest (centred on the Amazon basin), (2) the African rain forest, centred on the Congo basin, and (3) the Indo-Malayan rain forest (extending through the Malayan Archipelago from Sumatra in the West to Papua New Guinea in the East).

A significant proportion of deforestation also occurs in mountain ecosystems (which may have some tropical elements).[5]

Although the discussion concerning degradation or depletion of forests has so far centred mainly on tropical forests, it is important to stress that forests are also sometimes threatened in industrialized countries, by pollution and even by conflicting land use demands. The main concerns in industrialized countries as far as forest management is concerned are acid rain deposition, competing land use activities (for example agricultural and infrastructure), and trade-offs between economic (that is, jobs) and environmental ('birds and trees') demands.[6]

In addition, conflicts also arise between the need for highly productive monocultural forestry and the need for maintaining biodiversity (sometimes at the expense of productivity).

7.2   Diversity of conflicts

In order to assess IECs, they can be divided into three groups, each exhibiting a different aspect. (See Figure 11):

A—IECs related to access to, control over, and unsustainable use of forests, and to management of biodiversity

B—IECs resulting from externalities caused by using forest resources and/or by managing biodiversity

C—IECs resulting from incompatible goals over externalities, (caused by the use of other resources) which affect forests and/or biodiversity.

7.3 (A) IECs generated by access to, control over, and unsustainable use of forests, and management of biodiversity resources

Agricultural encroachment

Conversion of forests into crop land and pasture is a major cause of deforestation. To a considerable extent, forest clearing is taking place to meet the needs of subsistence farmers. The growing demand for food, due to increased population pressure, directly conflicts with the demand from the international community for forest conservation.

Nearly half of the forest clearing that takes place in the tropics each year is due to shifting cultivation by landless farmers. In Africa, 70% of the deforestation is due to shifting cultivation. In Asia, this figure is 50%. In South America, however, the need for pasture is the main factor leading to accelerated deforestation, and shifting cultivation accounts for only 30%.

Throughout the dry tropics, annual fires spread over huge areas of savanna, where the woody vegetation is of vital importance for securing supplies of food, fuel and fodder

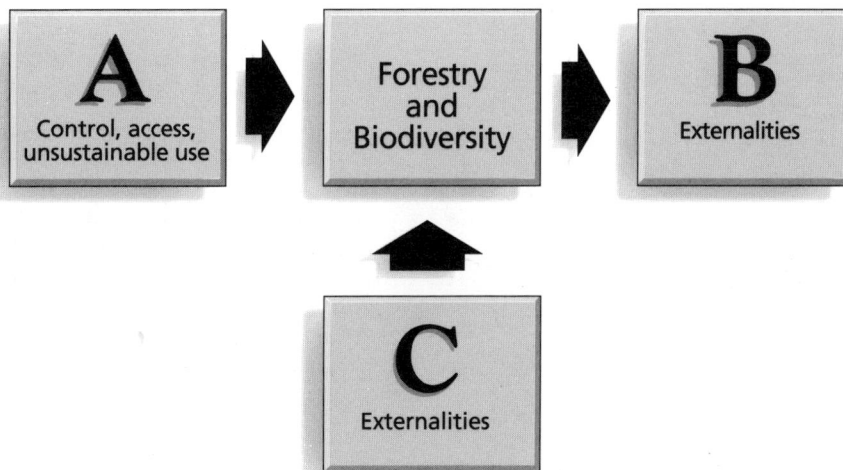

Figure 11.
The ABC model and forestry and biodiversity

A — Control, access, unsustainable use

Forestry and Biodiversity

B — Externalities

C — Externalities

nations is commercial logging. This causes an increasing number of conflicts which raise crucial questions about economic sustainability and environmental protection. At the heart of the problem is the increasing international demand for tropical hardwood, which is 14 to 16 times greater today than in 1950. Yet, the humid tropical forests contribute little more than one tenth of the amount of wood currently consumed worldwide for construction, pulp and paper and industrial purposes. According to the FAO, between 1958 and 1978 approximately one million square kilometres (385,000 square miles) of forestland (mainly in South East Asia and West Africa) was leased for tropical timber extraction.[7] Complicating the problem still further is the fact that in many developing countries, settlers and shifting cultivators enter the forests along logging roads after the log harvest, completing the process of forest clearance after the commercial trunks have been removed. The deforestation caused by subsistence farmers who practice shifting cultivation, and that resulting from timber operations, are therefore closely interlinked.[8]

Tropical forest ecologists insist that no commercial logging of tropical forests has proved to be sustainable from the standpoint of fully conserving the forest ecosystem.[9] This has led to conflicting reactions from both NGOs and native people in the exporting countries, (e.g., the conflict between loggers and native people in Sarawak, Malaysia); as well as from some countries importing tropical timber.

Calls for an end to logging in 'natural' forests by NGOs in South East Asia, have been backed by campaigns in Europe, Australia and the United States for bans on the import of products manufactured from un-

for rural communities, and for sustaining wildlife. Deforestation and loss of biodiversity are themselves sources of IECs. Conflicting interests occur at all levels. On an international level, an IEC may develop where international opinion is on one side (particularly the West, represented by environmental groups); and the developing countries are on the other side. The international community argues for a reduction in deforestation, because of the forest's ability to absorb greenhouse gases and its biodiversity (as expressed in the recent negotiations for the Convention on Protection of Biodiversity and the Framework Convention on Climate Change).

Commercial logging

Another major cause of primary forest destruction in both temperate and tropical

Box 22

Cattle Ranging in Botswana

Botswana has established three national parks, five game reserves, two educational reserves and numerous wildlife management areas, which together make up about 25% of the country's total land area. Some international environmental groups are concerned that, in spite of these conservation areas, Botswana's large animal wildlife population is decreasing, both in terms of number and species diversity.

Among other factors, the domination of the country's large cattle population seems to be one of the main reasons for this decrease in diversity, where most of the rural people are pastoralists.

Together with population growth, the peoples' economic, social and infrastructural needs are expanding. This leads to escalating pressure from an expanding livestock population, which is a major contributing factor to the ongoing loss of wildlife habitat. The black rhinoceros, roan antelope, oribi, waterbuck, sable antelope, klipspringer, white rhinoceros, mountain reedbuck, and puku were all considered to be endangered by the late 1970s, and the situation is even worse now.

This case is an illustration of a conflict of interest between international organizations (represented by international environmental groups) who wish to protect the "global commons", and national needs for economic growth (in this case through export revenue).

sustainable tropical timber resources. In response, Indonesia and Malaysia have entered into an official agreement to campaign jointly *against* calls for a boycott of products from unsustainable tropical timber sources. In the absence of selective bans, or at least accurate labels defining a product's origin and species, various means are considered. Some parties (particularly NGOs) argue that a complete consumer boycott should be implemented. Others, however, promote voluntary certification programmes and/or restrictions of legal imports (which, in turn, are likely to trigger trade disputes).[10]

The high degree of tension surrounding this conflict surfaced at the Tenth World Forestry Congress in Paris when a demonstration by some of the timber exporting states interrupted the negotiation of a reso-

lution text favouring restricted marketing of harvests of unsustainable species.[11]

It is expected that the centre of the world's tropical wood trade will shift from Asia to Latin America, which may increase the future potential for IECs in this region.

Over-harvesting

In the context of IECs relating to biodiversity, over-harvesting may involve the extraction of individual species at rates above their ability to reproduce. Examples are cattle ranging in Botswana, and the so-called 'Rhino case' (see Boxes 22 and 23 respectively).

Access to genetic resources

Plant germ plasm is not yet treated as a commodity. For more than two centuries, scientists from industrialized nations have

Box 23

The Rhino Case

The rhinoceros may be the most endangered large mammal. Recent estimates suggest an 85% decrease in numbers since 1970.

The Rhino Case represents the classic case of market demand arising out of a distant cultural tradition, and an illegal market developing in order to satisfy this demand. There have been two primary markets for rhino horn. North Yemen imported about half of the rhino horn available on the world market during the early 1980s. The handles of traditionally worn daggers (associated in local cultures with success and prestige) are carved out of the horn. Although North Yemen has made the import and use of the horn illegal, demand remains strong (driven by such a long tradition of use). North Yemen has reportedly devised a plan to deal with the problem. While daggers are still being carved from rhino horn, it is hoped that a switch to water buffalo horn will satisfy the market and eliminate the demand for illegal imports.

The second primary market has been Eastern Asia, where rhino horn is traditionally used in Oriental medicine. In most of these countries, importation of rhino horn was lawful until the early- or mid-1980s. Today, import into most countries is illegal, although it is not clear whether actual possession of rhino horn is illegal in all countries.

A major exporter of rhino horn was the country of Burundi, which became a member of CITES in 1988 after great pressure from a number of Western countries to control its trade in endangered species.

A major re-exporter of rhino horn to Eastern Asia is the United Arab Emirates, which, while previously a member of CITES, withdrew its membership in 1988. Because of the high value of the horn, its small size, and the few animals remaining, it has proved difficult to stop the trade while demand remains strong.

freely appropriated genetic plant resources from developing countries for use in plant breeding. The extraction of these materials has not been compensated, based on the widely accepted belief that germ plasm is the 'common heritage of mankind'. This point of view has been challenged by developing countries, raising the question of whether a particular nation's germ plasm should be treated as part of its national property, or not. (As clearly reflected in the negotiations for the Convention for Protection of Biodiversity under UNCED). The proponents of genetic industries argue that a legitimate distinction can be made between germ plasm considered as common heritage and that which is a commodity.

Economists have already started to call bio-technology 'the fourth industrial revolution' because of its promising results in agricultural production, the pharmaceutical industry and in finding substitutes for different kinds of raw materials. In the United States, biotechnology in the 1990s is regarded as a multi-billion dollar industry. The following claims are made:

■ Raw germ plasm cannot be assigned a price because of the lack of prior knowledge as to how useful any particular germ plasm accession will be.
■ Raw germ plasm only becomes valuable

after considerable amounts of time and money have been invested.

■ Collection of germ plasm does not actually deprive a country of anything.

On the other hand, developing countries express fears that they will not benefit from advances in biotechnology, which although originating from their nations, is developed elsewhere (see Box 24—Access to Genetic Resources: Ethiopia vs. Germany). They also fear that industrialized countries may become competitors in the supply of artificially produced germ plasm to the commercial seed industries.

Trade in endangered species

Trade in endangered species represents another cause of IECs, with conflicts present at two levels. Firstly there are conflicts at a local level (such as the local people's need for the income generated by hunting endangered species). The conflict of interest between the locals and the national government often triggers international attention from international NGOs. The second conflict level relates more explicitly to international conflicts, as outlined in the box describing the conflicts between Kenya and Djibouti (see Box 25) and between countries adhering to and not adhering to international agreements (e.g., the rhino case).

In this respect, the most important agreement is the Convention on International Trade in Endangered Species of Wild Fauna and Flora (CITES). This agreement is based on the fundamental principle that all trade affecting species threatened or potentially threatened with extinction must be subject to strict regulation, in order not to further endanger their survival. The contracting states must implement additional laws and regulations, coupled with

Box 24

Access to Genetic Resources: Ethiopia vs. Germany

The management of the "Ethiopian Gene Bank", which was originally constructed and financially supported by the German Development Agency (GTZ), has been controlled by Ethiopia for several years. GTZ funds have, however, continued to provide the hard currency necessary to maintain equipment. In return for the funding, Germany has requested a duplicate sample of Ethiopia's germ plasm, especially barley. Ethiopia agreed to this request more than a decade ago, but has not provided the material. Germany refused to continue financial support to the gene bank until it received its duplicate samples. The last GTZ official left Ethiopia on 15 June 1987, after two years of failed negotiations.

Technically, Ethiopia is prepared to make duplicates available, but points out that its access is to species which it is scientifically impossible to duplicate. Any division of seed samples would leave each party with genetically different material. Behind the dispute is Germany's economic interest in Ethiopia's barley, and Ethiopia's desire to retain sovereignty over its botanical assets.

Source: Rafi Communique, 1987

appropriate enforcement mechanisms on a national basis in order to be effective.

A major weakness associated with CITES and other international agreements is that any one nation can refuse to sign the convention (which thereby weakens the necessary international collaborative efforts—see Chapter Three).

Box 25

Kenya vs. Djibouti

Djibouti, which has not adhered to the Convention on International Trade of Endangered Species (CITES), serves as an important trade centre for endangered and rare species in the East African region. This undermines the efforts made by many countries (especially Kenya) to restrict poaching. By its stringent conservation efforts, Kenya has probably prevented the extinction of several species, and it has developed a tourist industry which is largely based on the country's rich wildlife resources.

This conflict depicts a regional problem, because by May 1989, only Kenya, Somalia and Sudan had become members of CITES. While being registered as a CITES member state in 1983, Sudan is still an important transit country for rhino horn exports. The conflict between conservation and short term utility maximization is closely linked to the unstable political environment in the East-African sub-region. Because of the fragile political situation between the countries in the Horn of Africa, little attention is paid to species protection.

Buffer zones

The establishment of protected areas alone can never fully conserve forests or prevent the extinction of species. In order to conserve a protected area, buffer zones or semi-protected areas are increasingly being used. Within the buffer zone, such sustainable uses as extraction of non-wood resources, game ranching, agro-forestry, aquaculture, and forest dwellers' reservations are taking place.

When buffer zones are well managed, they can strengthen conservation and decrease population pressure on the protected core. To be most effective, buffer zones need to surround the whole park. IECs might arise when protected areas are found close to international borders. If population pressure or economic interests begin to threaten the fringes of protected areas, conservation efforts on the other side of the border may be threatened (as in the case of Cameroun, where a planned protected area lies close to some developed areas near the border with Nigeria).

Recreation

A growing trend in industrialized countries is to attempt to gain access to more recreational areas in forests and mountains. In fragile ecosystems, this may cause severe damage and threaten biodiversity.

As forestry operations and recreational interests expand, conflicts are inevitable. Canada has some of the largest untouched wilderness areas left in North America, and calls for their preservation are increasing. As other land use interests emerge, so do conflicting demands about how to allocate and manage the land.

Until now, most of these conflicts have been at a national level, but many involve matters of international concern (e.g., in fragile ecosystems governed by many nations, such as the Spitzbergen archipelago).[12] In some instances, the inexorable spread of forestry operations and logging roads conflicts with hunting, orienteering and other recreational activities.

Some of the conflicts in British Columbia involve highly fertile sites containing Canada's largest stocks of Douglas Fir (*Nimpkish Island*), Western Red Cedar (*Meares Island*), and Sitka Spruce (*Tahsish*).

Box 26

The Tuna Case: United States versus Mexico

In 1990 the United States restricted the import of yellowfin tuna from Mexico, who then suffered heavily from loss in export revenue. The US import restrictions caused Mexico to search for other markets (which provoked a fall in in other countries' anticipated export revenue—for example, Senegal).

Mexico asked the Contracting Parties to the General Agreement on Tariffs and Trade (GATT) to establish a panel to examine the matter (under Article XXXIII:2. GATT is a multilateral treaty subscribed by 94 nations which together account for more than four-fifths of the world trade. Its basic aim is to 'liberalize world trade and place it on a secure basis').

Conflict issues

The purse-seine nets which many Mexican fishermen use to catch tuna, also catch and drown dolphins. The unintended catching of dolphins is a potential problem in the Eastern Tropical Pacific Ocean (ETP) where tuna and dolphins tend to congregate together. The US Marine Mammal Protection Act (MMPA) imposed import restrictions on tuna caught in purse-seine nets (in order to protect the life and health of dolphins).

Mexico argued that if the purpose of the MMPA was to protect dolphins (as the US claimed), then the MMPA should protect all dolphins regardless of the type of fishery, species of dolphin, fishing methods used, or geographical area. According to Mexico, this was not the case under the provisions of MMPA on which the restrictive trade provisions were based.

Conflict settlement

Since the outcome of the conflict would have important environmental effects and economic implications for a variety of commodities and sectors, GATT's panel members held intense negotiations.

The Panel established by GATT noted that the issues arose from the fact that the MMPA had jurisdiction only within the United States, and noted that import restrictions were contrary to the GATT Agreement (Articles XI and XX(b)). The United States was requested to bring its measures into conformity with its obligations under GATT.

A broader perspective on the case

Proponents of the environmental trade restrictions have noted that the GATT Agreement does not make provisions for environmental problems. They claim that the environment is now a global issue, and that GATT's provisions prohibiting nations from imposing environmental standards on others fail to take so-called global environmental goods into account. They also claim that environmental issues should be addressed internationally (not only at national levels).

Others claim that environmental issues can be used by protectionists on a wide range of issues.

7.4 (B) IECs caused by incompatible goals over externalities from the use of forests and biodiversity resources

This section outlines IECs emerging as a result of incompatible goals over the externalities from using the resource base (see Figure 11), such as loss of biodiversity and watershed degradation.[13]

Loss of biodiversity

The ecology of tropical and equatorial forests is distinguished from other types by its exceptionally high degree of biological diversity. The richness of these forests in terms of the number of species they contain is one of the main reasons why they have attracted particular attention, and why many people consider their protection to be of paramount importance.

As a result of deforestation, it is estimated that thousands of species are lost each year (the figures vary greatly within scientific literature). Many of these species have potential economic value and some are already important sources of food, medicine, genetic material, and chemical products.[14]

Watershed degradation

Forests help to regulate the hydrology of watersheds and river basins, such as those of the Ganges and the Amazon. When forests are cut, particularly on sloping land, water runs off unimpeded, taking large quantities of soil and nutrients with it, thus affecting the agricultural potential of the deforested area and often causing increased flooding and silt accumulation downstream. Social unrest has increasingly been associated with the effects of these processes (see further discussion in Chapter Six).[15]

7.5 (C) IECs over incompatible goals over externalities from the use of other resources

This section outlines IECs emerging as a result of incompatible goals over externalities from utilization of other resources which affect forestry and biodiversity resources, (for example, climatic changes, acid deposition, and economic development (see the ABC-model, Figure 11).

Climatic change

Changed precipitation patterns are a likely result of climatic changes, and the consequences for forests worldwide are likely to be profound. At this point in time, there is no scientific consensus on the exact effects of climatic change on forests and biodiversity. There are however, reasons to believe that the likely changes would trigger IECs.

It is expected that forest zones would migrate polewards in a global warming situation. If climatic changes are very rapid, forest zones may not be able to move at the same rate. The poleward edges of forest zones may alter in terms of species composition, and degenerate into shrub communities, resulting in a decline in the carbon stocks held in plants and soils, a decline that would in turn result in decreased atmospheric carbon storage. Such changes would have major effects on commercial forestry, timber supply, recreation and wildlife that depend on forest habitats, as well as on water supply and erosion rates. It is worth noting that no effective studies have been carried out on tropical forests (e.g., forest zone shift and changes in productivity).[16]

A major consequence of forest conversion would be its effect on local, regional and global climates (such as local alterations in air and soil temperature, relative

Box 27

Whaling: Norway and the International Whaling Commission

In June 1991, Norwegian whalers announced their intentions to resume commercial whaling operations, in spite of the International Whaling Commission's (IWC) moratorium. The position adopted by the Norwegian Fishermen's Union (det Norske Fiskarlag) triggered the international conflict over how whales should be utilized.

IWC was established in 1946 in order to find an internationally sustainable level of whaling. Whales had been under considerable pressure for several decades, and had suffered drastic decreases in stocks after whaling became industrialized. The Commission did not succeed in achieving its goals (mainly because only nations with commercial interests in whaling participated in the IWC). Pressure on stocks did not decrease until substitutes replaced the demand for whale-oil and other whale-derived products.

During the 1970s, the role of the IWC was altered as new member nations sought to focus more on the protection of whales. The number of nations taking part in the IWC rose from 25 to 40 in the course of just six years. The only nations continuing with commercial whaling were Norway, Japan, Iceland and the Soviet Union. Denmark, (Greenland), Canada and the United States were involved because whaling was a traditional source of national livelihood in certain local communities.

In 1982, the new situation within the IWC led to a commercial whaling moratorium which was scheduled to end in 1991. Norway did not sign this moratorium, but stopped commercial whaling in 1986. The objective of the moratorium was to encourage scientific research to determine whether the different stocks could sustain further exploitation without being threatened. In the summer of 1991, when the moratorium was due to end, the IWC decided to maintain it (because of lack of data). This moratorium included the Minke Whale (the only species commercially utilized by Norwegian whalers which, according to Norwegian research reports, could sustain hunting). At the meeting, the Norwegian Commissioner argued that the IWC had become an organization for protecting whales instead of one for managing resources.

Norwegian delegates from the Fishermen's Union protested against the decision to extend the moratorium. However, the Norwegian Government decided that the hunting of Minke Whales must be based on scientific data which will ensure rational, sustainable hunting, and that it will continue 'scientific hunting' until 1994. The Norwegian Government defended its position by arguing that existing stock assessments provided sufficient data to justify commercial whaling, and that Norway intends to continue its whaling practice until scientific evidence is provided (probably after 1994).

The IWC, meanwhile, after intense lobbying from international NGOs such as Greenpeace, is now concerned with 'humane' killing methods to avoid suffering when whales are hunted, and the threat of over-hunting.

—In June 1992, Norway resumed commercial hunting of Minke Whales.

Box 28

Air Pollution and Forest Decline

Around 1980, increased attention was drawn to the effects of air pollution on forests, after the former West Germany suffered sudden forest damage.

A combination of modern forestry practices and high levels of air pollution has caused severe damage to forests. Polluted air may affect trees both directly and indirectly. Direct effects include corrosion of the protective wax layer by the dry deposition of SO_2, acid precipitation or ozone. Indirect effects occur when the ground has become acidified, which consequently leads to a reduction in the supply of nutrients to the tree. The combination of both indirect and direct effects makes the tree more vulnerable to parasites such as fungi and insects, which very often are the ultimate cause of death.

The damage to Europe's forests resulting from sulphur emissions is estimated at US$ 30 billion a year (unless drastic action is taken to reduce emissions). The damage to forests caused by long-range transboundary air pollution has enormous potential for causing IECs.

Because polluting compounds remain airborne for several days, pronounced effects may occur up to a few thousand kilometres from the main emission areas. With the increased global trend towards industrialization, IECs related to transboundary air pollution and forest decline, with subsequent loss of biodiversity, will also emerge in developing countries. Conflicting interests have also been revealed between Great Britain and Norway, and the United States and Canada (see the ECE-Protocol discussion on transboundary air pollution in Chapter Eight).

humidity, and the amount of solar radiation received at ground level).

On a regional scale, deforestation influences water balance and causes an increase in streamflow and water yield from a watershed. Increase in streamflow following deforestation has been reported in Nigeria, East Africa, New South Wales, Australia, and the Amazon.

According to some scholars, the most direct effect of deforestation on global climate is that of increased *albedo* (the ratio of light received by a surface to the light energy reflected from it). Although deforestation increases albedo locally from a figure of 0.07 to 0.25, it is difficult to estimate global change in albedo by merely considering deforestation in the tropics.[17]

Forests also play an important role as a drain for carbon. Rainforests contain large amounts of carbon (which, when burned, is released into the air as carbon dioxide (CO_2)). The IPCC has estimated that 25% of the increase in atmospheric concentration of CO_2 is due to deforestation. The only short-term way of decreasing the concentration of atmospheric CO_2 is reafforestation, because new trees absorb CO_2 as they grow and incorporate the carbon into their cells.

Many IECs are related to deforestation and climatic changes. The negotiations under the auspices of the Intergovernmental Panel on Climatic Changes (IPCC, leading up to the Convention on Protecting the Global Climate during UNCED-

Box 29

Plano 2010: OECD countries versus Brazil

In 1986, the World Bank approved the first Power Sector loan to Brazil, for approximately US $500 million, in spite of opposition to the loan, based in part on environmental and social concerns.

In 1989 the Bank considered a second US $500 million Power Sector loan to finance Brazil's extensive energy project, Plano 2010, which involved building 125 dams, flooding 9 million square kilometres of land, including 260,000 square kilometres of tropical rain forest, and the resettlement of 500,000 people. Twenty-two dams would be located in the Amazon.

It was argued at that time by several representatives on the Bank's board (which was being lobbied by international environmental groups), that projects included in the investment plan would cause enormous destruction of natural resources and threaten the integrity and survival of indigenous groups, as well as causing unknown negative social implications for the people to be resettled.

Brazil, on the other hand, was facing a dilemma: should it generate much-needed national revenues (through industrialization), or should it try to ensure preservation of the environment? The country's debt burden forced it to try to implement the development plans. When a vote was carried out within the Bank, the result was that some OECD-countries voted against the loan, with reference to the Bank's Operational Manual on environmental and social implications. Brazil did not get the necessary financial resources to implement the energy project.

This situation is a typical example of the difficult issues related to international environmental concerns versus national demands for energy and for social and economic growth.

92), revealed incompatible goals between the main emitters of greenhouse gases and the net receivers. A possible solution to the conflict is compensation through providing additional (over and above traditional development assistance (ODA)) financial resources to developing countries for limiting increases in further emissions, or giving access to 'environmentally sound technology'. These conflicts of interest are also manifested between middle-income countries (such as India, Brazil, and China) and the least developed countries (e.g., Nigeria and Senegal) because continual and increased CO_2 emissions historically characterize rapidly industrializing countries.

Acid deposition

Acidification of the environment is today recognized as one of the most serious environmental problems, with severe consequences visible in the industrialized world today. It is most clearly manifested in highly industrialized regions (mainly Europe and parts of North America) as a fundamental alteration in the chemical cli-

Box 30

Mount Nimba: Guinea and Transnational Corporations (TNC) versus indigenous people and NGOs

The conflict over Mount Nimba exhibits features of a typical IEC: the challenge to make protection of a precious rainforest environment compatible with the generation of economic revenue for national governments (and, perhaps, their foreign investors).

Background

Mount Nimba comprises a mountainous area in the tropical rainforest shared by Guinea, Liberia and Ivory Coast in West Africa. With its geological traits, diversity of endemic species and a wide range of ecosystems, it was classified by Guinean legislation as a Strict Nature Reserve in 1944, and later as a World Heritage Site. In 1991, the Mount Nimba nature reserve was listed by UNESCO as a 'World Heritage Site in Danger', principally because of the threat posed by planned mining operations.

The area also contains possibly the world's largest unexploited source of iron ore. A consortium of French, US and Japanese mining and engineering firms have developed plans to open up an iron ore deposit on the Guinean side.

The governments of Guinea and Liberia are expected to receive an annual net revenue of US$ 20 million from the related mining activities.

Major Controversies

Four major controversies can be identified, related to economic, conservation, social upheaval and sovereignty issues:

The economic considerations are complex. The governments of Guinea and Liberia, and the transnational consortium have mutual economic interests in exploiting the ore. Until 1989, the Liberian sector of Mount Nimba was mined quite intensively by another consortium, but is not likely to be utilized any more. One European company has expressed interest in opening the Guinean iron ore deposit. The time factor is crucial, since the buying agent will not contract for deliveries from Mount Nimba unless output is guaranteed within the next year. The question of urgency also arises because the Liberian railroad may be destroyed due to vegetation growth and erosion unless maintenance is kept up (also complicated by civil war in Liberia).

The environmental implications are not yet fully established, but some representatives of the NGO community argue that damage will inevitably occur in the water catchment area (for instance through loss of vegetation and local climatic changes, pollution of water supplies, depletion of wildlife and loss of biological diversity).

The social upheaval problem stems from the implications of the project for nearly 30,000 people. Approximately 600 workers may be brought into an area which has a traditional subsistence economy and where there are already many refugees from the Liberian civil war. The discrepancies between salaried mine-workers and subsistence farmers are considered likely to create social conflicts and unrest.

The question of sovereignty is important since Guinea faces the balance between the need to protect the site with the opportunity to generate needed revenue. The government of Guinea has the authority to make the decision, but the trade-offs will be high with both options (pressure from outside to protect, or to develop, as well as internal pressure to exploit the country's resources). The case represents an example where an international institution may have acted as a facilitator or mediator by exploring ways to bridge conservation and development interests. The roles of the World Bank and UNEP are of interest in this context.

mate, and the associated changes in the chemistry and biology of surface waters and terrestrial ecosystems. In Europe alone, it is thought to have caused damage to almost 200,000 km² of forests, a large proportion of which are dead or dying. This total (an aggregate area equivalent to the area of Great Britain) amounts to some 13% of all forests in the region (see Chapter Eight for further discussion).[18]

Once considered to be exclusively a problem of industrialized countries, acid deposition is now seen as a potential scourge in areas where developing countries are being rapidly industrialized. Studies initiated by the Scientific Committee on Problems of the Environment (SCOPE) in co-operation with UNEP, have confirmed that acid deposition is a global problem.[19]

A main cause of acidification is anthropogenic emission of large quantities of sulphur and nitrogen oxides into the atmosphere. The proportions of the pollutants vary in time and space, and their relative stress-causing potentials are poorly understood: (1) sulphuric and nitric acids; (2) stresses imposed by gaseous pollutants on aerial plant parts; and (3) a broad range of responses to increased ecosystem loadings with nitrogen compounds.[20]

Economic development

Many of the sources of IECs reflect the dichotomy between economic development and protection of resources. There are several examples of development efforts which utilize water and mining resources and which have severe implications for forestry and biodiversity. The two cases outlined below, PLANO 2010: OECD countries vs. Brazil (see Box 29), and Mount Nimba: Guinea and TNCs vs. Indigenous people and NGOs (see Box 30),

reveal the complexity of interests and the number of adversaries involved. The Mount Nimba Case represents an example of how the international community is getting more involved in environmental issues even at local levels in many developing countries (which in turn often generates conflicts).

7.6   Case Study: Cameroun
Introduction

The increasing awareness of the industrialized countries of the North concerning national and global environmental problems has placed special focus on tropical and equatorial rain forests. The rain forests are considered by the North as a global heritage, playing an important role in the maintenance of such environmental qualities as biodiversity, air quality, moderation of climatic changes and sequestering of carbon dioxide. The South, where the rain forests are located, faces a dilemma as to whether it should utilize the forest resources and seize the economic benefits associated with them; or recognize the need for protection.

The issues

In recent years, Cameroun has experienced a major reduction in the trade of several of its most important export commodities, including coffee, oil, and cocoa. New opportunities for national development have been sought through improvement of its terms of trade. The forest areas, which are located in the southern part of the country, have in this context been seen as a means of reaching these goals through increased logging activities (see Figure 12).

For indigenous people, the rain forest and its ecosystem provide daily needs such as food, fuel and building materials; whereas non-indigenous people tend to consider the forest only in terms of maintaining local ecosystems. The range of interests in the rain forest is reflected by a variety of groups with divergent views.

Conflict Analysis
The Natural Resource System

Most of the nutrients in a rainforest ecosystem are tied up in the biomass rather than in the soil. Large scale removal of trees for agricultural purposes or commercial logging is not compatible with a sustained rain forest ecosystem. By the time such lands are abandoned, seed sources are so far away that the forest species cannot begin to grow again.

The Southern part of Cameroun belongs to the Guinea-Congolese ecological zone, the largest continuous rain forest block in Africa (see Figure 13). This area consists primarily of humid evergreen dense forest and semi-deciduous forest. The forests cover approximately 200,000 km².

This tropical forest is one of the most species-rich in the world, and Cameroun is classified by the World Bank and IUCN as one of the world's ten 'megadiversity-countries.' In the rainforest area, there are approximately 8,000 species of plants. There is also an extraordinarily rich species diversity, including a variety of primates and other large mammals, many of whom are listed by IUCN as rare, endangered, or threatened with extinction.

Figure 12. Map of Cameroun, the Congo, and the Central African Republic.

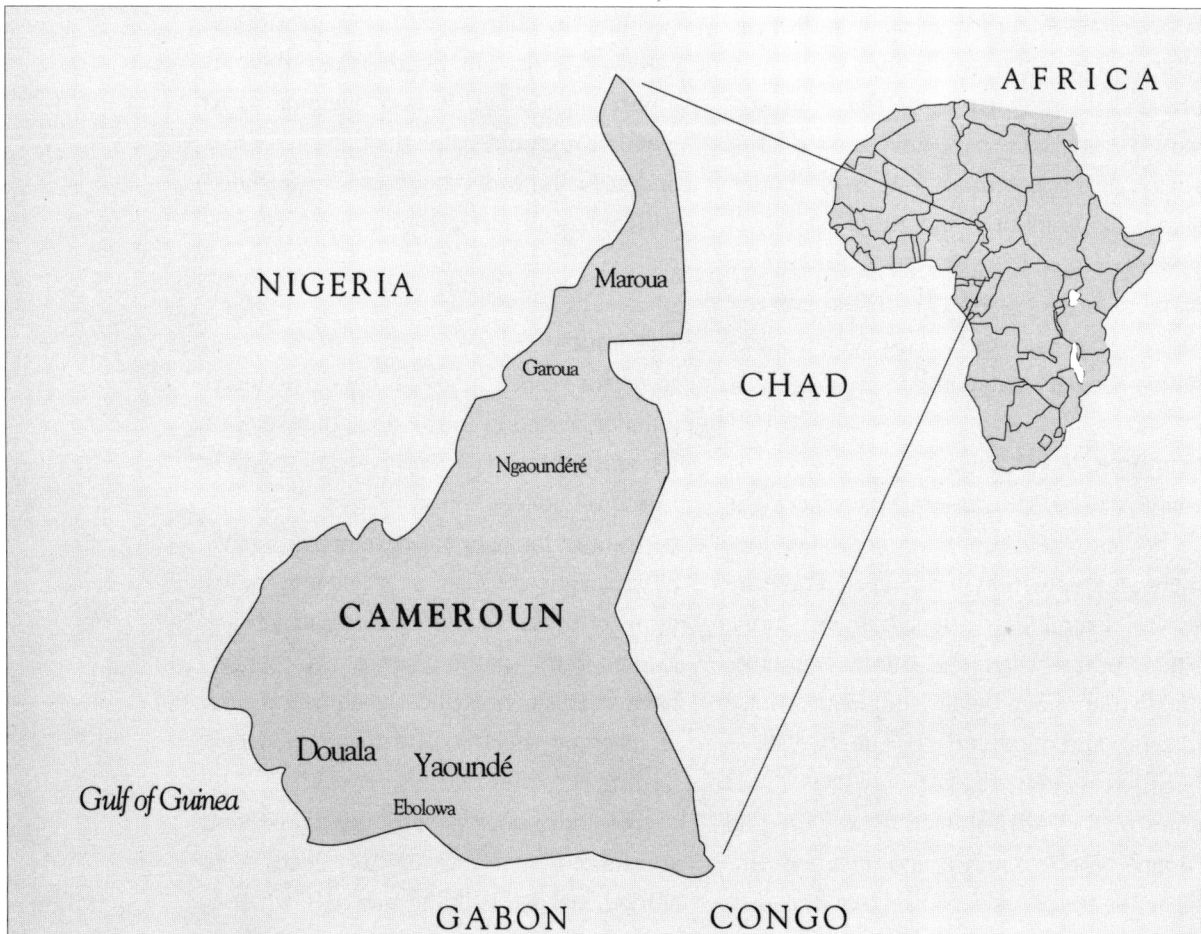

Demands on the resource system

The forest is divided into two major sectors as far as demands are concerned: the Niger-Cameroun-Gabon sector, which has high conservation priority and is highly endangered by logging and agricultural pressures; and the Cameroun-Congolese sector, which has lower, but still high, levels of biodiversity, and which because of its isolation is less at risk from logging, agricultural encroachment and poaching.

Fuelwood is Cameroun's primary energy source for cooking and heating, and its supply is clearly of great importance to the country. In the National Tropical Forestry Action Plan (TFAP), only three per cent of the total investment is dedicated to fuelwood and energy, but 'forest-based industrial development' may also affect the supply of fuelwood (see box on the National TFAP). In 1987, current consumption of fuelwood was estimated at about 10 million cubic metres per year.[21]

In order to analyse the different demands on the forest resource system, the following sections identify the respective positions and interests of the parties involved.

Positions and interests
The Local Level: Government vs. Indigenous People (see Figure 14)

The Government of Cameroun's intent is to invest in extensive logging activities in order to ease its difficult economic situation. In its Five-Year Plan (1986–91), it was stated that a great increase in exports of lumber and timber was expected to replace the country's lost income from other exports (including oil). Traditionally, the forest sub-sector has played an important role

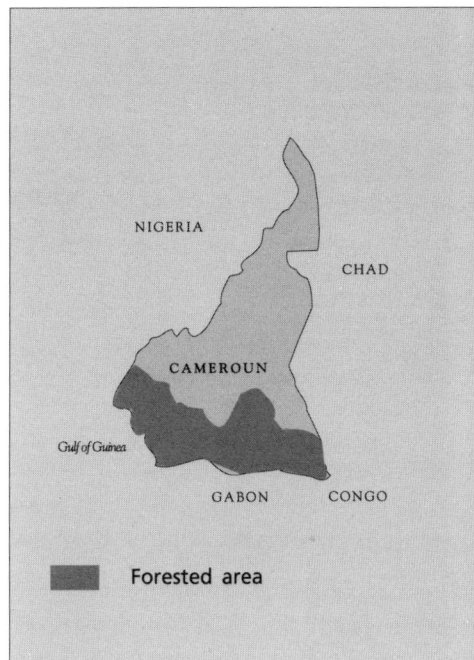

Figure 13. Map of the Tropical Forest Zone in the southern part of Cameroun

in the economic development of Cameroun. In 1987, the sector generated about five per cent of the country's export revenue.

In order to realize the Five-Year Plan, the Government of Cameroun has decided to implement the National Tropical Forestry Action Plan (National TFAP; see Enclosure 2), which was devised in 1988 through co-operation between the FAO, the World Bank and UNDP. This plan incorporates the idea of taking advantage of the great export potential represented by forest resources. One of the stated goals is that: "…Cameroun could thus become the most important African producer and exporter of forestry-based products from the start of the 21st century'.[22]

Such an objective would undoubtedly have far-reaching consequences for the rich biological diversity of these forests, and

133

Figure 14. Conflict levels with the actors

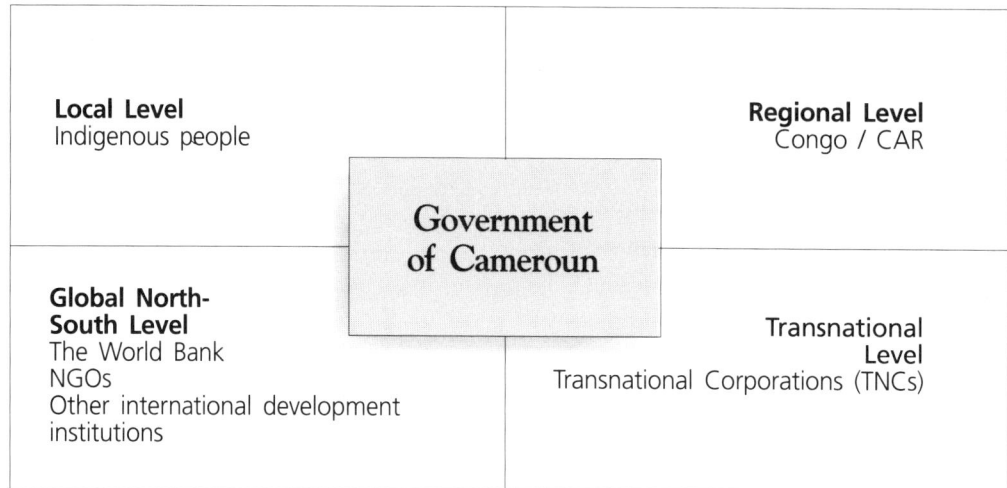

Local Level Indigenous people	**Regional Level** Congo / CAR
Government of Cameroun	
Global North-South Level The World Bank NGOs Other international development institutions	**Transnational Level** Transnational Corporations (TNCs)

would threaten several species with extinction. In order to prevent such a loss, the national objective is both to conserve national forests and increase sustainable forest productivity. However, within the government, conflicts exist between those who favour exploitation and those who support conservation.

Indigenous people

Among several ethnic groups, there are some 20–35 semi-nomadic Baka people who live in the South Eastern forests, while about 3,500 of the Bakola people live in the coastal South Western forests. Moreover, the forests in West Africa have more people living in them than in other tropical forest areas. The Baka and Bakola people have for generations developed a symbiotic relationship to the Bantu ethnic group. Cameroun is usually considered as the original homeland of the Bantu group, which after 200 BC migrated East and South, taking with them new crop varieties and iron-working methods. The people of the Bakola and Baka tribes have a culture based on hunting and gathering, which provides the basis for survival and trade with other

tribes. A greater degree of integration into Cameroun's economy, and/or an imposed limitation upon the forest areas they can use, is viewed as a threat to their culture and existence.

Regional Level: Cameroun vs. the Congo and the Central African Republic

The positions of the neighbouring countries, South-East of Cameroun (the Republic of Congo and the Central African Republic (CAR)), concern negative impacts on neighbouring countries' national reserves. East of Cameroun, the CAR has established a forest reserve, Dzangha-Sangha, and the Dzangha-Noloki National Park; while the Congo has proposed the Nouable Conservation Area through a Global Environment Facility (GEF)-financed programme (see Enclosure 1). The Dzanga-Sangha forest reserve contains a great diversity of flora and fauna, with lowland gorillas, forest elephants and chimpanzees among the many animal species.

Establishment of buffer zones on Cameroun's side of the border would reduce the chances of conflicting interests in these border landscapes.

134

Global Level: 'North' vs. Cameroun and Transnational Corporations

The international conservation interests are represented by different institutions, mainly NGOs, such as the Environmental Defence Fund. They argue that Cameroun has a global responsibility to protect its biological diversity and the subsistence base for its indigenous people. Seeking to ensure that developments in Cameroun are environmentally sound, EDF criticized the World Bank's National Forestry Development Project for over-emphasizing timber gathering (as opposed to conservation) and addressing the basic agricultural and fuelwood needs of Cameroun's rural population.

Another concern is that one of the goals of the forestry sector loan (to develop a coherent forest conservation and management policy by reorganizing and strengthening key institutions dealing with forestry issues), may be undermined unless it is co-ordinated within the structural adjustment process which the country is undergoing with the World Bank's support.[23]

Other institutions, such as the African Development Bank and the German bilateral development organization (GTZ), are actors in this conflict, since the environmental guidelines in these institutions may not correspond with the national priorities on extensive logging activities. In this context, the Global Environment Facility (GEF) may offer a means to resolve the incompatible goals between actors.

The international community's interest in tropical forests is due to its desire to protect genetic resources and ensure climatic stabilization. Genetic components from these forests may provide a very important resource in years to come.[24]

Relationships and explanatory factors

The forestry sub-sector has played an important role in the economic development of Cameroun. In 1987, the sector ac-

counted for about four per cent of GDP. It made up about ten per cent of the agriculture sector output, which in turn generated about five percent of export revenues, and provided full-time employment for some 20,000 people. There are about 20 million hectares of forest (consisting of 14 million hectares of tropical forest, and some 6 million hectares of transitional forest and woodland in the high savannah), of which only eight million hectares are currently exploited. Exports of wood products are mostly in the form of logs to the European market, which is expected to grow by two per cent annually until the year 2010. Sawn timber and plywood are better value-added products for export, but they must compete directly with South East Asian exports. Finally, Cameroun has the potential for producing semi-finished or finished wood products that can be exported to such nearby markets as Ghana.

The ongoing and planned logging activity favoured by the Government in Southern Cameroun will have great implications for the Baka and Bakola people. The Government has yet to address the issue of how the indigenous people can maintain their basic forest way of life. The greater part of Cameroun's forest area is owned by the state. The law requires that forests be converted to agricultural land before claims for land rights can be made. This provides an incentive for deforestation, but implies that the indigenous people no longer have legal rights to the forests and their way of life.

The Government's Five Year Plan (1986–1991) contains a strong environmental programme and the assistance of the international community has been sought to implement a programme of protection and conservation.

The role of international organizations

Cameroun is facing a dilemma. On the one hand, the country needs to maximize revenues from its resources, and on the other, it needs to protect its unique biodiversity. The World Bank's role is to help the Government pursue both objectives and advise it when making decisions involving trade-offs between these objectives. The World Bank is thus involved in Cameroun on several different levels:

—In November 1989, a structural adjustment loan of US$ 150 million came into effect. The primary objective of this loan is to assist Cameroun in overcoming its balance-of-payments deficit.

—Currently, a proposed forestry sector loan of US$ 30 million for a National Forestry Development Project is being prepared.

—In addition, a GEF-financed project of US$ 25 million for a National Parks and Reserves Ecological Protection project, aiming at protecting precious biodiversity, is proposed in the Southern area of Cameroun.[25]

There are also several other international institutions involved in Cameroun, with some conflicting interests since most of them include road construction among their aims:

—The *African Development Bank* (AfDB) is planning a US$ 65 million forestry sector loan to Cameroun to be implemented by the FAO for supporting increased timber exports. The AfDB is also preparing a US$ 135 million transportation sector loan to finance road building in the country's southern rain forests. This project is controversial because of the tension between conservation and development interests.

—German bilateral aid through the *Kreditanstalt fur Wiederausbau (KfW)* is building a major highway from Edea to Kribi which will have an influence on the GEF-supported Douala-Edea and Campo Wildlife Reserves, which in turn may lead to increases in migration to the area.

—A number of other planned road projects in Cameroun's rainforest areas (to be financed by the KfW, AfDB and the World Bank) may affect the GEF project.

—GTZ, a West German bilateral organization, is involved in several maintenance operations concerning roads in the Southern part of the country.[26]

—The Government is seeking international financing for a 500 km highway from Yokadouma to Kribi, which would traverse the forest. The government has apparently sought financing from Japan.

—Many logging companies operating in Cameroun, (mainly French, German,

Dutch and Italian), are running extensive operations in the areas close to the Congo and the CAR; the same areas which are inhabited by the Baka people.[27]

Escalation of Conflicts

The escalation of the various conflicts is hard to classify in clear terms. Determination of the level the conflict is at (e.g., incipient or latent) varies according to current negotiations and activities (see Chapter One, the Escalation Model, Figure 1). Nevertheless, by making a distinction between geographical levels, the following broad classification can be made:

Local Level: Indigenous People vs. National Government

This conflict is manifest and acknowledged, and the various development initiatives could certainly increase the polarization between the actors. There are, however, some interesting activities planned such as the GEF which could potentially combine protection and activities for the indigenous people with economic compensation for the governments.

The regional level in Cameroun and its two neighbouring countries may be characterized as an incipient conflict, since the core of the conflict, i.e., the logging on Cameroun's side of the border, does not represent an immediate threat to conservation efforts in the two neighbouring countries. Any logging closer than about 15 kilometres from the protected areas, however, could cause the potential conflict to escalate to a latent level, providing easy access for poachers to the natural parks and reserves on the other side of the border.

It is difficult to categorize and predict the escalation of IECs at a *global level*. There is, however, an increasing concern worldwide for the need to promote sustainable forestry and to protect biodiversity. This may indicate a further polarization between national sovereignty and the right to prioritize economic growth at the expense of protection and global concerns. At the same time, the Convention on the Protection of Biological Diversity, which was signed at UNCED (see Enclosure 2) reveals signs of a growing willingness from the North to transfer additional funds and technology (for example, through support of the GEF) for promoting protection and sustainable use of the global commons.

Options

Rational land use policies, including agroforestry and farm forestry for fuelwood production, can turn this threat to the environment into an economic opportunity. Fuelwood production, marketing and distribution could generate substantial income

for the rural population and, at the same time, could become a source of increased government revenues through taxation. The establishing of a large number of small-scale fuelwood plantations maintained by local communities, as well as a proper incentive structure for fuelwood production can create many possibilities for earning income in the vicinity of urban centres. In the countryside, on-farm forestry will avoid the need to search for fuelwood in more distant forests, and will ease the work load, especially for women, who are responsible for collecting and growing the food for their families. Instead, more time will be available for the cultivation of crops and other income-generating activities, while forests are protected from further encroachment.

7.7 Conclusion

Externalities of resource use (for example, loss of biodiversity and destruction of buffer zones) play an important part in creating and fuelling IECs. Increased recognition of the importance of these externalities as obstacles to long-term social, economic and environmentally-sound development is critical at a preventive stage.

The tropical and equatorial rain forest ecosystems are regarded as global commons because of their significance for global climatic patterns and their huge biological wealth. The 'common' concept used in connection to biodiversity and forestry issues differs to a certain degree from when it is used in connection to such resources as air and international waterways, because forests are located within sovereign states. Conflicts emerging from the utilization of these resources are basically national. It is the externalities of such utilization which often make the conflicts international.

The IECs in the case of Cameroun may be classified at three levels: (i) indigenous people versus the national government, (ii) regional level (Cameroun versus its two neighbour countries), and (iii) international interests (reflected by international environmental groups and other international development organizations) versus the national government's decision to exploit the country's own resources.

Chapter Eight

CASE STUDIES

8 Land resources

Marginal land—border landscapes—land-based effects of air pollution

THIS CHAPTER outlines systemic linkages between land resources and other economic, political, social and environmental factors related to international environmental conflicts (IECs). The main conflicts are between developmental and environmental requirements, in particular how to satisfy human needs while at the same time conserving land resources for future use. Land resources in marginal areas are chosen for study, since there are many current IECs associated with the use of these resources (especially in arid and semi-arid lands). Border landscapes represent a constant source of potential IECs over the use of their land resources. IECs associated with air pollution as a source of land degradation are also of particular interest, since some lessons have been learned in the prevention and resolution of such conflicts in Europe.

8.1 Introduction

Many IECs associated with the use of land resources began at a local level, but then escalated to an international level. This chapter represents only a selection of IECs related to land resources. There are many other examples which present a serious threat to land resources, such as global climatic changes, industrial accidents, and dumping of nuclear wastes.

Natural and man-modified semi-renewable and renewable land resources exhibit extensive interdependence within natural resource systems, as well as between social, political, economic and cultural systems. Non-renewable, exhaustible resources are extremely relevant to IECs. However, exhaustible resources tend not to be characterized by the same interdependence as that indicated for renewable resources, nor is the link to food and water so direct.

The close connection between water resources and food production makes *land security*[1] of vital national interest, since it affects the livelihood of the local people as well as international relations. Throughout history, there have been a vast number of local conflicts related to ownership, access to, or control of land.[2] In many instances, however, such conflicts are fuelled by external factors such as the international market price on agricultural commodities, which directly affects the income generation for local farmers, and subsequently changes the management of land resources (for example, market price on groundnuts and dryland degradation).[3]

One of the important causes of land degradation is the increasing pressure on land, and other closely interlinked factors such as population growth and increasing rates of consumption. This situation creates two closely connected sources of IECs: first, incompatible goals between users (from individual to national entities) because of scarcity, or inability to deal with scarcity successfully; second, incompatible goals between developmental and environmental requirements (in particular, satisfying human demands while at the same time pro-

tecting the environment for future generations). Many of the manifest IECs related to land resources clearly illustrate the difficulties in balancing the requirements of immediate and long term demands.

There is no way that any international organization can deal with land management in a comprehensive way on its own. Local and national entities play a vital role in land management policies, and most of them tend to operate along strictly sectorial lines, rarely taking such considerations as linkages and interactions into account.[4] Consequently, prevention and resolution of IECs related to land resources represent a great challenge to existing institutions.

8.2 Conflict analytical approach

In the following analysis, emphasis is put on the generation of IECs related to land resources, how the adversaries in IECs relate to each other, and which functions these relationships have in the prevention and resolution of IECs. The assessment of IECs is divided into the three aspect groups (see the ABC model, Figure 15).

A—This aspect deals with incompatible goals regarding access to, control over, and unsustainable use of land resources (as illus-

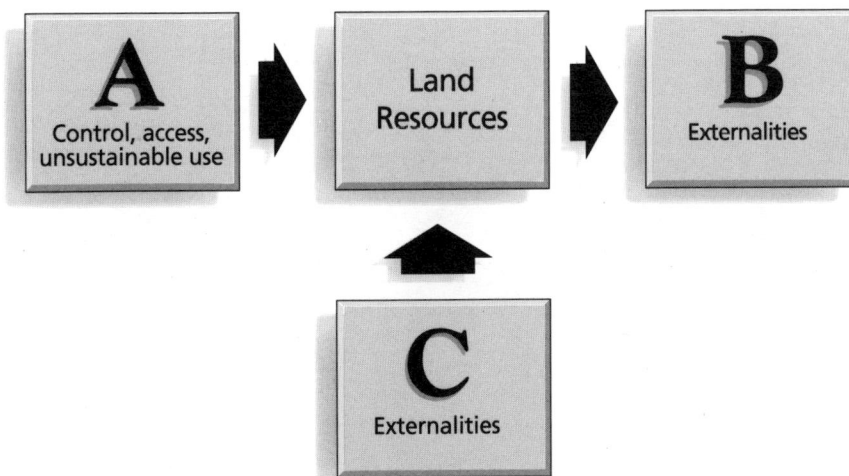

Figure 15
The ABC model and land resources

trated on the left hand side of Figure 15; marginal lands and border landscapes)

B—The next aspect deals with incompatible goals as a result of the negative side effects of utilization of land resources (marginal lands), and

C—The final aspect concerns negative side effects from use of other resources affecting land resources (the effects of air pollution on land, and the negotiations which were leading up to the UN Economic Commission of Europe Convention).

8.3 (A) IECs generated by access to, control over, and unsustainable use of land resources

This section briefly examines some IECs related to marginal lands.

IECs related to marginal lands

The implications of the low carrying capacity of land resources in drylands make them sensitive to stress, mainly through grazing and cultivation. Seasonal and annual mi-

gration has traditionally taken place in order to avoid 'ecological surprises' such as the sudden loss of soil fertility through severe water and wind erosion. The agroclimatic zones (for example, the Sahelian Sudanian zone in Sub-Sahara Africa) form a gradient in which migration is taking place (corresponding to the rainfall pattern in a North-South-North direction), in order to optimize use of scarce land resources[5].

Population growth and increasing development needs, combined with structural changes at a national level (such as urbanization) and the enforcement of international borders, restrict these movements.

Several IECs have been, and will continue to be, caused by an eroding resource base which leads to migration of people and their livestock—as illustrated by:

—*Mauritania vs. Senegal:* As degradation of rain-fed agriculture reduced in output, local people of both nations resorted to recessive utilization of land along the banks of the

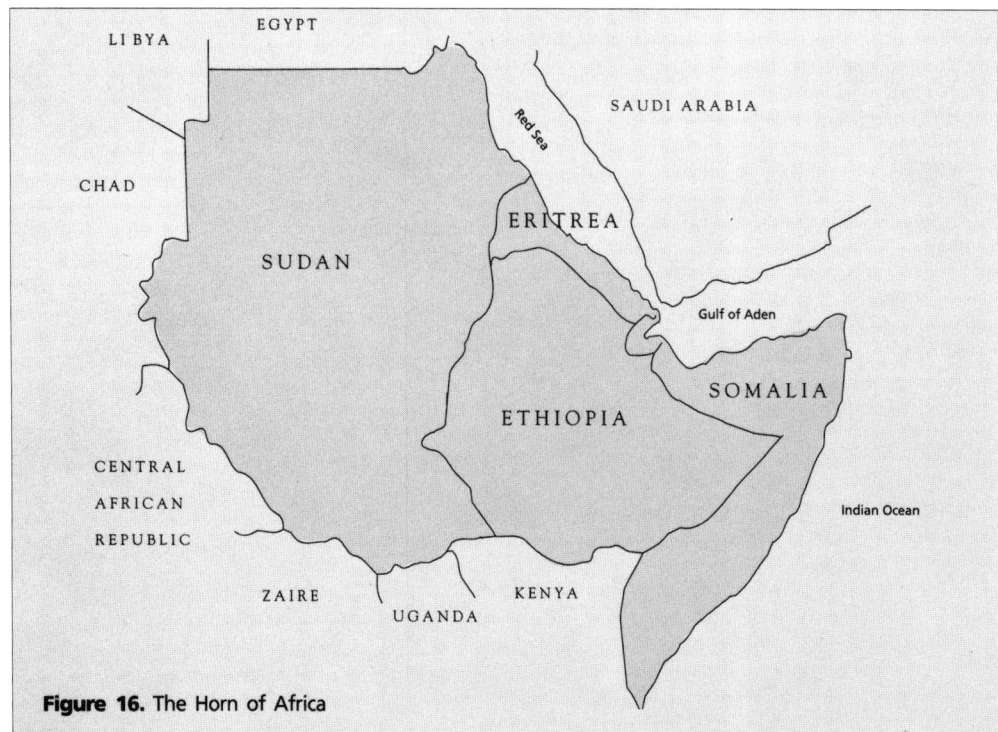

Figure 16. The Horn of Africa

Box 31

The Ogaden Conflict between Ethiopia and Somalia

The land and fossil resources along the border between Ethiopia and Somalia, especially in the Ogaden and Haud areas, have been the source of highly polarized conflicts since the mid 19th century. These territories represent important grazing fields and have for centuries been used extensively by pastoralists in the rainy season. The issue at stake is incompatible goals between user-groups in the utilization of these resources. In 1963 a local Ogadeni uprising, followed by overt actions against Ethiopia, was supported by Somalia. By 1977 Cuban and Russian troops were also involved in the Ogaden war.

Explanations of the economic interests involved in this conflict vary from pastoral grazing/welling rights; to distribution of trade profits and the utilization of the Wabi Shebbele and Genale rivers; to control over possible oil deposits. Recent Ethiopian estimates project that a large proportion of the national mineral oil needs will be met by extraction of the area's resources.

Competition between pastoral clans have caused conflicts in the area for centuries. Ethnic dispersion is another factor that must be taken into account in this case. There are ethnic Somalis living in Northern Kenya, Ethiopia and Djibouti.

The United States and the former USSR also exacerbated the conflict by supplying weaponry and technical and strategic facilities to the combatants.

Senegal river, which then turned into a highly polarized competition for land, and subsequently into an overt conflict (resulting in the death of approximately one thousand people);[6]

—*Lake Chad Basin* which is shared by Cameroun, Niger, Nigeria, and Chad provides another example of conflicting interests regarding control of shared river banks. Progress has been made in developing agreements between the states over the sharing of the basin.[7]

—*Mali vs. Niger*: where degradation of grazing land fuelled a latent ethnic conflict which resulted in military intervention near Gao in Mali.

An Example from the IGADD region of East Africa

The region with which the Inter-Governmental Authority on Drought and Development (IGADD) is concerned consists of the following countries: Ethiopia, Djibouti, Kenya, Sudan, Somalia and Uganda. This region of the African continent is often referred to as the *Horn of Africa* (although strictly speaking this refers only to Northern Kenya and Eastern Sudan, and not to Uganda).

The region is known to be severely affected by war and civil strife. Most of the countries are experiencing both civil unrest and ongoing conflicts with neighbouring countries. As a consequence of the many conflict situations, the Horn of Africa is also one of the areas of the world which is

Box 32

Somalia trading livestock grazed mainly in Kenya

The main issue in this conflict is that of incompatible goals between users of the same resource (namely, grazing land). The Somalis are forcefully arguing that ethnic Somalis have traditional grazing rights in Kenya, at the same time as Kenya is defending national sovereignty. The underlying interest for both adversaries is the need for income generation from the livestock trade.

Somalia is ecologically and historically a pastoral land. Some pastoral clans have traditionally utilized lands which do not belong to the internationally accepted Somalian territory. These lands are found in Northern Kenya, Eastern Ethiopia and Djibouti.

One obvious explanation of Somalia's firm stand is to be found in its production and economic structure, where more than 80 per cent of its export earnings stem from livestock. Conflicts of this kind are common throughout the IGADD sub-region, because the very nature of pastoralism forces its practitioners to follow ecological rather than international determinants.

most heavily affected by refugees fleeing from degrading land resources, and civil unrest. These problems are significant factors in the generation of IECs in the region.

The conflicts have deep-seated historical roots, and the contending interest groups involved are numerous and complex. They are all connected by ethnic bonds, ideological and religious loyalties and shared or competing territorial, politi-

cal and economic concerns. Colonial wars, Arab influence and conflicts between local ethnic groups have all helped to form the complex cultural context of the IGADD countries and their administrative borders.

There is a striking incongruity between the area's political and administrative borders, and its pattern of eco-regions. The pastoral lifestyle is an illustrative example: Pastoralists have adapted and synchronized their culture to the geographical and seasonal variations of the region. When the patterns of seasonal movement are broken up by political borders, conflicts and problems are likely to emerge. Conflicts between sedentary peasants and nomads are often known to occur when pastoral movements are restricted. Practically all the countries of the IGADD region have launched ambitious programmes with the aim of settling the nomads, but very often these have had unsatisfactory results. Even though it is difficult to establish causal relationships, there is no doubt that the *population / resource base ratio* for parts of the IGADD region is above a sustainable level. The arid and semi-arid lands of the region have never been able to support high populations, while the central highlands have been over-populated for centuries.[8]

Regional efforts to resolve IECs

IGADD was formed in response to initiatives by the United Nations and the Organization for African Unity in 1986. In 1991, IGADD issued a Plan of Action entitled "Forum on Environmental Protection and Development of Sub-Regional Strategy to Combat Desertification." [9] The process leading to the final report is remarkable in the sense that all member countries participated, even though some were at war with each other at the time.

The implementation of the strategy is, however, difficult. An additional step could include a critical assessment and identification of problems in IECs related to shared natural hazards and resources, such as locusts and other plagues, as well as water, grazing land and compliance with international environmental agreements.

IECs in border landscapes

International borders represent the area limit of the political organization of territory. The areas on both sides of a political border are called 'border landscapes'. Political boundaries are locations which both separate and link two nations. The way in which these border landscapes are used and perceived by people and by governments has various impacts on the environment. Where the pressure on land resources is heavy—usually in areas which are already politically sensitive—there is a higher risk for IECs to evolve and escalate.

Sometimes the international border runs right through land which has traditionally been perceived as one "unit" (for example, as described in the Ogaden conflict). The local inhabitants in such case often do not respect the international legal border as a limit for their resource use.

When dealing with an IEC related to border landscapes, it is often difficult to distinguish between the *reason* why the international border was drawn in a specific way (for example, because of the relationship between colonial powers) and what kind of *effects* this has on the local people, as well as on the state's foreign affairs. To further complicate the matter, international borders do not necessarily follow the traditionally perceived borders (as in the case of many of the former colonies in Africa).

The border landscape of Indonesia and Papua New Guinea is selected as an illustration of IECs that escalated because an international border runs through a shared local resource base.

An IEC between Indonesia and Papua New Guinea[10]

The situation is characterized by villagers from Papua New Guinea crossing the border to Indonesia in order to practise shifting cultivation by using the neighbouring country's land resources. The crossing might look 'innocent', but the Indonesian Government could interpret this as a threat to national security by a hostile regime.[11] The border agreement does not take into consideration the traditional land use patterns in the border areas. The local people in the border area have based their agricultural practice on using "their area" on both sides of the border.[12]

Four main sources for conflict can be identified:

i) *Border crossers*: Traditionally, villagers from the border area have crossed the international border from time to time to make use of the natural resources (such as sago, and hunting) and to visit relatives;

ii) *Border development*: which means settlements, local industries and other infrastructure;

iii) *Movement of the OPM*: guerillas cross into Papua New Guinea to escape Indonesian patrols; and

iv) *Military incursion*: Indonesian troops and aircraft have on several occasions crossed into Papua New Guinea in pursuit of OPM-groups.

Other sources of conflicts lie in the disproportionate relationship between the two countries in respect to their size, military capacity and factors indicated above. The IECs mainly originate from problems related to border crossers and border development.

The role of the UN

The UN system has intervened in the conflict between Indonesia and Papua New Guinea on several occasions:

i) UNDP has also been involved in the Papua New Guinea border landscape conflict, through a feasibility study of a joint border development programme.

ii) In 1984, the Indonesia—Papua New Guinea border landscape problem was also brought to the attention of the UN General Assembly with the intention of legitimizing the adversaries' positions.

iii) The UN High Commissioner for Refugees (UNHCR) has given assistance to Iranian nationals who have sought political asylum in Papua New Guinea.

In an IEC such as this, the UN's role in prevention and resolution has been minor, except for UNHCR's assistance to refugee camps. There may be a potential for third party assistance by, for example, UNDP, if accepted by the countries involved.

8.4 (B) IECs over incompatible goals over externalities from use of land resources

Some examples of IECs emerging as a result of externalities from the use of land resources are outlined (**B**—see the ABC-model). This category is illustrated by two cases, both from Africa:

Siltation of Sudanese irrigation schemes

In Sudan the water reservoirs and river channels Sennar, Roseires, Khasm and El Girba are significantly affected by high rates of siltation caused by intensified agricultural practices in Ethiopia. In addition, the Blue Nile, River Nile and Atbara River are affected, as well as the huge Gezira Scheme and other similar installations. The steady intensification of highland agriculture has led to heavy erosion and increased siltation. This has caused severe problems in countries bordering onto Ethiopia, thus representing a latent IEC.

At time of writing (1992), Ethiopia has not accepted any basin-wide agreement regarding the use of the Nile water.

Reduction of biotic production in Lake Turkana

The lowering of the water-level in Lake Turkana illustrates the international implications of land degradation in this region. The region's water demand is largely met by rivers originating in the Ethiopian highlands. Population growth and increased degradation of rain-fed agricultural areas leads to increased demands for irrigation water.

The Omo river, which flows southwards from Ethiopia and enters Kenya close to the Ugandan border, supplies more than 90% of the water inflow to Lake Turkana. Through its high production of limnic biomass, this lake has been important as a source of protein for many people. The lowering of the water level and the subsequent loss of biotic production present a latent threat to the stability of the region.

8.5 (C) IECs over incompatible goals over externalities from utilization of other resources

This section explores IECs emerging as a result of externalities from use of other resources, in this case, acid deposition stemming from industrial atmospheric emissions (see **C**, Figure 15).

Land-based effects of air pollution: the case of the UN Economic Commission of Europe (ECE)

The transnational nature of air pollution and its effects on land resources reveal interesting linkages between local problems and the need for international governance to solve them. Over the last 20 years, this nexus has increasingly been acknowledged as a result of transboundary acid deposition problems in both Europe and North America. The ECE-Convention on Long Range Transboundary Air Pollution (LRTAP) relates indirectly to the prevention and resolution of IECs over land degradation resulting from air pollution. Moreover, it is considered to be an example of a successful means to prevent and resolve IECs related to air pollution as a cause of land degradation.

Even though air is one of the most important common global resources, there is still no international convention concerned with air corresponding to for example, the UN Convention on the Law of the Sea (except for the framework convention on global climatic changes).

Air pollution is defined in the ECE-Convention as follows:

'Air pollution' refers to the introduction by man, directly or indirectly, of substances or energy into the air resulting in deleterious effects of such a nature as to endanger human health; harm living resources, ecosystems and material property; and impair or interfere with amenities and other legitimate use of the environment. 'Air pollutants' shall be construed accordingly;

'Long-range transboundary air pollution' means air pollution whose physical origin is situated either wholly or partly within an area under the national jurisdiction of one State, and which has adverse effects on an area under the jurisdiction of another State, at such a distance that it is not generally possible to identify or distinguish the contribution of specific individual emission sources or groups of sources.

According to the Regional Office for Europe of the World Health Organization (WHO), millions of Europeans live in areas with air pollution severe enough to cause thousands of premature deaths annually, and to make many more people chronically ill or disabled.[13]

Transboundary air pollution conflicts between the European states centres on several questions: How quickly should the emissions be reduced? How much reduction is necessary? Who should bear the extra costs? Air pollution can be considered as a reciprocal externality. The emitters of air pollution (whether individuals, companies or nations) impose the cost of the resultant degradation on all other users of air (including themselves).[14] Air pollution can also be considered as a unidirectional externality (for example, in cases where prevailing winds carry emissions away from the emitter so that the environmental damage is experienced almost entirely by others).

Effects of air pollution on land resources

The productivity of land resources relies to a large extent on external factors, such as nutrition circulation, agricultural techniques, and climate, including transpiration and evaporation. Air pollution is transferred to surfaces by two processes: (i) Dry deposition (the direct and relatively efficient transfer of gases); and (ii) Wet deposition (an indirect process whereby particles

of pollution and lesser proportions of gases are carried by raindrops, snowflakes or hailstones).[15]

Air pollution may consist of primary or secondary pollutants, gaseous or particulate. Primary pollutants are released directly into the atmosphere. Secondary pollutants are caused mainly by pollutants which have been transformed into secondary components through chemical reactions. An example of a secondary pollutant is ozone (O_3) which is a photochemical oxidant. When Nitrogen oxidants (NO_x) and Volatile Organic Compounds (VOC) are influenced by sunlight, photochemical oxidants are formed. Two important primary pollutants are Sulphur compounds (SO_x), which cause acidification, and NO_x which also causes acidification and is a necessary component to the formation of photochemical oxidants.

Air pollution is no new phenomenon. Wet deposition was reported by 1852, and as early as 1306,[16] regulations were made to reduce air pollution from sea colliers in London[17]. Until relatively recently, air pollution was considered to be mainly a local problem, located close to main emitters like brown coal fuelled industry. The solution to local pollution problems was the construction of higher chimney stacks, which transported emissions up into higher layers of the atmosphere, thereby moving the pollution problem away from the local source into other regions and nations.

Air pollution and damage to crops

Even though agricultural crops are sensitive to acid rain, the effect of acid rain on soil is small in comparison with the acidifying effects of intensive cropping, traditionally mitigated by the application of lime which also compensates for the acidification from air pollution.[18]

Acid rain in combination with ozone, however, has the effect of reducing plants' dry weight.

The main damage to agricultural crops from air pollution is caused by ozone, O_3. According to the USA's 'National Crop Loss Assessment Network', the United States loses an estimated US$ 3 billion per year through ozone damage to major crops.[19]

Some argue that increased CO_2 content in the atmosphere would increase the crop yield through the resultant increase in photosynthesis. This is, however, a controversial problem, and therefore the potential results of such a scheme are hard to estimate.

Air pollution and damage to lakes, rivers and groundwater

The acidification of lakes and rivers is closely connected with the effect of air pollution on soil, since much of the water has previously passed through the ground. The sensitivity of lakes and rivers depends on the acidity and amount of deposition, plus other factors such as the characteristics of the soil in the drainage catchment area; the canopy effects on the ground cover; and the composition of the bedrock.[20]

The acidification of a lake takes place in two main stages. In the first stage, there is still considerable resistance to acidification. By the second, all buffering ability has gone, and there are great seasonal variations in the acidification of the water.

Air pollution also increases the mobilization of aluminium and heavy metals in the soil, in addition to having direct effects on the groundwater.

Long range transboundary air pollution (LRTAP)

The subject of LRTAP was brought to the attention of the OECD Research Committee by the Swedish delegation in Paris in 1968. Seven years later, a final report from the OECD study concluded that long range transportation of pollution represented a serious, and growing, problem for the member countries.

When air pollution is transported more than approximately 100 kilometres away from the source before deposition, it is labelled Long Range Transported Air Pollution[21]. When pollution crosses borders before it is deposited it is called Long Range Transboundary Air Pollution (LRTAP), often referred to as 'acid rain'. The three main sources of emissions are industry, energy-production and transport. The main chemical components found in LRTAP are SO_x, NO_x, heavy metals and photochemical oxidants, mainly O_3 (ozone). The transport of emissions will vary markedly according to temperature, wind speed and direction; solar levels; intensity, duration and distribution of rainfall.[22]

The Convention

The ECE convention on LRTAP, also called 'The Geneva Convention,' was signed by 34 governments[23] and the European Economic Community in 1979, and has been in force since 1983. The signing of the Convention was considered by all participants to be an act of great significance for establishing effective intergovernmental co-operation to combat air pollution in the ECE-region.[24] The Convention provides a framework covering several pollutants and incorporating general undertakings by signatory states to limit emissions, and gradually reduce and prevent air pollution which could cross international boarders.

The Convention is the first internationally-binding instrument on a broad regional basis to deal with the problems of air pollution. Explicit reference was made to Principle 21 of the Declaration of the UN Conference on the Human Environment (Stockholm, 1972). The Convention functions as a framework which could be built upon with protocols, and serve as an example to other regional and bilateral agreements such as the 1991 bilateral agreement signed between the United States and Canada.

Escalation of LRTAP as an IEC

Several levels of conflicts were represented in the negotiations for LRTAP in Europe:

i) Net exporters vs. Net importers of air pollution,

ii) NGOs vs. Polluters such as industry, transportation and energy-production,

iii) NGOs vs. Net exporters, and

iv) Net importers vs. Transnational corporations (Polluters).

The focus in this context is on the parties involved in the conflicts between nations (i.e., net exporters and net importers).

In the 1970s, the parties were positioned as net exporters (e.g., former FRG, United Kingdom and Poland) *versus* net importers (e.g., Sweden, Norway, the Netherlands) of air pollution. These positions did not, however, reflect variations in the actual national emissions, nor the difficulty in identifying the original emissions source.

Today, the main adversaries are rather NGOs and industrial energy and transportation sectors (with national governments searching for compromises between adversarial positions of various interests groups through negotiations).

Box 33

Main points in the Economic Commission of Europe (ECE)-Convention on air pollution

Five main aspects of the Convention may be discerned:

i) The recognition (in the introduction to the Convention) that airborne pollutants are a major problem;

ii) the declaration that the parties would "endeavour to limit, and as far as possible gradually reduce and prevent air pollution" (article 2),

iii) the intention that they would use "the best available technology which is economically feasible" to protect people and their environment from air pollution (article 6),

iv) the intention to act together to work out guidelines and strategies for better control of emissions and pollutants (article 8), and

v) the intention to develop technical and scientific co-operation (e.g., the European Monitoring and Evaluation Programme (EMEP, cf. article 9, Source: Wettestad, 1991).

The scientific findings[25] in the late 1960s concerning the negative impacts of air pollution intensified the conflict. The main adversaries at that time were the Scandinavian countries, who expressed great concern about degradation of their land, forestry, and fresh water resources; and on the other side, the major emitters. The strategy of both parties was to continue research into air pollution, but their aims were, of course, poles apart. The Scandina-

Box 34

Protocols to the Economic Commission of Europe (ECE)-Convention on Air Pollution

As a basis for co-operative action, four Protocols to the Convention have been signed and one is being prepared:

i) 1984 **Protocol** on joint long term financing of the EMEP monitoring programme, ratified by 30 parties of the ECE-region and in force since 1988.

ii) 1985 **Protocol** on the reduction, by at least 30%, of SO_2 emissions or their transboundary fluxes, at the latest by 1993, ratified by 20 parties and in force since 1987. A revision of this protocol is in preparation.

iii) 1988 **Protocol** concerning the control of emissions of NO_x or their transboundary fluxes, ratified by 18 parties and in force since 1991. The aim of this Protocol is to freeze NO_x emissions at the 1987 level from 1994 onwards, and to negotiate subsequent reductions.

iv) **1991 Protocol** on the control of VOCs (Volatile Organic Compounds) or their transboundary fluxes, signed in November 1991.

v) Sweden and Canada are currently working on a proposal for a Protocol to control transboundary atmospheric transfer of persistent organic chemicals such as DDT, PCBs and dioxin.

vian countries wanted to prove that the increased acidification was a result of emissions from foreign sources. At the same time, the countries being accused of contributing to air pollution wanted to prove that air pollution was not the main reason for the increased acidification.

The initial scientific findings triggered extensive research into the causes and consequences of air pollution. The subsequent findings contributed to raising the political and public awareness of air pollution.[26]

Regional 'Security' and Air Pollution—the Role of the Conference on Security and Co-operation in Europe (CSCE) and ECE

The Swedish government used the UN Conference on the Human Environment in 1972 to present its growing concern over air pollution.

After the adoption of the Final Act of the Conference on Security and Co-operation in Europe (CSCE) in Helsinki in August 1975, the former USSR Secretary General Brechznev proposed three 'all-European' Minister- level conferences on energy, transportation, and the environment. The initiative for the negotiation process was taken in the favourable European political climate.[27] The Scandinavian countries suggested LRTAP as the theme for the conference.[28] An interesting observation is that the former Soviet Union's initiative for an environmental conference in 1976 was not necessarily due to a genuine concern for the environment. The environment was rather seen as a 'neutral' theme which could provide a chance to have high-level meetings between East and West. Paradoxically, the *dominant* wind direction over Europe does not give LRTAP any major East-West dimensions, although the main polluters were located in the East.

Box 35

Why ECE was chosen for implementing the CSCE's Final Act

Some of the reasons for choosing ECE instead of CSCE for implementing the Final Act include:

i) ECE had traditionally been the appropriate arena for discussing issues involving OECD-countries, the former USSR and Eastern European countries. In 1976, when Brechznev proposed the high level meeting, ECE already had 30 years of experience of East-West co-operation;

ii) ECE already had a principal subsidiary body (the Senior Advisers to ECE Governments on Environmental Problems) qualified to deal with environmental questions;

iii) ECE operates on the principle of consensus; and

iv) ECE has a permanent "machinery."

Subsequently, during the preparation for the conference, it became obvious that the conflict was not mainly between East and West, but rather along a North—South axis (Northern vs. Central and Southern Europe). In general, Northern interests could be said to be represented by Scandinavian countries who are the recipients of airborne pollution originating in Central Europe. Those nations traditionally are most dependent on fossil fuel, especially coal, (the UK, FRG and the US) opposed a convention on LRTAP.

In 1977, there was no longer any doubt that long-range transportation of SO_2 and air pollution did occur across Europe[29]. In April 1978, at the first CSCE follow-up meeting after the Final Act, the ECE Exec-

utive Secretary reported on the progress made in the ECE with regard to the pertinent provisions of the Final Act, as well as the possibilities open to the ECE for contributing further to the implementation of the Final Act.[30]

The International Conference on Acidification

Time went by and there were not enough ratifiers to the Convention to bring it into force. The 'pushers' for binding protocols on reduction of emissions were not satisfied with the situation. As a result, the Swedish government took the initiative to arrange the Stockholm International Conference on Acidification in 1982.

A major change in the negotiation at the Conference took place when the former FRG announced a change of position. Overnight, the balance of power shifted dramatically; the United Kingdom had lost its main ally in the political fight to slow down the implementation process of the Convention. This development gave the EEC political leverage to take action to reduce the level of atmospheric emissions within their jurisdiction. The final statement was strong and positive, and concluded that further concrete action was required to reduce SO_2 and NO_x emissions. By early 1983 the goal of the Stockholm Conference, to enhance the ratification of the Convention, was attained.

Progress and expansion of the negotiations

The next phase is dominated by the signing and ratification of various protocols which enforce binding agreements on the parties to the Convention. The Convention has thus changed its character from a framework convention to an instrument for concrete actions which could improve air quality in the ECE-region.

During the ECE Executive Body's third meeting in Helsinki in July 1985, the Protocol on the reduction of SO_2-emissions by at least 30% by 1993 at the latest was signed. The United Kingdom and the United States argued, however, that there were still too many scientific uncertainties, and that more research was required.[31] The United Kingdom has since then been criticized more or less openly by signatories to the 1985 Protocol for not attending. The United Kingdom has, however, promised to cut their SO_2 emissions by 30 per cent by 1999.[32]

While international negotiations for the 1985 Protocol were taking place, scientific interest in air pollutants shifted focus from SO_2 emissions to NO_x emissions due to new studies on forest damage, which suggested that NO_x might play a more significant role than SO_2 in causing some forms of biological damage.[33] This was quickly followed by a switch in the political debate and in the main concern of the NGOs, and the demand for an additional protocol on NO_x emissions grew.

The preparation of the NO_x Protocol went rather smoothly, and in November 1988, 25 parties signed the Third Protocol to the Convention (which is, however, thought to be inadequate by many parties). A number of countries have therefore declared their intention to reduce national emissions by a further 30 per cent from the agreed level, not later than 1998.

It was also agreed between the signatories of the 1988 Protocol that a second stage would be negotiated, once the Protocol had come into force, to take into account internationally accepted 'critical loads'.[34] The critical load principle refers to the amount of pollution the natural resource system can absorb without experiencing degradation. While earlier protocols aimed at a flat-rate percentage reduction of specified air pollutants, the focus is now on the determination of agreed critical loads as a basis for air pollution control measures (which could mean that some countries will have to reduce emissions more than others).

The Vienna follow-up meeting to the CSCE in January 1989, specifically addressed co-operation on LRTAP within the framework of the Convention. The participating states called upon contracting and signatory parties to the 1985 Protocol on SO_2 emissions, and recommended further steps to reduce sulphur emissions. The CSCE meeting welcomed the 1988 NO_x Protocol, and recognized the need for developing arrangements to reduce emissions of other relevant air pollutants such as hydrocarbons and VOCs.[35]

From Regional to Global Conflicts

A shift of emphasis from traditional, regional air pollution problems, to the issue of global atmospheric pollution occurred in the late 1980s. Growing international concern over potential climatic change (resulting from emissions of greenhouse gases in the atmosphere) led to the establishment of the joint WMO/UNEP Inter-Governmental Panel on Climatic Changes. As a result, the 44th UN ECE Session in April 1989 decided to undertake a review of its programmes, activities and discussions in order to find possible contributions from the ECE to the prevention of Climatic Change. [36]

The Fourth Protocol to the Convention was signed on 19 November 1991 in Geneva, by 21 states. This Protocol aims to control and reduce the emissions of Volatile

Organic Compounds (VOCs). VOCs include organic compounds of an anthropogenic nature (other than methane) which are capable of producing photochemical oxidants such as ozone by reacting with nitrogen-oxides in the presence of sunlight. The signatories have agreed to one of three ways to control and reduce their annual emissions of VOCs or their transboundary fluxes. This gives the various signatories an opportunity to choose the way most suitable for their level of industrial development. In addition to the articles on the reduction and control of emissions, the Protocol also includes articles on exchange of technology in order to reduce emissions of VOCs; on research and monitoring; and on information exchange between the signatories.

The willingness of the emitters to adopt pollution reducing policies and technologies has prevented the IEC from escalating to an overt behaviour conflict. Criticism from non-governmental organizations, and the nations which receive the largest amounts of LRTAP, however, suggests that the measures may be inadequate for resolving the IEC of air pollution.

Lessons Learned

What can be learned from the negotiations of the Convention, is that acceptance of research and monitoring results by the international political system requires the involvement of scientific groups from a number of countries. Even though it is not always necessary to organize the research and monitoring internationally, evaluation of the results must be a joint effort. To achieve political or diplomatic progress in the field of the environment, scientific results must be provided which all parties involved can accept.[37]

The negotiation process which took place within the framework of ECE (resulting in the Geneva Convention on Long Range Transport of Air Pollution (LRTAP)), shows that when the involved parties have a mutual relationship within an institution, as in the case of ECE, the chance to prevent and resolve the conflict is greater than when there is no such established relationship.

Monitoring of the environment seems to be an effective tool for ensuring the prevention of IECs and compliance with agreements. The monitoring data gives all parties in the IECs information on both current and past situations, which is vital if agreements are to be reached during negotiations.

Chapter Nine

CASE STUDIES

Secondary effects of degradation: environmental refugees[1]

9

THIS CHAPTER deals with environmental refugees as a source of IECs caused by the secondary effects of environmental degradation or disruptions. The causal linkages between the degradation of natural resources and cross-boundary movement of people are complex, but of great interest in the context of IECs.

9.1 Introduction

Still controversial, the term 'environmental refugee' was popularized with the release of the 1985 UNEP report entitled 'Environmental Refugees' by Essam El-Hinnawi.[2] Describing the growing incidence and numbers of people displaced by environmental degradation, El-Hinnawi's 1985 report drew attention to the important and complex challenges that such problems present to the international community.

Use of the term 'refugee' to describe people who are displaced for environmental

reasons is problematic. Such persons are often in desperate need of assistance, and they may cross national borders in search of safe refuge. There are also increasing numbers of *internally* displaced people who have left their homes for environmental reasons, but who do not satisfy the traditional eligibility criteria for refugee status. The definitional issue demands special consideration, because the operable international definitions of 'refugee' do not necessarily cover such persons.

Nevertheless, numerous articles have appeared since 1985 that have further popularized the term 'environmental refugee'. Environment related movement may be caused by factors that are coercive (or otherwise involuntary) and may result in transboundary movements. In some cases this may parallel historical conditions, thus giving rise to protected refugee status. Most cases of such movement do not, however,

satisfy such criteria. Lack of agreement in the international community concerning the status of persons displaced for environmental reasons is reflected in the literature that has appeared since El-Hinnawi's report. Vague mandates, poor co-ordination, competing interests and agendas, and inadequate funding have also complicated the task of clearly identifying both the scope of the problem and the appropriate international institutional responses.

The continuing debate over terminology notwithstanding, there is a growing consensus that the number of 'environmental refugees' around the world is increasing. UNCED's Agenda 21[3] makes frequent reference to the complex links between population, environment and development, and the increasing challenges posed by environment-related migration and displacement issues, and emphasizes the increasing importance of these issues to the world community, for whom the challenge entails both assistance and protection for these refugees.

The environmental aspect is also found at both ends of the displacement problem: although 'environmental degradation' can be a *cause* of displacement, it also can be a *result* of movement of people who are displaced for other reasons.

This chapter focuses on the environmental degradation and disruption that lead to 'environmental refugees'.

A great deal of further research is needed to assess the scope of the problem and its complex causes; to provide estimates of numbers of environmental refugees; and to identify those locations most likely to be affected.

9.2 IECs and environmental refugees

Environmental refugees have been classified as a D-type conflict, which means that they are a secondary effect of degradation of natural resources (see Figure 17).

When analysing IECs stemming from movements of environmental refugees, the complex set of causes of the movement has to be considered. Many IECs originating from the movement of environmental refugees are related to access to, control over and unsustainable use of natural resources, especially land and water resources.

Inadequate production systems, such as traditional land practice combined with population growth, increase the competi-

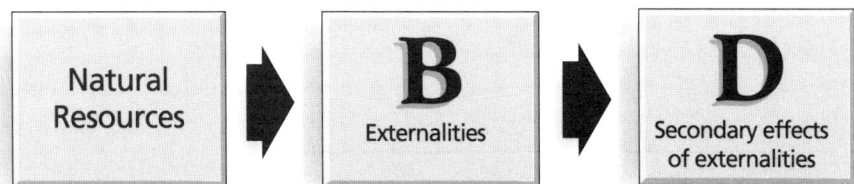

Figure 17. The ABC(D) model: IECs as secondary effects of degradation of natural resources

tion for (i.e., the pressure on) land resources. Few nations have areas of productive land which are not already under intensive cultivation.

A large group of internally displaced people within a nation can be a serious threat to national security. A nation with a large group of internally displaced people is more exposed to a declining economy, and destabilization/deterioration in its social and political structure. The outcome of such situations is often open conflicts, either in the form of internal disorders, or in tension and hostilities with other nations in the case of cross border migration.

When environmental refugees cross an international border in search of safety, the problem often becomes an IEC. Developing countries are the main receivers of environmental refugees. Most of these countries have a tradition of accepting environmental refugees from neighbouring countries. As the number of environmental refugees grows, however, the pressure on the land resources in receiving nations increases drastically as a result. This has led to open conflicts between locals and immigrants. Conflicts between environmental refugees and governments often arise from increased populations in slum areas, which increase the proportion of the nation's population considered to be impoverished. Examples of overt conflict behaviour between environmental refugees and local populations include the clash between Assamese farmers and Bangladeshi refugees in India and the conflict between Ghanaians and environmental refugees from Sahel in Accra and Tuaregs (see Box 36).

9.3 Driving forces behind the environmental refugee problem

The close interaction between environmental disruption and degradation, and mismanagement of natural resources; combined with poverty, oppression and violence, make it hard to isolate environmental roots or immediate causes of the refugee problem. Any attempts to make such distinctions must take into account both short and long-term historical factors.[4]

Clearly, sudden *environmental disruption* or *long-term degradation* must be understood in a socio-economic, cultural, and political context. The close links between social order, internal stability, and resource utilization need to be examined with care when drawing distinctions between 'man-made' and 'natural' disasters or degradation. This distinction has sometimes been made for the purpose of establishing appropriate institutional responsibility and answering the related questions of protection and assistance. While an earthquake may be an unequivocal 'natural disaster', the heavy loss of life following a drought or a famine may be explained by basic economic problems and social development as well as in the context of the background of armed conflict or serious internal disturbance.

Cases of movement of people caused solely by environmental factors are rare. It is sometimes the case that blaming movement on 'environmental' conditions is used as an excuse to divert public attention from a political or economic situation. However, it is generally accepted that most cases of environmental disruption and degradation are caused by human activities and not due to natural processes alone.[5]

The driving forces outlined above are the coerced or involuntary nature of the displacement; transboundary movement; and the need for protection arising from life-threatening environmental conditions. Except for an indication of cross-border movement versus internally displaced people, it has been difficult to assess these concerns directly in the case studies. This situation illustrates the need for more research and understanding of the driving forces behind the movements, and to what extent they exhibit a need for assistance and/or protection.

This chapter **does not** attempt to indicate whether or not the environmental refugees in question in the following case-studies would or would not fall within any of the existing international definitions of refugees or within the definition given by UNHCR's mandate. Rather, it attempts to provide examples of both the types and the severity of problems involved with migration resulting from environmental degradation or disruption.

Historically, the principal causes of environmental migration and displacement have been:

i) Natural disasters, such as drought/famine, floods, tropical cyclones, earthquakes and volcanoes (these are often exacerbated by human activities)

ii) Degradation of land resources (for example, marginal lands)

iii) Involuntary resettlement or relocation of people (for example, resulting from the construction of large dams)

iv) Industrial accidents (for example, Bhopal or Chernobyl)

v) Aftermath of war (as, for example, in Afghanistan)

Some models of potential climatic changes also point to unprecedented human displacements around the world (potentially in coastal areas and marginal agro-climatic zones), as briefly outlined at the end of this chapter.

Natural disasters

A natural disaster may be defined as:
'an event, caused by disruptive changes in the physical environment, concentrated in time and space, in which a community undergoes severe damage and endures such losses to its members and physical appurtenances that the social structure is disrupted and fulfilment of all or some of the essential functions of the society are prevented.'[6]

A complex chain of causes and effects exists between man-made and natural disruption and degradation, which makes differentiation between them difficult. Natural disasters may, however, be divided into the following categories:
—Seismic hazards (earthquakes and volcanoes)
—Mass movement hazards (rockfalls, landslides, snow avalanches)
—Atmospheric hazards (tropical cyclones, severe summer and winter storms) and
—Hydrological hazards (floods and droughts). [7]

Floods, hurricanes and earthquakes are the most frequently reported natural disasters.[8] The high-risk nations, based on deaths per million inhabitants, are Bangladesh, Guatemala, Nicaragua, Honduras, Iran, Peru, New Guinea, Haiti and South Korea.[9]

Another type of natural disaster which affects large groups of people is drought, particularly in Sub-Saharan Africa. The drought affecting Southern Africa in 1992 put more than 40 million people at risk of starvation and disease.[10]

The increased numbers of natural disasters over the last three decades may be explained in part by the fact that popula-

Box 36

Nomadic groups in West Africa

Many environmental refugees from Mali, Burkina Faso and Niger who were first displaced by the Sahelian drought in 1973—74, and again in 1984, were forced to seek sanctuary in Ghana. The traditionally self-sufficient nomadic groups of the Fulanis and Tuaregs from West Africa were forced to leave their homelands because of a prolonged drought which killed almost all their livestock, destroyed their way of life and resulted in famine.

For the Tuaregs, increased cultivation of marginal land by other ethnic groups has meant loss of pasture, while restrictions in movements across national boundaries and unsuccessful settlement schemes have considerably reduced the land area available to them, further increasing their vulnerability to drought. The Fulanis, on the other hand, have been more settled than the Tuaregs. A modern monetary economy and border-crossing restrictions that hamper flexible pastoralism have made them more heavily dependent on agriculture and caused them to settle more permanently, which makes them, too, highly vulnerable to drought (Trolldalen, 1991). Most of the environmental refugees in West Africa have moved out of the more marginalized Sahelian zone to areas with greater productive carrying capacity, especially the Guinean zone and its coast (Essuman-Johnson, 1991).

Great ethnic tensions have, however, arisen between local people and refugees from neighbouring countries, which have resulted in violent conflicts, for example in receiving areas such as Accra, Ghana. (Essuman-Johnson, 1991).

tions have tended to concentrate in areas vulnerable to natural disasters because of land degradation. Improved monitoring systems and global communications have also resulted in unprecedented reporting of such disasters.[11]

The world community has also become more aware of the link between the frequency and severity of natural hazards and environmental degradation caused by population growth, scarcity of land resources, and exceeding the biological carrying capacity of ecosystems through industrialization and pollution.[12]

In the 1970s and 1980s, natural disasters killed 3 million people and affected 820 million globally, but no data exists to indicate what proportion of these people be-

came environmental refugees.[13]

Degradation of land resources

Recognized as the principal factor behind the ever-growing migration from native homelands, land degradation drives people from their native homelands in search of more fertile lands that can sustain their basic needs. Population pressure and international economic factors often encourage farmers to apply agricultural techniques which are not sustainable (abandoning methods such as crop rotation, fallowing and terracing). Fallowing and crop rotation have historically permitted farmers to grow crops on marginalized land, but increasing population and economic pressures (potentially in drylands and mountain areas) have

Box 37

Land resources in Haiti

Many of the Haitian refugees in the United States are peasant smallholders who have experienced an eroding land resource base caused principally by removal of the vegetation cover (Kurlansky, 1989).

One contributing factor to land degradation in Haiti is the 'Napoleon inheritance system', which is a remnant of French colonial rule. According to the Napoleon inheritance code, each child has the right to an equal share of its parents' land, which has resulted in the partitioning of the farmland into thousands of small fields, too small to make a living for a family. The need to feed families year after year from these minuscule plots rules out the use of traditionally practised crop rotation to conserve land, while a rapidly growing population puts additional pressure on strained land resources. Today Haiti has more than 200 people for every square mile of land; in North America the average is 30 people per square mile. Estimates given by USAID predict that the population will double in 25 years (Kurlansky, 1989).

Preventive efforts may include land reforms, which ensure that each land unit is sufficiently large to enable sustainable agricultural production, and soil conservation projects which could help prevent further waves of environmental refugees.

forced cultivators to shorten rotation cycles. In developing countries, increasing population pressure and the loss of topsoil seem to go hand in hand, and force formerly self-sufficient rural societies into cycles of poverty and food shortages.

Marginalized people in developing countries are more vulnerable to land degradation than others, since they do not have the economic or technological means to prevent land degradation processes (for example, erosion of soil; changes in, or removal of, vegetation cover; changes in hydrological regime; or changes in soil and water chemistry). When such degradation occurs in industrialized countries, some type of 'security system' usually exists which may assist injured parties, and thereby prevent them from becoming environmental refugees. The risk of becoming a displaced person is greater in developing countries, however, since large populations often live in areas which are prone to natural disasters (as, for example, concentrated settlements on the banks of the rivers in Bangladesh).[15] The effects of hurricane 'Andrew' which hit south Florida in the summer of 1992 highlight the fragility of even the most sophisticated 'security systems' in the industrialized world and the vulnerability of all people to the danger of massive environmental disasters.

Involuntary resettlement

Many infrastructural activities (for example, industry, dam and road construction) that entail land acquisition sometimes involve involuntary resettlement. Most irrigation, hydro-electric power and water supply projects, and some urban, transport and industry projects, can only be implemented if people are resettled from land required for

Box 38

Refugee Movements in the Horn of Africa

Ethiopia, Eritrea, Tigray, Eastern-Sudan, Somalia, Djibouti and Northern Kenya constitute the 'Horn of Africa.' This region is well known for being heavily affected by refugee movements. The area has seen years of war, as guerilla movements have fought governments, and neighbouring countries have clashed, and in this context it is difficult to determine whether people are 'political' or 'environmental' refugees. In a statement made in 1984, UNHCR said that there had been no political event in Africa during the previous two years significant enough to account for major new refugee movements (suggesting that movements that were occurring in this period must have been due to other reasons such as falling land productivity). (Timberlake, 1988). In June 1988, the US Embassy in Addis Ababa reported that one million inhabitants of the highlands of Ethiopia were about to move, due to famine conditions. Since then, droughts have caused waves of environmental refugees in this region, and appear to be continuing to do so.

Preventive action taken by UNHCR through financial support for 'durable solutions' seems to be fruitful. At its annual Executive Meeting in late 1983, UNHCR acknowledged the environmental factors relevant to the refugees by allocating one third of its $400 million budget to 'durable solutions', which imply development and preventive aid instead of more common short term relief (Timberlake, 1984).

The Inter-Governmental Authority on Drought and Development (IGADD) provides another example of a regional preventive effort to promote proper management of land and water resources.

civil works. Involuntary resettlement is complex because lost income sources such as farmland, forests, pastures, markets and other production resources must be replaced or compensated with equally productive alternative assets, if affected people are to reconstruct their lives and restore economic productivity. Careful planning is needed for acquisition of even small strips of land where the loss would make farming inviable, or where people would lose their homes and shops to make way for highways or transport lines.

Involuntary resettlement has been one of the most controversial components of development assistance. A major reason has been the failure to appraise resettlement plans in this field. This has often led to inadequately designed and underfinanced resettlement initiatives, which turned into relief rather than development operations. The environmental impact of poor resettlement operations is impoverishment and the environmental degradation that often accompanies poverty.

The risk of impoverishment in forced resettlement operations is high because of the loss of a productive resource base. In addition, unlike voluntary settlement, which involves self-selected, younger families, involuntary resettlement compels everyone to move. This means that the resettlement communities must support not only the able bodied, but also less produc-

Box 39

Bangladesh

The environmental refugees of Bangladesh can be divided into two groups: **(i)** those having to move because of floods and other natural disasters, and **(ii)** those having to move because of land degradation within Bangladesh.

Bangladesh has 115.6 million inhabitants (1990) most of whom live in flood-prone areas. In the past, massive floods have hit Bangladesh roughly twice a century. Now, the 'abnormal' floods occur almost annually, killing thousands and leaving millions displaced. The increased magnitude and frequency of the floods is exacerbated by watershed degradation in the up-stream countries (Nepal and Bhutan). Watershed degradation takes place when the vegetation cover is removed, and the soil in the watershed loses its sponge-like retaining effect on the rainwater.

The increasing number of people vulnerable to floods in Bangladesh is not only due to watershed degradation in the Himalayas, but also to the fact that areas which in the past were considered too dangerous for settlement are now being used as residential areas because of growing population pressures (Ives and Pitt, 1990).

Population growth is the main reason for today's pressure on land resources (Bangladesh has an annual population growth rate of 2.7%, and is expected to have 235 million inhabitants by 2025, see Sadik, 1991).

In addition, the number of environmental refugees forced to move by degraded land resources is growing. Some resettle within Bangladesh, while others cross into India. Much of the cross-border movement has been into the Indian republic Assam, where Assamese and Bangladeshi farmers have found themselves in direct competition over land resources. In 1983, tension between local Assamese and Bangladeshi farmers erupted into violence, which resulted in the deaths of 3000 people (Timberlake, 1984).

tive people, such as the old, the incapacitated and the unskilled. Moreover, wealthier and better-educated families tend to move to better areas, taking with them important sources of local investment capital and socio-economic support, leaving a disproportionately poor community to be resettled.

Industrial accidents

Industrial accidents with a heavy environmental impact are becoming a potential main cause of environmental refugees in industrialized and developing countries. On July 10, 1976, the population of Seveso (700) was evacuated as a result of the accidental discharge of dioxin following an explosion.[16]

On August 7 1978, 240 families were evacuated from Love Canal, New York, due to leakage from corroded drums containing industrial wastes buried in the 1940s and 1950s.[17]

At Chernobyl power station in the former USSR, on April 26, 1986, one of four nuclear reactors experienced a cata-

Box 40

South Asia

Many environmental refugees are located in India, Bangladesh, Sri Lanka, Bhutan, Pakistan and Afghanistan. As elsewhere, there is little reliable data available to give an reliable estimate of the numbers of such refugees. Some monitoring and research has, however, been undertaken on involuntary displacement due to development projects.

The majority of the environmental refugees are internally displaced, but there is some cross border movement. India, for example, has received environmental refugees from both Nepal and Bangladesh (Raju and Maloney, 1992).

The environmental refugees that were created by the construction of a dam on the Kaptai Lake in Bangladesh are one example of cross-border migration due to lack of resettlement schemes after a development project. The Kaptai Lake is one of the few places where the Bangladeshi landscape provides facilities for construction of dams for hydroelectric power projects. When the lake was flooded in the 1960s, more than 100,000 people were forced to leave (ibid, 1991).

India is another South Asian nation which has a large number of displaced people due to unsatisfactory resettlement policy. The Indian Social Institute has estimated that 15.5 million Indians have been displaced by development projects. Dams, reservoirs and canals alone have contributed to the displacement of 11 million, of whom only 2.75 million have been resettled. The rest (8.25 million) have had to 'find their own way,' which for the majority means either in slum settlements in cities or as poor day workers in the countryside (ibid).

strophic melt-down as a result of experiments conducted on it during a routine maintenance shutdown. The reactor building was partly destroyed by explosives and fire, which released large clouds of radioactive material. At least 135,000 people were evacuated from the site, and 31 were killed.[18] Thousands of local inhabitants were subsequently resettled in less contaminated areas.[19]

Industrial accidents with heavy environmental effects also take place in developing countries, the most well-known example of which is the Bhopal accident. In this Indian city, on December 3, 1984, an accident in a pesticide factory owned by Union Carbide India released a cloud of methyl isocyate, killing at least 7000 people[20] and injuring approximately 200,000. [21]

There is always a danger of industrial accidents with local, national and international environmental effects.

The accident triggered a massive exodus from Bhopal. This accident illustrates the

Box 41

The Risk of Environmental Refugees in Central and Eastern Europe

A brief review of the potential risk of environmental refugees in Central and Eastern Europe[23] needs to apply a broad perspective due to the lack of earlier research on the topic in this region, and thus, the general lack of accurate data. For the purpose of gauging the scale of the potential risk of environmental refugees in the region, examples of past and recent trends are provided. Most of the region is densely populated, which presents a huge potential for migration.

One should bear several things in mind in this context: that the perception of environmental hazards varies among nations and groups within nations; that economic stagnation and the dismantling of the political and existing economic system are ongoing; and that radical change of vital social and economic facilities, and lack of institutional capacity make the marginalized sectors of the population most exposed when environmental disruption and degradation occur.

Hazards and pollution related to nuclear power stations

In recent years, nuclear power stations have been considered to be the most serious threat both to the environment and to human health in Central and Eastern Europe. Accidents, or unsafe handling of radioactive material in nuclear power plants, have affected people directly through exposure to radioactivity, or indirectly, through for example, crops and drinking water which have been contaminated.

After the Chernobyl disaster in 1986, at least 135,000 people were evacuated and resettled from the most contaminated area. In the village of Polesskoje, 55 kilometres away from Chernobyl, just outside the 'official' devastated area, sociologists have carried out a research project on how the behaviour of the village's 27,000 inhabitants has been affected by the nuclear catastrophe. The study revealed that those who were well off, and had better access to information about the consequences of the melt-down in the reactor, moved away. Those who stayed behind are strongly marked by hopelessness and despair (Herrmann, 1992).

In Central and Eastern Europe there are 32 nuclear power stations, altogether 70 operable reactors, with 36 more under construction and a further 45 planned. This represents a quarter of the total in Europe (World Nuclear Industry Handbook, 1991).

Despite having a smaller proportion of reactors, Central and Eastern Europe is considered to have a significantly higher risk of accident than the rest of Europe. This is partly explained by the difference in construction of nuclear power plants (Central and Eastern European reactors lack an outer containment, a 'hood'—which is found in Western installations.[24] It is not known whether this 'hood' has any effect in the case of an accident such as Chernobyl, since there have not been any accidents of this proportion in any of the West European reactors).

Some observations indicate that the installations and their risk management procedures decay as the economy declines, which points to an increased threat of new nuclear disasters in the former Soviet Union.[25]

There have been several reports of smaller accidents and malfunctions in the same kind of reactor as that which caused the disaster at Chernobyl. These Light Water Cooled Graphite Reactors (LWGRs) are found on five sites in addition to Chernobyl.[26]

A leakage at one of the reactors in St. Petersburg on March 24, 1992, which received much publicity in the press, is only one of many incidents.

Ignalina is another nuclear power station with LWGR reactors, which has received attention due to several malfunctions. Several 'awkward episodes' have been reported unofficially from the Ignalina plant.[27] Most of the LWGR reactors are located in densely populated areas with 50–100 inhabitants per square kilometre. The population density is significantly higher in St. Petersburg city, which alone has a population of 5 million, while the surrounding areas have an additional 1.7 million inhabitants.[28] These figures give an indication of how many environmental refugees might be caused by a similar disaster in one of these reactors.

Several incidents of malfunctions have also been reported from Bulgarian installations.[29]

A recent report from the International Atomic Energy Agency (IAEA) in Vienna, singles out the nuclear power station in Kozloduy, Bulgaria, as the world's most dangerous nuclear power plant. (Barmetter, 1992)

Nuclear Waste

Not only the reactors themselves are a potential cause of new environmental refugees, but the handling of their radioactive waste is also critical. Until recently, nuclear waste generated by the Soviet-designed reactors used to be taken back to the Soviet Union. Under the former "state concept," used fuel was not classified as waste, but was reprocessed. There are three known sites in the former Soviet Union for nuclear waste management. (Barker, 1991)

Chelyabinsk is located on the far Eastern side of the Urals, in the province of Chelyabinsk. The other two, Krasnoyarsk and Tomsk, are located further East on the Siberian taiga.

At the end of 1991 the civil atomic power authorities of the former Soviet Union announced that they would no longer handle waste from foreign reactors, despite their contractual obligations. As a consequence of this, radioactive waste must be stored by the individual nuclear plant operators. The IAEA is concerned that in a situation lacking a central regulatory authority, individual plant operators will not take the necessary safety and environmental precautions. IAEA officials describe the situation as an 'invitation for disaster.' (Land, 1992)

Air pollution

'The Black Triangle' (comprised of South-Western Poland, North-Western Czechoslovakia and the South-Eastern part of Germany), is an area which is identified as an environmental 'hot spot' by environment and health studies. (Hertzmann, 1990) In the Katowice-Krakow area of Poland, the ground water and soil have been polluted for 200 years by intense industrial activity. (Livernash, 1992). Then, as today, local brown coal was the main energy source. The combination of the concentration of industry and the choice of fuel results in some of Europe's highest SO_2 emissions and depositions. (Iversen et al., 1991) The region's reliance on coal has inflicted a heavy toll on the atmosphere, and thereby on the population's health. Out of 33 industrialized countries, life expectancy is the shortest in the Central and Eastern European countries. Air pollution is a major cause of this situation. (Levy et al., 1992)

In the commentary to Czechoslovakia's Clean Air Act, it is stated that the air pollution in the Czech Republic is so high that it places the area among the most polluted territories in Europe. (Pape et al., 1991b) The quality of the air in North-Western Bohemia is also unhealthy, as it is in heavily populated areas such as Prague and Ostava. In 1990, the Czechoslovakian Federal Committee for the environment published a study on the state of the country's environment. The study concludes that there has been a substantial increase in emissions over the last few years. Half of the population in the Czech republic, and a third of the Slovakian population, is living in areas with notably low air quality. (ibid.)

precarious nature of a city where many of the inhabitants live in close proximity to a variety of potentially toxic industrial installations.[22]

So far, the number of people who have had to leave their homes because of industrial accidents has not reached the same proportions as those fleeing from land degradation, but nevertheless environmental accidents have a significant potential for creating more displaced persons.

Aftermath of war

Wars affect the environment both directly and indirectly. The direct effects may be short-term, in which case the environment may be restored almost to its original condition, and those who migrated because of war may return. The effects may, however, endure, in which case refugees will stay away longer and many may never return.[30]

Indirect effects include the remnants of war (for example, unexploded mines, bombs and shells) which may hinder the rehabilitation of affected areas. These areas, particularly in developing countries, are often far removed from any hope of rehabilitation and their original inhabitants are forced to seek refuge elsewhere.[31]

Afghanistan has, for example, experienced a decline in productive land area due

to war. When the farmers fled, many fields were abandoned and left exposed. The Afghan soil is very vulnerable to water and wind erosion. When irrigation systems broke down from lack of maintenance and war destruction, large areas of productive land had to be abandoned. The loss of productive land is one of the causes of the refugees in Pesawar in Pakistan.[32]

Another area which has fostered environmental refugees is Egypt's North-Western desert and the Libyan desert. In this area nomads have been driven from areas they frequented for generations, by remnants of the Second World War.[33]

More recently, examples are areas in Cambodia and Vietnam where areas remain uninhabitable, or at least without significant investment in rehabilitation of the environment for the foreseeable future.

Climatic changes

Within the scope of this paper, it is impossible to make predictions as to potential future causes of environmental displacement of people. There are however, some general traits in the global environment which might significantly affect movements of people in the future, sudden 'environmental surprises' like changes in world fresh water resources, or the widely-predicted global climatic changes (see a more thorough discussion of such changes in Chapter Six).

Sea level rise is *potentially* the most important single factor causing new groups of displaced people. Any sea level rise would be caused by the greenhouse effect, which contributes to global warming. Several different estimates as to the degree of future sea level rise have been put forward. The worst-case IPCC scenario predicts a 110 cm sea level rise by the year 2100, while a more

Box 42

The Maldive Islands

The Maldevian archipelago, only a few metres above sea level, is seriously threatened by sea level rise. If and when the level rises, sea water will enter ground water inland and increase the salinity of the Maldevian soil. At the same time, the archipelago will experience more frequent and serious intrusions by the sea, with the salinated soil eventually becoming covered by sea water. Initially, people will experience a reduction in the production capacities of their farmlands, and later, they will literally see their homes being swallowed by the ocean. The Maldevian population of 202,000 will be forced to abandon their country and thus add to the increasing number of environmental refugees .

conservative scenario predicts a rise of 31 cm.[34]

Potential global climatic changes may force new sections of the world's population into involuntary migration. A potential sea level rise of one metre worldwide could result in millions of new environmental refugees. Such a rise in sea level could affect all land up to the five metre contour line, if maximum storm surges and the effects of salt water intrusion along river mouths are taken into account.[35] The affected area would be about 5 million km², or about 3 per cent of the global land area, containing one third of the world's total cropland. This would have severe implications for nations like Sri Lanka, Bangladesh and the South Pacific island states, as well as for the Netherlands, Denmark, Japan and the United States.

Defences may be constructed to keep sea water out of productive areas and settlements; or the land may undergo a change of use, or be abandoned altogether. In the poor regions of the South, migration seems to be the only option.

Many densely populated areas and as many as one billion people could be affected. In this context, it is alarming to note that the main current migration direction, in a global perspective, is from inland areas towards the coast, in parallel and related to the movements from rural to urban districts.

9.4 International response to environmental refugees

The complex nature of causes of environmental degradation leading to human displacement and migration means that the need for protection and assistance varies at a regional, national and local level. Despite such differences, there is a need for a thorough discussion of the term 'environmental refugees': and subsequently an international and national acceptance of their existence and living conditions. The following text attempts therefore to highlight some of the critical points in this discussion.[36]

Problems of definition

The terms most frequently used to describe persons displaced by environmental factors —'environmental refugees', 'ecological refugees', 'resource refugees', 'environmental migrants'—reflect the lack of clear focus on the problem. Such phrases do not correspond to internationally agreed terms and criteria historically applicable to 'refugees'. Reflecting the lack of consensus over the correct term to apply to these people, the competing phrases have come into fashion in various circles in indiscriminate ways (mainly since 1985 and the appearance of El-Hinnawi's report which popularized the term 'environmental refugee'). However, despite widespread popular use, there has been little use or acknowledgment of the terms in legal and institutional contexts.

Indiscriminate use of the terms has caused some confusion over their exact meaning, and the major issues of concern to the category of people in question. Ideally, to advance international understanding and discussion of the problem, it is necessary to define the characteristics of people displaced by environmental factors; to identify their assistance and possible protection needs; and to outline the possible options for resolving migration and displacement problems caused by environmental factors. Although the discussion is outside the scope of this study, one may argue that the term 'environmental refugee' refers to a category of displaced persons that *supplements* the categories of people defined in the 1951 Convention Relating to the Status of Refugees (hereafter called 'the 1951 Convention'). The creation of a new category of 'environmental refugees' should *not* compromise the status and standing of the refugee definition in the 1951 Convention.

A working definition of 'environmental refugee' should reflect two factors. First, it should refer to persons who are *coerced* or *forced* to leave their homes for environmental reasons that threaten their lives. Second, in the context of IECs, it should be limited to persons who have crossed an international border (that is, persons who are *outside their country of nationality or origin*). These two points are expanded upon below.

Coercion

The definition proposed by El-Hinnawi in 1985 incorporates the principle of *coercion*:

"Those people who have been *forced* to leave their traditional habitat, temporarily or permanently, because of a marked environmental disruption (natural and/or triggered by people) that jeopardized their existence and/or seriously affected the quality of their life." (Emphasis added)

"Environmental disruption", El-Hinnawi explained, refers to "physical, chemical and/or biological changes in the ecosystem or the resource base that render it, temporarily or permanently, unsuitable to support human life."

Although it is unclear whether El-Hinnawi's definition of 'disruption' also describes gradual environmental deterioration, the operative word is 'coerced' (in contrast to voluntary or non-coerced movements).

At about the same time as the 1985 UNEP report, the UN General Assembly Group of Governmental Experts on Averting Mass Refugee Flows identified *coercion* to be a **decisive** factor in differentiating between the types of movements it sought to address, and traditional migrations and other voluntary movements of people.[37]

The distinction between *coerced* and *voluntary* movement of people should be taken to imply that in the first case, the people in question are in special need of help from the international community in terms of prevention and protection as well as assistance, because of their own government's unwillingness or inability to provide protection and help; whereas in the second case, the migrants may qualify for assistance, but not for preventive actions or protection.

In practice, however, the distinction

between coercion and pressure falling short of coercion may be hard to discern. Moreover, the fact that a movement may not have been coerced does not necessarily mean that there is no problem warranting prevention, protection or assistance. Environmental disasters resulting in mass movements rarely stem from natural causes alone. Rather, they typically reflect a combination of natural causes that are exacerbated by human activities (see earlier discussion). This complex sequence of causes cannot be overlooked and is being increasingly recognized.[38]

Externally displaced

El-Hinnawi's 1985 definition also includes persons who are displaced *internally* (that is, *within* their country of nationality or origin). It must be kept in mind that there are significant political and legal differences which have historically distinguished 'refugees' (or persons displaced *externally*) from persons displaced *internally*. In part, the distinction is based on the different legal status of the citizen and the alien. The difference is especially significant in relation to such international legal principles as freedom of movement and sovereignty.

Assistance and protection

Ideally, one of the most important means to prevent IECs is development assistance to refugees in departing areas. Realistically, however, in most cases, assistance can only be given in receiving areas, where the needs are enormous. The issue requires renewed thinking on ways to improve the international assistance system. Being a much less problematic area of international action, from a political point of view, than international protection, it should be possible to develop a system which addresses the assistance needs of persons displaced both internally and externally for environmental reasons.[39] Inter-agency co-ordination is required in such a system.

In most cases, the need for protection is clearly of vital importance for environmental refugees. There seems, however, to be a tendency to assume that environmental refugees are not in need of protection. As observed in the 1991 report of the Working Group on Solutions and Protection of the Executive Committee of the United Nations' High Commissioner for Refugees: 'Persons fleeing natural or ecological disasters normally have a need for relief assistance rather than protection.'[40]

Such an observation by the Working Group can only serve to hamper the development of protection standards for this category of people. Because large groups of environmental refugees are in situations where environmental degradation or disruption give rise to protection needs, this statement needs some further explanation and refinement.

A legal response to environmental refugee protection must address the following issues: First, whether there is a right of access to, and of refuge in a country other than the country of origin; and, second, what the standards of treatment are for those seeking refuge.

It is an open question as to how far an international obligation to protect environmental refugees should go, when the persons in question may be said to lack protection from their own government when it comes to imminent harm caused by environmental factors.[41]

The basic standards for the treatment of refugees in situations of 'temporary refuge' (set out in 1981 by the Executive Committee of the UNHCR Programme, and endorsed in the same year by the United Nations General Assembly), are of great interest.[42] These minimum standards represent an important consensus in the ongoing development of international legal principles with regard to modern refugee problems. Part II, Section A, paragraphs one and two of this Conclusion state: 'In situations of large-scale influx, asylum seekers should be admitted to the state in which they first seek refuge…in all cases the fundamental principle of non-refoulement, including non-rejection at the frontier, must be scrupulously observed.'

The standards of treatment and protection need further development within the framework of universally accepted human rights and humanitarian law.[43] Efforts have been made to clarify the rights of individuals as well as the obligations of states, but there is still a need for more study on this issue. The level of standards of protection should be considered in the light of the presumed "temporary" nature of the situation. If residence becomes lengthy, a higher set of standards could be considered.

Possible solutions

In the context of environmentally-induced displacement, the magnitude of the problem alone would suggest that prevention as well as remedy, particularly voluntary return, should be seen as the most pertinent aspects of the solution.

However, in practice, the options available may be much more limited than in the case of traditional categories of refugees, such as for persons covered by the 1951 Convention. In the same way as causes of ecological disaster are considered to be man-made, (there are almost always man-made elements in the chain of causation), they are also likely to be seen by governments as temporary causes of displacement. This factor, in addition to the large numbers of persons displaced by such disasters, makes it quite unlikely that governments worldwide will accept third country resettlement as a solution. In most cases even local integration in the region may not be a realistic option. Local integration generally will only achieve success when the receiving country is strongly committed to integration, and adequate resources are available to meet the integration needs. Yet, for many reasons, the massive (and ever-growing) scale of the present worldwide problem of coerced migration has already led many governments to restrict, as far as possible, the reception of refugees in general.

Although this general trend can be open to considerable criticism, there is no doubt that *preventive* approaches, as well as voluntary return, should be considered the preferred response to the problem. International legal and ethical issues, as well as practical international relations concerns, provide strong arguments for the international community to accept and apply this policy, which would undoubtedly have important implications for the management of IECs.

The international community's ability to protect and assist environmental refugees relies on states' willingness to recognize the coerced cross-border movements caused by environmental disruption or long-term degradation as a severe human and political problem.

Endnotes

Preface

1. As outlined in WCED (1987): Our Common Future.
2. UNCED took place in Rio de Janeiro, Brazil in June 1992.
3. UN General Assembly (1989): United Nations Conference on Environment and Development (paragraph 12 w), Report A/44/246/ Add.7, UN, New York.
4. The May 1989 NATO Declaration of Heads of State or Government, acknowledging the threats to international peace and security posed by environmental degradation, resource conflicts and economic disparities, called for new efforts to "settle disputes peacefully, and search for solutions to those issues of universal concern, including poverty, social injustice and the environment, on which our common fate depends."
5. The UN system means its main organs, agencies and specialized organisations (see Chapter Two for further discussion).
6. The World Bank Group (IBRD, IFC, MIGA, IDA, and ICSID) and the International Monetary Fund (IMF).
7. South Commission (1991): The Challenge to the South.
8. As defined by OECD as Overseas Development Assistance (ODA).
9. "Additional funds" means funds in addition to traditional development assistance as defined as ODA.
10. Ecosystem analysis as interpreted by Trolldalen (1991).

Chapter One

1. One of the most prominent authors who has raised such issues is Arthur Westing through his three publications: Westing, (ed.) (1986), (1989), and (1990).
2. Based on the three concepts developed by Wiman, 1991.
3. UNCED (1992), Framework Convention on Climate Change.
4. See Sand (1990).
5. Brundtland Commission = World Commission on Environment and Development (1987) with its report "Our Common Future," and further stated in London April 24, 1992.
6. See e.g., Forrester, (1970), Goldsmith et al., (1972), and Meadows et al., (1972).
7. On a global scale, the relationship between supply cost and stocks is unproven and improvable given past cost trends. Work has shown that the average cost of resources has actually fallen markedly in relative terms over time. Although in the early 1970s it appeared that this trend would not continue, it has in fact done so. Measured both in terms of the cost of labour input and against the cost of remanufactured goods, resources are now cheaper than in 1975 (Barnett et al (1984); see also Rees (1990)).
8. See e.g., Baumol and Oates (1988) for a more in depth discussion.
9. This is mainly due to lack of data on IECs in existing conflict data-bases. The following data-bases have been examined:
ICSPR 5303: Conflict Management by International Organizations, 1945—70
ICSPR 8303: Alker, H.L. & Sherman, F.L.: International Conflict Episodes, 1945—1979
ICSPR = Inter-University Consortium for Political and Social Research.
10. See Winman (1991) and his reasonings on environmental complexity, response and management practice.
11. See Mitchell (1981) and Kremenyuk (1991).
12. The Global Environment Facility (GEF) is a tripartite agreement between the World Bank, UNDP, and UNEP governing a fund for covering the incremental cost related to environmental components of development initiatives with a regional or global impact (protection of forestry, biodiversity, statospheric ozone, and water systems).

Chapter Two

1. See Fig. 2 on the UN family.
2. See also Riggs and Plano (1988).
3. See Schrijver (1989).
4. Except in the case of Security Council Resolution 668 concerning condemnation of Iraq's invasion in Kuwait in 1990.
5. See Riggs and Plano (1988).
6. See also Kaufman (1988).
7. UN Document E/1990/14, 22 January, 1990, Basic Programme of Work of the Council: Implementing of Council Resolutions 1988/ 77 and 1989/114.
8. See also Schrijver (1989).
9. The UNCED process referred to this in Conference paper: A/CONF/151/PC/80.
10. See Schrijver (1989).
11. An assessment of the ICJ function and fulfilment of its intentions draws on: Riggs and Plano (1988).
12. ICJ's organization and power are set forth in the UN Charter, Articles 92 and 96, but are contained in the ICJ Statute, a multilateral treaty that serves as its basic constitution.
13. As argued by Riggs and Plano (1988).
14. WCED (1987).
15. Statue of the International Court of Justice, Article 26, paragraph 1.
16. Report from the ICJ to the 41st Session of the UN General Assembly, 1985.
17. Mathews: A Strong Secretary General to Reshape the UN (*Washington Post*, January 28, Washington DC, 1987).
18. The UN Charter XV Article 99 (and 98).
19. UNEP, GC (1991).
20. UN General Assembly Resolution 37/10, UN, New York.
21. Stein (1991)
22. Ibid.
23. The IMF and World Bank were established under the Articles of Agreement drawn up at the Bretton Woods Monetary and Financial Conference in 1944.
24. The World Bank has in recent years: created a central Environmental Department as well as regional environmental units; increased staff resources assigned full-time to the environment about tenfold over staffing five years ago; developed Environmental Assessment

Procedures for application in all projects with any likely kind of environmental implications; prepared Environmental Issues Papers for most of its active borrowers, and assisted them in developing national Environmental Action Plans; set up an Environmental Technical Assistance Program to speed up preparation on environmental projects; set up a Global Environment Facility together with UNDP and UNEP to cover additional costs compared to lending and traditional development assistance related to protection of the statosphere, global climatic changes (forestry), biodiversity, and international water systems (see further discussion in Chapter Seven, Enclosure 1); and finally initiated a number of regional studies and programs.

25. The shift of the World Bank's environmental strategy took place in 1987/88; see Warford & Ackerman (1988).
26. See Kirmani (1990) and Michel (1967).
27. See discussion of this tripartite agreement between the World Bank, UNDP, and UNEP in Chapter Seven, Enclosure 1.
28. Based on consultation with the Legal Department in the World Bank.
29. The box is largely based on a paper given by Parra (1987).
30. Personal communication with Mr. Kenneth Piddington (former Director of the Environment Department of the World Bank (October 1992)).
31. See Biswas (1983).
32. See Bowett (1982).
33. Biswas (1983).
34. CSCE (1990).
35. Ibid.
36. An example of this is shown in the request from the Secretary General of the UN to the CSCE to be more actively involved in monitoring the embargo imposed on Serbia by the UN Security Council. CSCE was further requested to play a more active role with the EC in resolving the conflict (The Times, August, 1992).
37. The Vatican State is increasingly paying attention to environmental concerns, as recently revealed in a statement by Pope John Paul II (January 1, 1990): 'Peace with God and the Creator—Peace with All of Creation.'
38. One important general principle of humanitarian law in this context is *"the right of parties to the conflict to choose methods or means of warfare is not unlimited."* (In accordance with Protocol I of the 1977 Geneva Convention.)
39. See also Porter & Brown (1991).
40. Nitze (1991).
41. As shown in many of the examples in Kaufman (1989).
42. Zartman (1991) and Raiffa (1982).
43. See Mitchell (1981).
44. See UNITAR (1991).

Chapter Three

1. UNEP (1989a).
2. Döös (1991).
3. Coordination of Environmental Emergencies
The United Nations Conference on Environment and Development (UNCED) 1992 agreed that an international 'Green Cross' organization should be established (the mandate is not yet clearly defined). The background for this can be traced back to a proposal tabled at the UN General Assembly in 1988 (and in the following year in ECOSOC), by the former General Secretary M.S. Gorbachev of Soviet Union to establish a UN Center for Emergency Assistance. The main focus of the Center was to send experts on very short notice to damaged areas, and give advice and support on how to handle emergencies. It was suggested that such a group include lawyers to consider legal problems from transboundary conflicts (i.e., that a dangerous action register should be added to the portfolio of the Center).

In Nairobi, 1991, support for a coordinating role of UNEP on environmental disasters (man-made and natural disasters) was given to the Executive Director. Apart from the need for traditional emergency assistance as urgent supplies of food shelter and medical attention, a proposal to strengthen UNDRO, or even UNDP on a regional basis with ecologists and environmental engineers giving advice on clean-up measures has been put forth.

The distinction between the 'Green Cross' and the UN Center for Emergency Assistance is not yet quite clear, and there is a growing concern that there might be overlapping mandates between the two organizations.
4. Nanda (1990).
5. Barker (1991).
6. See for example the World Bank's World Development Report, 1992 (on Environmental issues).
7. CITES = Convention on International Trade in Endangered Species.
8. UNEP (1989b).
9. As revealed through the Preparatory Committee meetings and under the Conference in Rio, June 1992 (UNCED).
10. Scott and Trolldalen (1992).
11. UNEP (1987b).
12. UNCHE (1972).
13. Trail Smelter: UN, Reports on International Arbritral Awards (UN IAA), Vol. 3 (1949).
14. Lac Lanoux: U-N. I.A.A., Vol 12 (1957).
15. Gut Dam arbitration in Erades (1969).
16. Vicuña (1991).
17. Nanda (1990).
18. UNCHE (1972).
19. Levy (1987).
20. Ibid.
21. UNEP (1991).
22. Ibid.
23. UN IAA, Vol. 3 (1949).
24. UNECE (1990).
25. UNEP (1991).
26. Ibid.
27. Ibid.
28 Ibid.
29. Ibid.
30. The Hague Declaration stems from a ministerial meeting of invited countries in 1990. Prime Ministers Rocard (France), Rubbens (the Netherlands) and Gro Harlem Brundtland (Norway) facilitated the meeting.
31. U.S. General Accounting Office (1992).
32. See e.g., Fisher (1981).

33. See Bingham, 1985
34. The importance of this is underlined in the non-compliance procedures under the Montreal Protocol which prescribe a right for the Implementation Committee to receive, consider and report on any information or observations with regard to the Member States' implementation of the provisions of the Protocol. This implies that the public, media, organizations or individuals and scientists, etc., in addition to governments, can bring information of interest in relation to states' compliance with the Montreal Protocol to the Implementation Committee.
35. The compliance control mechanisms in the Montreal Protocol are closely related to the principle of the necessity to apply preventive measure. A Legal Expert group has been asked by the parties to the Montreal Protocol to develop a list of measures which will be used in non-compliance situations. These measures vary from a gentle form, which concentrates on transfer of financial or technical assistance to parties facing problems, to issuing warnings and finally to decisions on suspensions from certain rights and privileges under the Protocol.
36. UNCED, 1992: *The Rio Declaration.*
37. As for example argued by North American environmental NGOs in the case of Norway which started up commercial whaling, and the demand put forward by the NGO community in the U.S. that Norwegian export products should be boycotted by consumers.
38. The Hexagonal countries include Austria, Czechoslovakia, Hungary, Romania, the former Yugoslavia, and Poland.

Chapter Four

1. Ecosystem analysis is here defined as a combination of General Systems Theory and Ecosystemology as interpreted by Trolldalen (1991).
2. See also: Hammond, Munpower, & Smith (1977).
3. See also: Purkitt & Dyson (1985).
4. As for example shown in Fraser & Hipel (1984).
5. Examples of different types of integrations include: *economics and environment* (e.g., Daly & Cobb (1991), or World Bank Environment Working Paper Series 1992), *social transformation and the environment* (e.g., Mortimore (1990)), *environmental impact assessments* (e.g., as presented at the Earth Summit, Rio (1992)), *natural hazards and the environment* (e.g. Kreimer and Munasinghe (1991)).
6. See Burton, ed. (1990).
7. As argued by Trolldalen (1991).
8. See Straszak (1983).
9. Ibid.
10. See Russwurm (1976).
11. As developed by von Bertalanffy (1968).
12. See Ashby (1958).
13. As set forward by Langton (1972).
14. See also Burton ed. (1990).
15. See further discussion in Lutz & El-Serafy (eds.) (1988).
16. As defined by Trolldalen (1991).
17. See, e.g., Malthus (1798), Ehrlich (1968), Forrester (1970), Goldsmith *et al.* (1972), and Meadows *et al.* (1972).
18. See, e.g., Clark (1949), Brown (1956), and Maline (1972).
19. See, e.g., Boserup (1981).
20. See e.g., Ohlin (1967).
21. Kennedy (1990).
22. World Bank, UNDP, UNEP, 1991: Global Environment Facility = GEF, is a tripartite agreement between the World Bank, UNDP and UNEP governing funds for covering the incremental costs related to environmental components of development initiatives with a regional or global impact (protection of forestry, biodiversity, statospheric ozone, and water systems).
23. See, e.g., Johnston (1990).
24. A stricter definition will point out that technology can be included as a subsystem in the various types of production systems. The techno-subsystem is tied to the utilization of the resources, where production is the outcome of this utilization (cf. Trolldalen (1991): pp. 14-19).
25. *Environmentally-sound technology* is a problematic term, but nevertheless a frequently used notation in the UN vocabulary.

Chapter Five

1. Rogers (1991).
2. WMO, 1992: International Conference on Water and the Environment, Development Issues in the 21st century, Dublin.
3. Rogers (1991).
4. World Resources Institute et al (1992).
5. United Nations (1986).
6. United Nations (1986).
7. Scientific American, Managing Planet Earth
8. US Geological Survey (1983).
9. Hillel (1987).
10. Reij (1989).
11. See Fowler (1955), Knauth (1960), and Baxter (1955).
12. Trolldalen (1992).
13. World Bank's Operational Directive No. 4.0, Annex B.
14. World Bank (1989).
15. Burbridge et al. (1988).
16. Trolldalen et al. (1992).
17. Burbridge et al. (1988).
18. It is estimated that about 200 million people are infected with schistosome parasites and the disease is a threat to about 600 million. Its vector snails are commonly found in Africa, parts of Latin America and the Far East. Malaria is even more widespread with about 100 million new cases per year and 365 million people living in malaria-infected areas.
19. Trolldalen (1992).
20. Scudder (1985).
21. Scudder (1980).
22. David (1976).
23. Lee (1989).
24. See Convention and Statute Relating to the Development of the Chad Basin, signed at Fort Lamy on May 22, 1974 (UNEP).
25. Act Regarding Navigation and Economic Cooperation between the states of the Niger Basin, signed at Niamey on 26 October 1963 (UNEP).

26. See Convention Establishing the OMVS (Organisation pour la Mise en Valeur du Fleuve Senegal), signed at Noukachott on 17th December 1972 (OMVS).
27. Convention and Statute Relating to the Development of the Chad Basin, signed at Fort Lamy on 22 May 1974 (UNEP).
28. See Agreement on the Action Plan for the Environmentally Sound Management of the Common Zambezi River System, signed at Harare on 28 May 1987.
29. International Law Commission (1991).
30. The length and catchment area of the Zambezi are controversial. Welcomme (1977) claims that the length is 2574 km, Balon & Coche (1974) 2494 km, Balek (1977) 2600 km and Beadle (1932) 3000 km. The catchment area varies from 1,193,500 sq.km (Balon & Coche 1974) to 1,570,000 sq.km (Balek 1977).
31. Rough estimate based on data from the 'Nordic Mission.'
32. Balon & Coche (1974).
33. Schulze & McGee (1978).
34. SADCC/UNEP (1991).
35. Sponsored by the Nordic Development Aid Organizations, with representatives from the four Nordic countries and a representative from SADCC.
36. The report outlined recommendations regarding relevant institutional and legal arrangements for implementation of the ZACPLAN related to establishment of an interim commission which should include the same organizational structure as other sectorial commissions within SADCC, and that SWCLU should be reinforced by a separate coordination unit, Zambezi Coordination and Planning Unit (ZCPU). This unit was either to be subordinated under the SWCLU, or to be a complete separate unit located inside the Zambezi basin. In addition, the report recommended establishment of a Steering Council with representatives from the donor countries, SADCC, and UN organizations. The Steering Council was to have an advisory role. The costs of establishing the ZCPU were to be paid by Nordic donor countries.

Not all the delegates of this missions report agreed to the recommendation of the institutional arrangements. Some of the delegates found the organizational options unnecessarily voluminous and not in line with the present situation.

Disagreements between the Nordic experts delayed publication of the report for more than half a year, and disagreements between representatives of the Nordic Mission and between the Nordic Mission and SADCC/SWCLU, and also between UNEP and SADCC/SWCLU, resulted in the Nordic countries losing their donor interests related to the ZACPLAN in 1989.

Chapter Six

1. United Nations, General Assembly (1991): A/Conf.151/PC/69, p. 4,
2. See United Nations (1984).
3. See Couper (1989).
4. Much of this information is based on Couper (1989).
5. See for example Wolpin (1990).
6. Couper (1989).
7. FAO estimate in Hinrichson (1990).
8. A joint facility by IMCO/FAO/UNESCO/WMO/WHO/IAEA/UN/UNEP.
9. Adapted from GESAMP: UNEP (1982).
10. See Annex III B of LBS-Protocol (1980).
11. Magrath & Doolette (1989).
12. IPCC (1991).
13. Ibid.
14. Ibid. and Oerlemans (1989).
15. IPCC (1991).
16. Hekstra (1989).
17. Hashimoto & Nishioka (1991).
18. Haas (1990) and United States Senate, Subcommittee on Ocean and Atmosphere of the Committee on Commerce (1972).
19. Based on Chemical Week, Dec. 8, 1976: 65-67.
20. Hinrichson (1990).
21. See some of the reasonings in Haas (1990).
22. FAO (1972).
23. Status of signatures: (UNEP/WG.25/Inf.3, Annex 2). States:
Algeria, Cyprus, Egypt, France, Greece, Israel, Italy, Lebanon, Libya, Malta, Monaco, Morocco, Spain, Syria, Tunisia, Turkey, Yugoslavia, EEC.
24. As summed up by Haas (1990).
25. UNEP/IG.6/3, 1977, Documents prepared for the 1977 Athens Intergovernmental meeting.
26. Paris Convention on Protection of the Marine Environment against Land-Based Sources (1974).
27. As quoted in Kuwabara (1984).
28. Kuwabara (1984).
29. UNCHE (1972).
30. See Article 192 of the Convention.
31. See Hinrichson (1990).
32. World Resources Institute et al. (1989) and Grenon & Batisse (eds.) (1989).
33. Greenpeace: Undated booklet from Mediterranean Sea Project
34. This excludes forests, cropland, and pasture.
35. Grenon & Batisse (1989).
36. World Resources Institute et al. (1992).
37. Ibid.
38. Haas (1990).
39. EEC (1976): The Council Directive of 4 May on Pollution Caused by Certain Dangerous Substances Discharged into the Aquatic Environment of the Community.
40. International Registry of Potentially Toxic Chemicals (1978): Data Profiles for Chemicals for the Evaluation of Their Hazards to the Environment of the Mediterranean Sea, Vols. 1 and 2, Geneva.
41. Haas (1990).
42. UNEP (1979): WG. 17/4: (Inventory of areas of disagreement).
43. UNEP (1982): Convention for the Protection of the Mediterranean Sea against Pollution and its related protocols.
44. UNEP (1982): Convention for the Protection of the Mediterranean Sea against Pollution and its related protocols.
45. (a) The Mediterranean Sea Areas as defined in article 1 of the Convention; (...the Mediterranean Sea Area shall mean the maritime waters of the Mediterranean Sea proper, including its gulfs and seas, bounded to the west by the meridian passing through Cape Spartel

Lighthouse, at the entrance of the Straits of Gibraltar, and to the east by the southern limits of the Straits of Dardanelles between Mehmetcik and Kumkale Lighthouses.)
(b) Waters on the landward side of the baselines from which the breadth of the territorial sea is measured and extending, in the case of watercourses, up to the freshwater limit;
(c) Saltwater marshes communicating with the sea.

Chapter Seven

1. World Bank (1990).
2. UNEP/FAO (1982).
3. See World Bank (1990).
4. See UNEP/FAO (1982).
5. Ives & Pitt (1988).
6. See World Bank (1990).
7. UNEP/FAO (1982).
8. Repetto (1987).
9. Lee Talbot, ex-director of the IUCN.
10. Colchester (1990).
11. The Tenth World Forestry Congress assembled more than 2,500 participants from 136 countries September 17-20, 1991.
12. Kaltenborn (1991).
13. Some of the effects of deforestation on the climate are well known, and so is the climates influence on the forests. For practical purposes these issues will be treated in the next section (C).
14. World Bank (1990).
15. Ives & Pitt (1988).
16. Andrasko (1990).
17. Lal (1989).
18. Meyers (1989).
19. UNEP News, (November/December 1987).
20. UNECE (1990).
21. TFAP (1990).
22. Collins (1990).
23. This situation is similar in many other countries where structural adjustment loans are not linked directly to sectors (e.g., forestry and agriculture).
24. As reflected in Prep. Com. IV before UNCED: A/conf.151/pc/109, A/conf.151/pc/100/Add.9.
25. The national TFAP for Cameroun has been used as a framework, but the World Bank has stated that this loan foresees a much lower level of exploitation than envisaged. Also, unlike the TFAP proposals which included a major road system, no new road construction is envisaged under the project now being prepared.
26. Environmental Defense Fund: Back-to-office-report from Cameroun by the Environmental Defense Fund (Washington, D.C.), June 23 to July 2, 1990.
27. The proposed GEF-financed operation would provide the government with some resources to implement parts of its stated conservation policy, and possibly act as an incentive to the government to make the sometimes difficult choices between maximizing the country's income and protecting the environment.

Chapter Eight

1. Land security defined as in Blaikie & Brookfield (1987).
2. See for example, Blaikie & Brookfield (1987).
3. There seems to be clear linkages between dryland degradation and regions where groundnuts constitute a major part of national revenue, such as in the Gambia; see an evolutionary study of this interrelationship in Trolldalen (1991).
4. See also Preparatory Committee III for UNCED (A/CONF. 151/PC/63), as stated in 'Land Resources'.
5. See, e.g., Bie (1989), Nelson (1989) and Trolldalen (1991).
6. Salem-Murdock & Horowitz (1991).
7. UNDP (1979).
8. Hutchinson, ed. (1991).
9. IGADD (1991).
10. Data for this section is taken from May (1991).
11. Papua New Guinea's former defence minister Epel Tito and former defence chief Ted Diro have been quoted as saying (in 1982) that Indonesia probably had plans to take over Papua New Guinea 'one day' (May, 1991). Threats are thus felt by both parties.
12. The Indonesian—Papua New Guinea border is defined by an Australian—Indonesian border agreement signed in 1973 (May, 1991). The agreement has been renegotiated in 1979 and 1984 with minor, but significant, amendments. As in other countries where the borders are the product of arbitrary decisions made by past colonial regimes, language groups and traditional rights to land as well as relations of kin and of trade extend across the border.
13. Prep. Com. for UNCED (1991), third session (A/CONF/151/PC/59) 'Protection of the Atmosphere, Transboundary Air Pollution.'
14. Landin (1986).
15. UN ECE (1986).
16. Park (1987).
17. French (1990).
18. Brunstad ed. (1991).
19. Mac Kenzie & El-Ashry (1988).
20. UN ECE (1990).
21. Brunstad ed. (1991).
22. Rees (1990)
23. List of governments includes: Austria, Belgium, Bulgaria, Byelorussia (SSR), Canada, Czechoslovakia, Denmark, Germany, Finland, France, Greece, Hungary, Iceland, Ireland, Italy, Liechtenstein, Luxembourg, Netherlands, Norway, Poland, Portugal, Romania, San Marino, Spain, Sweden, Switzerland, Turkey, Ukrainian (SSR), former USSR, United Kingdom, USA, The Vatican, former Yugoslavia, and the EC.
24. UN ECE (1986).
25. Wettestad (1991).

26. As early as the 1960s and the early 1970s, i.e., before the Brezhnev proposal, the Soviet Union had tried several times to get a policy-relevant matter on the ECE's agenda, a case which would enhance the ECE's political authority (Chossudovsky (1988)).

27. In the preparation process for the high level meeting on environment, transboundary air pollution commended itself to virtually all countries as one of the few topics fully meeting the criteria set out by the ECE's annual meeting in 1976 (Chossudovsky (1988)).

28. Conversation with Jørgen Wettestad, FNI, Sept. 1991 by N.M. Birkeland).

29. Park (1987).

30. Chossudovsky (1988).

31. Park (1987).

32. Alm (1989).

33. Park (1987).

34. The principle of 'critical loads' or 'carrying capacity' of natural resources systems, such as water or air, is becoming accepted in international agreements. In recent years policy-makers have increasingly moved toward accepting the concept of using critical loads and critical levels of air pollutants as a tool for formulations of both national and international pollution control programmes.

    The precise definition of critical loads remains a matter of some discussion, but is essentially embodied in the following statement: "The highest deposition of acidifying compounds that will not cause chemical changes leading to long term harmful effects on ecosystem structure and function" (Nilsson and Greenfelt (1988)).

    The concept of critical levels of air pollutants has been embodied in establishment of air quality standards and guidelines by various organizations e.g., the International Union of Forest Organisations. The development of critical levels as a tool for international air pollution control policy is essentially based on findings of a workshop held in Bad Harzburg, in the framework of the Convention. Here, short- term and long term critical levels for O_3, SO_2 and NO_2 were defined.

35. UN ECE (1990).

36. Ibid.

37. See also Persson (1989).

Chapter Nine

1. Note of clarification: for the sake of simplicity. This study makes use of the term 'environmental refugees'. It is, however, important to note that the qualifications made of this term in the text.

2. El-Hinnawi (1985).

3. See also UNGA (A/Conf.151/PC/100/Add.2).

4. Trolldalen (1992).

5. See for example Fields (1985).

6. Revised after UNDRO (1989).

7. Smith (1992).

8. Rossi, Wright, Weber-Burdin, & Pereira (1983).

9. Smith (1992).

10. Statement by Lionel Rosenblatt, executive director of Refugees International in a Congressional hearing, May 6 1991, concerning the drought in Southern Africa.

11. Smith (1992).

12. Kreimer & Munasinghe (eds.) (1991).

13. Smith (1992).

14. See Brown & Wolf (1984).

15. Trolldalen (1991).

16. Allaby (1991).

17. Ibid.

18. Ibid.

19. Ibid.

20. The official number is 2800, but the number of death shrouds sold immediately after was 7000. Private agencies in the area put the estimates even higher (see Maloney, 1991).

21. Allaby (1991).

22. El-Hinnawi (1985).

23. 'Central and Eastern Europe' includes Russia (west of the Urals), Estonia, Latvia, Lithuania, Byelorussia, the Ukraine, Romania, Bulgaria, Hungary, Czechoslovakia, and Poland.

24. Consultation with Finn Ugletveit, Senior Health Physicist, National Institute of Radiation Hygiene, Norway, 22nd April 1992 (by N.M. Birkeland).

25. Edvard Stang, researcher at the Center for Technology and Culture, University of Oslo (Aftenposten, 26.04.92).

26. These five sites in addition to Chernobyl are: Ignalina (Lithuania), St. Petersburg, Smolensk, Obninsk, and Kursk (all in Russia).

27. Consultation with Liucija Baskauskas, Prorector, Vytautas Magnus University, Kaunas, Lithuania, 7th November 1991 (by N.M. Birkeland).

28. Diercke Weltatlas (1988) and the 1989 USSR census; in Soviet Geography, Vol.30.

29. Consultation with Finn Ugletveit, Senior Health Physicist, National Institute of Radiation Hygiene, Norway, 22nd April 1992. (by N.M. Birkeland).

30. El-Hinnawi (1985).

31. Westing (1990).

32. Iglebæk (1991) and personal communication with the Norwegian Church Aid/Norwegian Refugee Council's Residential Representative in 1989 in Pesawar.

33. El-Hinnawi (1985).

34. Intergovernmental Panel on Climate Change (1990).

35. Hekstra (1989).

36. This part is largely based on Trolldalen et al. (1992).

37. Report of the Group of Governmental Experts on International Cooperation to Avert New Flows of Refugees, UN Doc. A/4/324 (1986).

38. The 1986 UN General Assembly Group of Governmental Experts report referred to above, which observed that "mass movements could be attributed to one or several causes and factors."

39. See Suhrke (1992).

40. Report to the UNHCR Executive Committee, Forty-second session, Doc. EC/SCP/64, (Sub-paragraph h).

41. See further discussion in Trolldalen et al. (1992).

42. UNHCR (1991).

43. Of particular importance is for the country of refuge to safeguard the right to life and to respect the prohibition of torture and cruel, inhumane and degrading treatment.

Enclosures

Chapter Five: The largest international rivers of the world (countries within the river basin)

1. Amazon: Bolivia, Brazil, Colombia, Ecuador, French Guyana, Peru, Surinam, Venezuela. Rivers touches Colombian border, branches to Ecuador, ex. Curaray River. Basin borders on French Guinea, Surinam, and Venezuela

2. Amur: China, Mongolia, USSR. Forms part of border between China and Russia. Breaks off into two branches, one of which goes into Mongolia

3. Brahmaputra: Bangladesh, Bhutan, China, India

4. Columbia: Canada, United States

5. Congo or **Zaire:** Congo, Zaire. Forms part of this border. Tributaries run from Angola, Cameroon, Central African Republic.

6. Danube: Albania, Austria, Bulgaria, Czechoslovakia, France, Germany, Greece, Hungary, Italy, Poland, Romania, Russia, Switzerland, former Yugoslavia. Forms parts of border between Bulgaria-Romania, Hungary-former Yugoslavia

7. Elbe: Czechoslovakia, Germany

8. Ganges: China, Bangladesh, India, Nepal. Branches from main river system into Nepal. Smaller River Alaknanda flows from China into Ganges at western tip

9. Indus: Afghanistan, China, India, Pakistan

10. Mekong: Cambodia, China, Laos, Thailand, Union of Myanmar, Vietnam. Forms parts of border between Laos-Thailand, Laos-Union of Myanmar.

11. Mississippi: Canada, United States

12. Niger: Algeria, Benin, Burkina Faso, Cameroon, Cote d'Ivoir, Guinea, Mali, Niger, Nigeria. Forms part of border between Benin-Niger

13. Nile: Burundi, Central African Republic, Congo, Ethiopia, Egypt, Kenya, Rwanda, Sudan, Tanzania, Uganda, Zaire

14. Orinoco: Colombia, Venezuela. Forms part of Colombia-Venezuela border

15. Parana: Argentina, Brazil, Paraguay. Forms part of Argentina-Paraguay border

16. Rhine: Austria, France, Germany, Liechtenstein, Luxembourg, The Netherlands, Switzerland. Forms parts of borders between Austria-Liechtenstein, France-Germany, France-Switzerland

17. Salween: China, Thailand, Union of Myanmar. Forms parts of borders between Thailand-Union of Myanmar, China-Union of Myanmar

18. Shatt-al Arab (Tigris, Euphrates, Karun): Iraq, Syria, Turkey

19. St. Lawrence: Canada, United States

20. Uruguay: Argentina, Brazil, Uruguay. Forms part of Argentina-Uruguay border. Flow from Brazil

21. Yukon: Canada, United States

22. Zambezi: Angola, Botswana, Malawi, Mozambique, Namibia, Tanzania, Zambia, Zimbabwe. Forms parts of border between Zambia-Zimbabwe, Namibia-Zambia

(Revised after Rogers, 1991)

Chapter Seven, Enclosure 1
The Global Environment Facility (GEF)

As the degradation of tropical forests continues, and as other local, national, and international problems threaten the global environment, new efforts are being made to decrease the impacts on the global commons.

Industrialized countries have recognized their responsibility for action. The developing countries are also aware of the threat which environmental degradation poses at the local, national and global levels, but due to their economic situation they are not able to prioritize these problems.

As a measure to contribute to solutions to these problems, a Global Environment Facility, GEF, was established as a tripartite pilot-venture between UNDP, UNEP and the World Bank. Its purpose is to mobilize new and genuinely additional financial resources to cover the incremental costs of developing countries in addressing environmental problems of global significance and nature: climate change, biodiversity, ozone depletion. Some areas for inclusion in GEF are projects related to desertification, water, etc., insofar as they can be subsumed under the main areas of responsibility.

GEF, with its US$ 1.3 billion fund, covers four types of global environmental concerns:

1. Reducing and limiting emission of greenhouse gases which cause global warming.
2. Preserving the earths biological diversity and maintaining natural habitats.
3. Arresting the pollution of international waters.
4. Protecting the ozone layer from further depletion.

The three cooperating agencies determine whether a project qualifies for GEF support, and ensure that it protects the global environment in a cost-effective, technologically sound way, while respecting the interests of the country's people. A project should contribute to the understanding of global environmental problems and their solutions, while also focusing on training and other human resources development activities.

In order to qualify for funding from GEF, a project must relate to at least one of its four specific areas of concern. A further qualification is that a project would not be economically viable without GEF support. There is also a provision that only those nations that are parties to the Montreal Protocol on ozone-depleting substances are eligible for GEF funds addressing ozone protection.

Three types of investments are made which generate both domestic and global environmental benefits. These are:

1. The project is economically viable in terms of domestic benefits and costs to the country itself. Such projects will only receive financial funds when it is clear that the operation in question would not proceed without GEF involvement.
2. The investment is not justified in a country context if the full costs are borne by the implementing country. If the projects are made attractive to the implementing country by concessional assistance by GEF, and meet the demand for cost-effectiveness, GEF involvement will make the project attractive.
3. The investment is justified in a country context, but the country would need to incur additional costs to bring about additional global benefits. The additional costs of accommodating global concerns would be eligible for GEF funding, if they are cost-effective.

Funds from GEF, which are additional to other development programmes, should complement, but not substitute for, action that can be supported under existing programs.

At the first stage of project identification, UNEP will provide scientific and technological guidance for identifying and selecting projects. UNDP will coordinate the financing of preinvestment activities required for adequate 'upstream' work (for example, assistance to choose among technologies, and identify specific investment requirements and sites). The World Bank will normally be the executing agency for such activities, with involvement from UNEP and other specialized agencies.

Project proposals will be of two main types: new projects by governments or by NGOs with government endorsement and modifications to existing projects currently under consideration of the World Bank and eventually by other funding institutions.

To be selected for GEF funding, project proposals should:
1. be consistent with global environment conventions;
2. be consistent with the country-specific environment strategy or program. Countries will need to have, or be willing to develop a policy, regulatory, and institutional framework relating to the project

issues, within which the particular GEF operation would be carried out;

3. utilize appropriate technology from the spectrum of available options, and;

4. be both cost-effective and of high priority from a global perspective.

GEF seems to be one of the most important mean available for the UN system and the Bretton Woods institution in management of IECs.

Chapter Seven, Enclosure 2

Convention of biological diversity

The international recognition of the need to protect the global biodiversity has lead to a comprehensive negotiation process for a Convention on Biological Diversity. The Convention was signed under UNCED in Rio in 1992.

UNEP, assisted by FAO and IUCN, was the secretariat under the negotiations for a convention on biological diversity.

The negotiators were working under a mandate to view the problems in a broad socio-economic context. During the negotiations, it has become clear that the main goals vary from a strict protection of biodiversity based on ethical values, to the importance of survival of ecological systems, to concentrating on human needs and welfare. Furthermore, lack of knowledge of the consequences of loss of biodiversity makes it difficult to define goals that all parties can agree upon.

The industrializing countries, especially those from Latin America, focus strongly on national sovereignty and their rights to the management of the natural resources within national borders. The balance between sovereignty and global responsibility is one of the main problems in the negotiations.

Some developing countries, rich in biological diversity, express a need for compensation for any use of their genetic resources involving technological and economic resources.

The US has raised doubts about whether it is possible to include access to biological resources in private property. However, questions regarding property rights and patents are dealt with in other forums such as the General Agreement on Trade and Tariffs (GATT), World Intellectual Property Organization (WIPO) and United Private Ownership (UPOV), and have therefore not been brought up to the surface in the negotiations.

The issue of transfers of financial resources is certainly critical in the negotiations, and countries with a well developed industry based on genetic resources from developing countries may have to contribute more than the other nations.

The developing counties regard access to know-how in the field of biotechnology as one of the main issues in the negotiations.

This raises the difficult question of the distinctions between country of origin and the country which holds the resources today. Another difficulty involves how to include the 'gene-poor' countries of the South.

The role of UN and especially UNEP has been crucial—and is clearly an example of successful involvement of the UN system and its agencies in conflict management of IECs.

Bibliography

Allaby, M., 1991: *Dictionary of the Environment*, 3rd Edition. New York University Press, New York.

Alm, H., 1989: Emissions Are Falling, But Is It Enough? *Acid Magazine*, No. 8.

Amy, D.J., 1987: *The Politics of Environmental Mediation*, Columbia University Press, New York.

Andrasko, K, 1990: Global Warming and Forests: An Overview of Current Knowledge, *UNASYLVA*, Vol. 41, 1990/4.

Arad, R.W., Arad, U.B., McCulloch, R., Piñera, J. & Hollick, A.L., 1983: *Sharing Golbal Resources*, 1980's Project/Council on Foreign Relations, McGraw-Hill Book Company

Ashby, W.R, 1958: *An Introduction to Cybernetics*, John Wiley & Sons, New York.

Asian Development Bank, 1990: *Economic Policies for Sustainable Development*, Asian Development Bank.

Balek, J., 1977: Hydrology and Water Resources in Tropical Africa. Development in Water Science, 8, Elsevier, Amsterdam. In; Pinay (1988).

Balon, E.K. & Coche, A.G, 1974: Lake Kariba: One Man-Made Tropical Ecosystem in Central Africa. *Monographiae Biologicae*, 24, W. Junk Publisher. In: Pinay (1988).

Bardach, J. E. 1989: Global Warming and the Coastal Zone, *Climatic Change* Vol. 15.

Barker, K.,1991: Reprocessing and HLW Management in the USSR, *Nuclear Engineering International*, Vol.36.

Barmetter, S., 1992: Etwa so sicher wie ein atomgetriebner Leiterwagen, *Die Weltwoche*, nr. 17, 23 april 1992, Zürich.

Barnett, H.J., Van Muiswinkel, G.M., Shechter, M. & Myers, J. G. 1984: Global Trends in Non-Fuel Minerals. In: Simon & Kahn eds. (1984).

Barnett, T.P., 1984: The Estimation of "Global" Sea Level Change: A Problem of Uniqueness. *Journal of Geographical Research* 89.

Baumol, W.J. & Oates, W.E., 1988: *The Theory of Environmental Policy*, Cambridge University Press, Cambridge (2nd edition).

Baxter, R.R., 1955: "The Indus Basin", in Garrettson *et al.* (1967).

Beadle, L.C., 1932: Scientific Results of the Cambridge Expedition to East African Lakes in 1930-31 IV. The Waters of Some East African Lakes in Relation to their Fauna and Flora. *J. Limn. Soc. (Zool.).* 38, 157-211. In: Pinay (1988).

Bergesen, H.O., Norderhaug, M. & Parmann G., (eds.), 1992: *Green Globe Yearbook 1992*, Fritjof Nansens Institute, Oxford University Press, Oxford.

Bingham, G., 1985: Resolving Environmental Disputes: A Decade of Experience.

Bie, S., 1989: *Dryland Management Techniques*, Environment Department Working Paper Series, World Bank, Washington DC.

Binswanger, H.P., 1989: *Brazilian Policies that Encourage Deforestation in the Amazon*, Environment Department Working Paper No.l6, The World Bank, Washington DC.

Biswas, A. K., 1983: Shared Natural Resources, In; Dupuy (1983).

Blaikie, P. & Brookfield, H. (eds.), 1987: *Land Degradation and Society*, Methuen & Co., London.

Boserup, E., 1981: *Population and Technology*, Blackwell, Oxford.

Botkin, D., Caswell, M., Estes, J. & Orio, A., (eds.), 1989: *Changing the Global Environment: Perspectives on Human Involvement.* Academic Press, Inc., San Diego.

Bowett, D.W., 1982: *The Law of International Institutions*, Stevens & Sons, London.

Brown, H., 1956: *Challenge of Man's Future.*, Viking, New York.

Brown, L.R. and Wolf, E.C., 1984: *Soil Erosion: Quiet Crisis in the World Economy*, World Watch Paper 60, World Watch Institute, Washington DC.

Brown, L. et al., 1992: *State of the World 1992*, World Watch Institute, Washington, DC.

Brunstad, H., (ed.), 1991: Forurensingstrussler mot grunnvann, Bind II, NTNF, Ås.

Burbridge, P.R., Norgaard, R.B., and Hartshorn, G.s., 1988: Environmental Guidelines for Re-settlement Projects in the Humid Tropics, *Environment and Energy Paper* 9, FAO, Rome.

Burton, J. (ed.), 1990: *Conflict: Human Needs Theory*, St. Martin's Press, New York.

Caldwell, L.K., 1984: *International Environmental Policy: Emergence and Dimen-sions*, Duke University Press, Durham, North Carolina.

Campos, S., 1989: *Management of the Zambezi Basin: Social, Political and Economic Considerations.* Working Paper, International Institute for Applied Systems Analysis (IIASA), Laxenburg.

Carpenter, S.L. & Kennedy, W.J.D., 1990: ROMCOE: Managing Environmental Conflict in the 1980´s, ROMCOE.

Carroll, J.E., 1986: *Environmental Diplomacy: An Examination and a Prospecitve of Canadian—U.S. Transboundary Environmental Relations*, University of Michigan Press, Michigan.

Carter, R.W.G., 1988: *Coastal Environments*, Academic Press, London, New York.

Cernea, M.M. (ed.), 1985: *Putting People First, Sociological Variables in Rural Development*, Oxford University Press, New York.

Charnock, A., 1983: Maqarin deadlock forces major revision of Jordan's water plans, In; *World Water*, Vol. 6, Liverpool.

Choudhury, G.R. & Khan, T.A., 1983: Developing the Ganges basin, In; Zaman, M. et al (ed.)
Chossudovsky, E.M., 1988: *"East-West" Diplomacy for Environment in the United Nations*, UNITAR, Geneva.

Clark, C., 1949: The World's Capacity to Feed and Clothe Itself., *The Way Ahead*, Vol. II, no. 2.

Colchester, M., 1990: The International Tropical Timber Organization: Kill or Cure for the Rain-forests? *The Ecologist*, Vol. 20, No. 5, September/October1990.

Collins, M., 1990: *The Last Rain Forest. A World Conservation Atlas*, Oxford University Press, New York.

Conference on Security and Cooperation in Europe (CSCE), 1990: *The Charter of Paris for a New Europe*, Paris.

Conference on Security and Cooperation in Europe (CSCE), 1991: *Report of the CSCE Expert Meeting on Peaceful Settlement of Disputes*, Valletta.

Cooley, J.K., 1984: War over Water, In; *Foreign Policy*, Vol. 54, Washington

Couper, A. (ed.), 1989: *Atlas and Encyclopedia of the Sea*, The Times Ltd.

Daly, H.E. & Cobb, J.B., 1990: *For the Common Good: Redirecting the Economy Toward Community, the Environment, and a Sustainable Future*, Beacon Press, Boston.

David, L. 1976: *River Basin Development for Socio-Economic Growth*: General Report in UNDP (ed.)

(1976).

Diercke Weltatlas, 1988: Westermann GmBH, Braunschweig

Döos, B., 1991: *Environmental Issues Requiring International Action,* International Institute for Applied Systems Analysis, Laxenburg

Druckman, D. & Zechmeister, K., 1973: Conflict of Interest and Value Dissensus, *Human Relations* 26.

Dupuy, R.-J. (ed.), 1983: *The Settlement of Disputes on the New Natural Resources,* Martinus Nijhoff Publishers.

Dzúrova, D., Kara, J. and Karel, K., 1990: *Environment and Health in Czechoslovakia.* Paper presented at the Conference on Public Health and the Environmental Crisis in Central Europe, Woodrow Wilson International Center for Scholars, Smithsonian Institution, Washington DC, April 30—May 2, 1990.

Egler, F.E., 1970: *The Way of Science. A Philosophy of Ecology for the Layman,* Hafner, New York.

El-Ashry, M. T. & Gibbons, D.C., 1986: *Troubled Waters, New Policies for Managing Water in the American West,* World Resources Institute, Washington.

El-Ashry, M. T., 1990: *Issues in Managing Water Resources in Semiarid Regions,* World Resources Institute, Washington.

El-Hinnawi, Essam, 1985: *Environmental Refugees,* UNEP, Nairobi.

Erades, L., 1969: The Gut Dam Arbitration. *Nederlands Tijdschrift voor Inter-nationaal Recht,* vol. 16.

Erlich, P.R., 1968: *The Population Bomb,* Ballantine Books, New York.

Essuman-Johnson, A., 1991: *Environmental Refugees in Ghana. The Politics of Assistance to Sahel Refugees.* Paper presented at the international conference on Refugees Crisis Geographical Perspectives on Forced Migration, Kings College, London (18-20 September).

Falkenmark, M., 1986: Fresh Waters as a Factor in Strategic Policy and Action, In; Westing (ed.) (1986).

FAO, 1972: *State of the Marine Pollution in the Mediterranean,* GFCM, FAO, Rome

Fields, R.M., 1985: *Refugees from Environmental Degradation: The Truth behind African Migration.*

Fisher, R., 1969: *International Conflict for Beginners,* Harper & Row, New York.

Fisher, R., 1981: *Improving Compliance with International Law,* The University Press of Virginia, Charlottesville.

Folke, C. & Kålberger, T., 1991: *Linking the Natural Environment and the Economy: Essays from the Eco-Eco Group.* Kluwer Academic Publishers, Dordrecht, the Netherlands.

Forrester, J.W., 1970: *World Dynamics,* Wright-Allen Press, Cambridge, Mass.

Fowler, F.J., 1955: The Indo-Pakistan Water Dispute, *Yearbook of World Affairs.*

Fraser, N.M. & Hipel, K.W., 1984: *Conflict Analysis—Models and Resolutions,* North-Holland, New York & Oxford.

French, H., 1992: Strengthening Global Environmental Governance, in Brown *et al.* (1992).

French, H., 1990: *Cleaning the Air: A Global Agenda,* World Watch Report No. 94, Washington DC.

Friday, L. & Laskey, R., 1989: *The Fragile Environment,* Cambridge University Press, Cambridge.

Garrettson, A.H., et al., 1967: *The Law of International Drainage Basins,* Dobbs Ferry, New York.

Gartland, S., 1990: *Practical Constraints on Sustainable Logging in Cameroon,* paper presented at the

Abidjan Conference on Forest Conservation in West and Central Africa, Nov. 1990.

GESAMP (IMO/FAO/UNESCO/WNI/WHO/IAEA/UN/UNEP Joint Group of Experts on Scientific Aspects of Marine Pollution), 1990: The State of the Marine Environment, In; *UNEP Regional Seas Reports and Studies.*

Gjessing, J., 1988: Environment and sustainable development, *N.Geogr. T.42.*

Glos, G.E., 1961: *International Rivers—A Policy-Oriented Perspective*, University of Malaya, Singapore.

Godana, B.A., 1985: *African Shared Water Resources. Legal and Institutional Aspects of the Nile, Niger, and Senegal River Systems*, Lynne Rienner Publications Inc., Boulder, Colorado.

Goldsmith, E., Allen, R., Allaby, M., Davoll, J. & Lawrence, S., 1972: Blueprint for Survival, *Ecologist*, reprinted, Harmondsworth, Penguin.

Grenon, M. & Batisse, M. (eds.), 1989: *Futures for the Mediterranean Basin. The Blue Plan*, Oxford University Press, Oxford.

Grigg, D., 1985: *The World Food Problem*, Basil Blackwell, Oxford.

Haas, P.M., 1990: *Saving the Mediterranean: The Politics of International Environmental Co-operation*, Colombia University Press, New York.

Hammond, Munpower, & Smith, 1977: Linking Environmental Models of Human Judgement: A Symmetric Transaction on Systems, Man and Cybernetics. SMC Vol. 8, no. 5.

Harris, D.R. (ed), 1980: *Human Ecology in Savanna Environments*, Academic Press, London.

Hashimoto, M., and Nishioka, S., 1991: Potential Impacts of Climatic Change on Human Settlements; the Energy, Transport and Industrial Sectors: Human Health and Air Quality, In; Jäger & Ferguson (1991).

Hekstra, G.P., 1989: Global Warming and Rising Sea Levels: The Policy Implications, *The Ecologist*, 1989 Vol. 19, no. 1.

Herrmann, G., 1992: Kein Leben im Schatten des toten Reaktors, *Die Weltwoche*, nr. 17, 23 April 1992.

Hertzmann, C., 1990: *Environment and Health in Czechoslovakia*, University of British Columbia, Canada.

Hillel, D., 1987: The Efficient Use of Water Irrigation, *World Bank Technical Paper* No. 64, World Bank, Washington, DC.

Hinrichson, D., 1990: *Our Common Seas: Coasts in Crisis*, Earthscan Publishers, London.

Hulm, P., 1989: *A Climate of Crisis*, UNEP & ASPEI.

Hutchinson, R.A. (ed.), 1991: *Fighting for Survival—Insecurity, People and the Environment in the Horn of Africa*, IUCN/ World Conservation Union. Gland.

Iglebæk, O., 1991: Mye en krig om jordsmonn, *På Flukt* 2/91.

Intergovernmental Authority on Drought and Development (IGADD), 1991: *IGADD's Plan of Action. Forum on Environmental Protection and Development of Sub-regional Strategy to Combat Desertification*, NORAGRIC, Agricultural University of Norway, Ås.

Intergovernmental Panel on Climate Change (IPCC), 1991: *Climate Change, The IPCC Scientific Assessment*, Cambridge University Press, Cambridge..

International Law Commission (ILC), 1991: The Law of the Non-Navigational Uses of International Watercourses, ILC, 43rd Session, *Environmental Policy and Law*, 21/5/6.

Iversen, T. (et.al), 1991: *Calculated Budgets for Airborne Acidifying Components in Europe, 1985,*

1987, 1988 and 1990. EMEP Technical Report no. 91, Meterological Synthesizing Centre—West, The Norwegian Meterological Institute, Oslo.

Ives, J. & Pitt, D.C., 1988: *Deforestation: Social Dynamics in Watersheds and Mountain Ecosystems,* Routledge, London.

Jackson, C.I., 1990: A Tenth Anniversary Review of the ECE Convention on Long Range Transboundary Air Pollution, *International Environmental Affairs,* Institute for Research on Public Policy, Ottawa, Vol. 2, No. 3.

Jacobsen, J., 1988: Envrionmental Refugees: A Yardstick of Habitability, *World Watch Paper* 86, World Watch Institute, Washington DC.

Johnston, R. J., 1990: *Environmental Problems: Nature, Economy and State,* Belhaven Press, New York.

Jörnstedt, O., 1991: Green Taxes Gaining Ground in Sweden, *Enviro Magazine,* No. 11..

Jäger & Ferguson, 1991: *Climatic Change: Science, Impacts and Policy,* Second World Climate Conference, WMO, UNEP, UNESCO, FAO, ICSU, Cambridge University Press, Cambridge.

Kaltenborn, B.P., 1991: *The Role of Environmental Setting Attributes in Tourism and Outdoor Recreation Planning. A Case Study for Svalbard in the Norwegian High Arctic.* Dept. of Geography, University of Oslo / NINA, Lillehammer

Kaufmann, J. 1988: *Conference Diplomacy—An Introductory Analysis,* UNITAR, Martinus Nijhoff Publishers, Dordrecht (2nd edition).

Kaufmann, J., (ed.), 1989: *Effective Negotiations - Case Studies in Conference Diplomacy,* UNITAR, Martinus Nijhoff Publishers, Dordrecht.

Kennedy, P., 1990: *The Rise and Fall of Great Powers,* Vintage Books, New York.

Kimball, Lee A., 1992: Forging International Agreement: *Strengthening inter-governmental institutions for environment and development,* World Resources Institute, Washington DC.

Kirmani, Syed, S., 1990: The Experience of the Indus and the Mekong, *Water International,* Vol. 15, No. 4.

Knauth, A.W., 1960: The Indus River System, *Proceedings of the American Society of International Law,* Vol. 54, 1960.

Koskenniemi, M., 1991: Peaceful Settlement of Environmental Disputes, *Nordic Journal of International Law.*

Kreimer, A. & Munasinghe, M.(eds.), 1991: *Managing Natural Disasters and the Environment.* Environmental Policy and Research Division., Environment Department, World Bank, Washington DC.

Kremenyuk, V.A. (ed.), 1991: *International Negotiation: Analysis, Approaches, Issues,* Josscy-Bass Publishers, Oxford.

Kurlansky, M., 1989: *Haiti's Environment on the Edge, International Wildlife,* U.S. Committee for Refugees, World Refugee Survey.

Lal, R., 1989: Soil Degradation and Conversion of Tropical Rainforests, In; Botkin *et al.,* eds. (1989).

Land, T., 1992: Nuclear Waste Seeks Home, *Nature,* Vol. 355, 13 Feb. 1992.

Landin, B., 1986: *Om Trær Kunne Gråte,* Gyldendal Forlag, Oslo.

Langton, J., 1972: Potentialities and Problems of a System Approach to the Study of Change in Human Geography. *Process in Geography,* Vol. 4.

Lee, K., 1989: Columbia River Basin. Experimenting with Sustainability: *Environment*, Vol. 31. No. 6, July/August 1989.

Levy, R. E., 1987: International Law and the Chernobyl Accident: Reflections on an Important, but Imperfect System, *Kansas Law Review*, Vol. 36.

Levy, B. & Hertzmann, C., 1992: Environment and Health in Central Europe, In; WRI *et al.* (1992).

Livernash, R. 1992: Regional Focus: Central Europe, In; WRI *et al.* (1992).

Lutz, E., & El-Serafy, S. (eds.), 1988: *Environmental and Resource Accounting and their Relevance to the Measurement of Sustainable Income*, World Bank, Washington DC.

Lyman, F., 1990: *The Greenhouse Trap: What We're Doing to the Atmosphere and How We Can Slow Global Warming*, World Resources Institute, Beacon Press, Boston.

Mac Kenzie, J. & El-Ashry, M., 1988: *Ill-Winds*, World Resources Institute, Washington DC.

Magrath, B. & Doolette, J.B., 1989: Strategic Issues for Watershed Development in Asia, *Environmental Working Paper*, No. 30, Environment Department, World Bank, Washington DC.

Mahar, D. J., 1989: *Government Policies and Deforestation in Brazil's Amazon Region*, The World Bank, Washington DC.

Malin, K.M., 1972: Food Resources of the Earth, *WPC/WP/187* (in Russian).

Maloney, C., 1991: Environmental and project displacement of population in India, In; *Development and Deracination, Field Staff report*, No. 14, Universities Field Staff international & The National Heritage institute, Sausalito.

Malthus, T.R., 1989: *Essay on the Principle of Population.*

Mathews, J.T., 1989: Redefining Security, *Foreign Affaires*, Spring 1989.

Mathews, J., 1991: A Strong Secretary General to Reshape the U.N., *The Washington Post*, Jan. 28, Washington DC.

May, R.J., 1991: The Indonesia—Papua New Guinea Border Landscape; in Rumley, & Minghi (eds.)

McNeely, J., et al., 1990: *Conserving the World's Biological Diversity*, IUCN, WRI, CI, WWF-US, The World Bank, Washington, DC.

Meadows, D.H., Meadows, D.L., Randers, J. & Behrens, W., 1972: *The Limits to Growth*, Universe Books, New York.

Meyers, N., 1989: The Future of Forests, In; Friday & Laskey (1989).

Michel, A.A., 1967: *The Indus River*, Yale University Press.

Milliman, J.D., Broadus, J.M. & Gable, F., 1989: Environmental and Economic Implications of Rising Sea Level and Subsiding Deltas: The Nile and Bengal Examples, *AMBIO No. 18.*

Mine Watch, 1991: Briefing Note of June 30., London.

Mine Watch, 1992: Briefing Note No. 17, London.

Mitchell, B., 1989: *Geography and Resource Analysis*, 2nd edition, Longmann Scientific & Technical, Essex, U.K.

Mitchell., C.R., 1981: *The Structure of International Conflict*, The Macmillan Press, London.

Nanda, P., 1990: Trends in International Environmental Law, *California Western International Law Journal*, Vol. 20.

Naveh, Z. & Liberman, A.S., 1984: *Landscape Ecology - Theory and Applications*, Springerverlag, New York.

Nelson, R., 1989: *Dryland Management: The Desertification Problem*, Environment Department Working Paper No. 3, World Bank, Washington DC.

Nillsson, S. & Sallnäs, O., 1990: Air Pollution and European Forestry: Policy implications based on simulation markets. *Unasylvia* 163, Vol. 41.

Nilsson, J. & Greenfelt, P., 1988: *Critical loads from suphur and nitrogen:* Report from a workshop held at Skokloster, Nordic Council of Ministers, Copenhagen.

Nitze, W. A., 1991: Improving U.S. Interagency Coordination of International Environmental Policy Development, *Environment*, Vol. 33, No. 4.

Nordic UN Project,, 1991: *The United Nations Issues and Options*, the Nordic UN Project, Almquist & Wiksell International, Stockholm.

Nye, J.S., 1971: *Peace in Parts: Integration and Conflict in Regional Organization.*, Boston, Little, Brown.

Oerlemans, J., 1989: A Projection of Future Sea Levels, *Climatic Change*, Vol. 15 No. 1—2.

Ohlin, G., 1967: *Population Control and Economic Development.*, OECD, Paris.

Olson, M., 1965: *The Logic of Collective Actions*, Cambridge, Harvard University Press.

Organization for Economic Cooperation and Development (OECD), 1991: *The State of the Environment*, Paris.

Pape, R., 1991a: As it is Now, *Acid News*, no. 3, Oct, 1991.

Pape, R., 1991b: Preparing for Clean Up, *Acid News*, no. 3, 1991.

Park, C.C., 1987: *Acid Rain: Rhetoric and Reality*, London.

Parra, A., 1987: *The Role of the World Bank in the Settlement of International Investment Disputes.* Paper presented to the ABA National Institute on the Resolution of International Commercial Disputes, Miami, Florida..

Persson, G., 1989: Editorial, *Acid Magazine*, No. 8.

Pinay, G, 1988: *A Hydro-Bibliographical Assessment of the Zambezi River System: A Review*, Working Paper, International Institute for Applied Systems Analysis (IIASA), Laxenburg.

Porter, B. & Brown, J.W., 1991: *Global Environmental Politics*, Westview Press, Boulder, San Francisco, Oxford.

Potapchuk, W. R., 1990: Processes of Governance: Can Governments Truly Respond to Human Needs?; in Burton ed. (1990).

Purkitt, H. & Dyson, J., 1985: Analyzing Global Systems: A Problem-Solving Perspective and Some Suggested Applications, *Systems Inquiring: Applications, Society for General Systems Research*, Internsystems Publications, California.

Rafi Communique, 1987: *A Report on the Security of the World's Major Gene Banks.*

Raiffa, H., 1982: *The Art and Science of Negotiations—How to Resolve Conflicts and Get the Best Out of Bargaining*, Harvard University Press, Cambridge.

Raju, K.V. & Maloney, C., 1992: *Environmental Refugees in India.* A paper presented at Refugee Policy Group´s international conference: 'Migration and Environment', Nyon.

Rees, J., 1990: *Natural Resources, Allocation, Economics and Policy* (2nd ed.), Routledge, New York.

Reij, M. 1989: Strategies for Initiating Sustainable Moisture Conservation Programs in Semi-Arid West Africa, In; Trolldalen, ed. (1990).

Repetto, R., 1987: Creating Incentives for Sustainable Forest Development, *AMBIO*, No. 16.

Riggs, R.E. and Plano, J.L., 1988: *The United Nations and World Politics*, Dorsey Press, Chicago.

Rogers, P., 1991: *International River Basins: Pervasive Unidirectional Externalities*. Paper presented at a conference on "The Economics of Transnational Commons." Universita di Siena, Italy, Apr. 25-27, 1991.

Rosenau, J.N., 1983: New Natural Resources as Global Issues; in Dupuy, ed. (1983).

Rossi, P.H., Wright, J.D., Weber-Burdin, E., & Pereira, J., 1983: *Victims of the Environment: Loss from Natural Hazards in the United States, 1970–80*. Plenum Press, New York and London.

Rumley, D. & Minghi, J. (eds) 1991: *The Geography of Border Landscapes*, Routledge, London.

Russwurm, L.H., 1976: *A System Approach to the Natural Environment*. Methuen, London.

Sadik, N., 1991: *Population and the Environment: the challenges ahead*, UNFPA, New York.

Salem-Murdock, M. & Horowitz, M., 1991: Hidden Costs of River Basin Development, *Dryland Bulletin*, IIED, London.

Sand, P., 1991: *New Approaches to Transnational Environmental Disputes*, UNCED, Geneva.

Sand, P., 1990.: *Lessons Learned in Global Environmental Governance*, World Resources Institute, Washington DC.

Schrijver, N., 1989: International Organization for Environmental Security, *Bulletin of Peace Proposals*, Vol. 20 (2).

Schulze, R.E. & McGee, O.S., 1978: Climatic Indices on Classifications in Relation to the Biogeography of Southern Africa, In; Pinay (1988).

Scott, P.T. & Trolldalen, J.M., 1992: *International Environmental Conflict Resolution; Proceedings of WFED's seminar Feb. 10, 1992 prior to UNCED's Prep.Com. Meeting IV*, Holmenkollen Park Hotel Rica, Oslo.

Scudder, T., 1980: River Basin Development in African Savannas, In; Harris, ed. (1980).

Scudder, T. 1985: A Sociological Framework for the Analysis of New Land Settlements, In; Cernea, ed. (1985).

Second World Climate Conference, 1991: *Climate Changes Science, Impacts and Policy*, WMO, UNEP, UNESCO, FAO and ISCU, Cambridge University Press, Cambridge, New York

Secretariat of the Independent Commission on International Humanitarian Issues, 1986: *The Vanishing Forest*, Zed Books Ltd, London and New Jersey.

Simon, J.L. & Kahn, H. (eds.), 1984: *The Resourceful Earth*, Oxford, Blackwell.

Smith, K, 1992: *Environmental Hazards, Assessing Risk and Reducing Disaster*, Routledge, London.

South African Development Coordination Conference (SADCC), 1989: *Zambezi River System Action Plan--Implementation of Category I Projects*, ZACPRO's 1-8 SADCC Coordination Unit, Soil and Water Conservation and Land Utilization Sector (SWCLU), Maseru.

South African Development Coordination Conference / United Nations Environment Programme (SADCC/UNEP), 1991: *ZACPLAN—Zambezi River System Action Plan, ZACPRO 5—Development of a Basin-Wide Unified Environmental Monitoring System Related to Water Quality and Quantity*.

South Commission, 1990: *The Challenge from the South*, Oxford University Press, Oxford.

South Commission, 1991: *The Challenge to the South*, Oxford University Press, Oxford.

Stein, R.E. & Cormick G.W., 1991: Elements of a United Nations Environment and Development Dispute Prevention and Settlement Service.. Paper presented for the consideration of the Preparatory Committee and Secretariat of the United Nations Conference on Environment and Development, July 1991.

St. meld. nr. 7, 1983—1984: Om Norges deltakelse i Konferansen om Sikkerhet og Samarbeid i

Europa (KSSE). Oppfølgingsmøte i Madrid 1980—83, *NOU*, Oslo.

Stocklasa, J. & Duinker, P.N., 1988: Social and Economic Consequences of Forest Decline in Czechoslovakia, IIASA, Laxenburg.

Strahler, A.N. & Strahler, A.H., 1987: *Modern Physical Geography*, Third Edition, 1987.

Straszak, A., 1983: Systems Issues Analysis Framework for International Conflict Resolution Technology. Supplementary Ways for Improving International Stability, In; *Proceedings of IIASA Workshop*, Laxenburg, Pergamon Press, New York.

Stromayer, K.A.K and Ekobo, A., 1991: *Biological Surveys of Southeastern Cameroon.*, June 1991. Study conducted by Wildlife Conservation International (WCI) under contract to the European Community. Unpublished paper.

Suhrke, A., 1992: Towards a Comprehensive Refugee Policy: Conflict and Refugees in the Post-Cold War World, paper prepared for UNHCR/ILO Joint Meeting in Geneva, on International Aid Strategies to Reduce Emigration Pressures. May 1992.

Susskind, L. & Cruikshank, J., 1987: *Breaking the Impasse: Consensual Approaches toResolving Public Disputes*, Basic Books, New York.

Swedish National Environmental Protection Board: Acidification and Air Pollution. (pamphlet, undated)

Third World Guide 91/92, 1990: Instituto del Tercer Mundo, Uruguay.

Timberlake, L. & Tinker, J., 1984: *Environment and Conflict, Earthscan Briefing Document No.40,* 88 International Institute for Environment and Development, London.

Trexler, M.C., 1991: *Minding the Carbon Store. Weighing U.S. Forestry Strategies to Slow Global Warming*, World Resources Institute, Washington.

Trolldalen, J.M. (ed.) 1990: *Professional Development Workshop on Dryland Management*, Departmental Working Paper, no. 33, World Bank, Washington DC.

Trolldalen, J.M. & Bie, S., 1990: *Dryland Management Guidelines*, Environmental Working Paper, Environment Department, World Bank, Washington DC.

Trolldalen, J. M., 1991: On the Fringe, *Occasional Paper Series*, no. 10. NORAGRIC/University of Oslo, Ås/Oslo.

Trolldalen, J. M., 1992: Damming the Future?—The Bridge Barrage Project in the Gambia, *Resource and Environmental Geography, Series A*, no.4, Department of Geography, University of Oslo, Oslo.

Umbricht, V.H., 1989: *Multilateral Mediation—Practical Experiences and Lessons*, UNITAR, Martinus Nijhoff Publishers, Dordrecht.

Unesco/United Nations Environment Programme (Unesco/UNEP), 1990: *The Impact of Large Water Projects on the Environment.* United Nations Educational, Scientific and Cultural Organization, Paris.

United Nations, 1984: Urban and Rural Population Projections 1950—2025 (the 1984 Assessment) UN, New York.

United Nations (UN), 1986: Report of the Group of Governmental Experts on International Cooperation to Avert New Flows of Refugees. Doc. A/4/324.

United Nations (UN), 1986: *Urban and Rural Population Projections 1950—2025. The 1985 Assessment*, New York.

United Nations (UN), 1986: *A Report of the Secretary General on the UN International Drinking Water Supply and Sanitation Decade*, New York.

United Nations (UN), 1990: Basic Programme of Work of the Council: Implementing of Council Resolutions 1988/77 and 1989/114. Document E/1990/14, 22 January, 1990.

United Nations Conference on Environment and Development (UNCED), 1992: *Agenda 21* UNCED Secretariat, Geneva.

United Nations Conference on Environment and Development (UNCED), 1992: *Convention on Protection of the Global Biodiversity*, UNCED Secretariat, Geneva.

United Nations Conference on Environment and Development (UNCED), 1992: *Framework Convention on Climatic Change*, UNCED Secretariat, Geneva.

United Nations Conference on the Human Environment (UNCHE), 1972: *The Stockholm Declaration, The Final Act at the United Nations Conference on the Human Environment*, United Nations, New York.

United Nations Development Programme (UNDP) (ed.), 1976: *River Basin Development: Policies and Planning*, New York.

United Nations Development Programme (UNDP), 1979: *Lake Chad Basin Development Study*, Intermediate Report, Office for Project Execution, UNDP, New York.

United Nations Economic Commission of Europe (UN ECE), 1986: Transboundary Air Pollution, Effects and Control., *Air Pollution Studies* No.3. UN, New York.

United Nations Economic Commission of Europe (UN ECE), 1990: Effects and Control of Transboundary Air Pollution, *Air Pollution Studies* No. 6, UN, New York.

United Nations Economic Commission of Europe (UN ECE), 1990: *The Bergen Ministerial Declaration on Sustainable Development in the ECE Region*, United Nations Economic Commission of Europe, Geneva.

United Nations Environment Programme (UNEP), 1982: *The Health of the Oceans*, UNEP Nairobi.

United Nations Environment Programme (UNEP), 1986: *Assessment of the Present and Future Actions Related to the Zambezi Action Plan*, Mission of Experts to the Zambezi Countries.

United Nations Environment Programme (UNEP), 1987a: *Agreement on the Action Plan for the Environmentally Sound Management of the Common Zambezi River System—Final Act*, Harare, May 26–28, 1987.

United Nations Environment Programme (UNEP), 1987b: *The Montreal Protocol on Substances that Deplete the Ozone Layer, Final Act*, United Nations Environment Programme, Nairobi. Revised in Helsinki 1990.

United Nations Environment Programme (UNEP), 1989a : *Environmental Perspectives to the Year 2000 and Beyond*, United Nations Environment Programme, Nairobi.

United Nations Environment Progrmme (UNEP), 1989b : *Convention on Control of Transboundary Movement of Hazardous Wastes and their Disposal (the Basel Convention)*, United Nations Environment Programme, Nairobi.

United Nations Environment Progrmme (UNEP), 1989c: *Project Identification and Reformulation Mission—Zambezi Action Plan* (Main Report).

United Nations Environment Progrmme (UNEP), 1991: *Register of International Treaties and Other Agreements in the Field of the Environment*, United Nations Environment Programme, Nairobi.

United Nations Environment Programme / Food and Agriculture Organization (UNEP/FAO), 1982: *The Global Assessment of Tropical Forest Resources*, Nairobi, April 1982. GEMS pac information series no. 3.

United Nations Environment Programme, Governing Committee (UNEP, GC), 1991: Report of the Governing Council on its Work on its Sixteenth Session, UNEP, Nairobi.

United Nations General Assembly (UN GA), 1989: United Nations Conference on Environment and Development, paragraph 12 w, Report A/44/246/Add.7, UN, New York.

United Nations High Commission on Refugees (UNHCR), 1991: EXCOM Conclusion No. 22 (XXXII), UNHCR, Geneva.

Untawale, M.G., 1990: Global Environmental Degradation and International Organizations, *International Political Science Review*, Vol. 11, No. 3.

UNITAR, 1991: *Environmental Negotiations and Dispute Resolution*, Proceedings from UNITAR's Expert Meeting, UNITAR, Geneva.

U.S. General Accounting Office, 1992: International Environment: International Agreements Are Not Well Monitored (GAO / RCED-92-43) January 1992.

U.S. Geological Survey, 1983: National Water Summary.

Vicuña, F.O., 1991: State Responsibility, Liability and Remedial Measures under International Law: New Criteria for Environmental Protection (DRAFT).

Vellinga, P. & Leathermall, S. P., 1989: Sea Level Rise, Consequences and Policies, *Climatic Change*, no. 15.

von Bertalanfly, L., 1968: *General System Theory: Foundations, Development, Applications*, George Braziller, New York.

Warford, J. & Ackerman, R., 1988: Environment and Development: Implementing the World Bank's New Policies, *Development Committee*, No. 17, World Bank, Washington DC.

Warrick, R. A. & Oerlemans, H. 1990: Sea Level Rise, In; WMO, UNEP (IPCC), *Climate Change*.

WCED, 1987: *Our Common Future*, Oxford University Press, Oxford.

Welcomme, R.L., 1977: Some Factors Affecting the Catch Tropical River Fisheries, In: "Symposium on River and Floodplain Fisheries in Africa", Bujumbwa, CIFA Technical Report No. 5, 266-275, In: Pinay (1988).

Westing, A. (ed.), 1986: *Global Resources and International Conflict—Environmental Factors in Strategic Policy and Action* PRIO/UNEP, Nairobi.

Westing, A., (ed.), 1989: *Comprehensive Security for the Baltic—An Environmental Approach*, PRIO/ UNEP, Nairobi.

Westing, A., (ed.), 1990: *Environmental Hazards of War—Releasing Dangerous Forces in an Industrialized World* PRIO/UNEP, Nairobi.

Wettestad, J., 1991: *The Effectiveness of International Resource Cooperation: Some Preliminary Findinings*, Fridtjof Nansens Institute, Oslo.

Wiman, B.L.B., 1991: Implications of Environmental Complexity for Science and Policy—Contribution from Systems Theory, *Global Environmental Change*, Vol. 1, no. 3.

Wolpin, M.D., 1990: *Third World Military Roles and Environmental Security*, International Peace Research Institute, Oslo.

World Bank, 1989: The Large Dam Controversy, ENV/Tech. Dep./Afr., World Bank.

World Bank, 1990: *Forest Policy: An Approach Paper*, October 18.

World Bank, 1992a: *The World Bank and the Environment—Fiscal 1992*, World Bank, Washington DC.

World Bank, 1992b: Environment Working Paper Series.

World Bank, UNEP, UNDP: Global Environment Facility, Report by the Chairman to the April 1992 Participants' Meeting GEF-Secretariat, World Bank, Washington, DC.

World Bank's Operational Directive no. 4, Annex B.

World Nuclear Industry Handbook ,1991. Reed Business Publishing Group, Sutton

World Resources Institute, et al., 1989: *World Resources 1988-89*, Basic Books, Inc., New York.

World Resources Institute et al., 1990: *World Resources 1990-91*, Oxford University Press, New York, Oxford

World Resources Institute, 1991: *Individual Profiles of UN System Organizations*, Institutions Project, Background Paper No. 2.

World Resources Institute, et. al., 1992: *World Resources 1992-93*, Oxford University Press, New York/ Oxford.

Wright, R.F., 1983: Acidification of Freshwaters in Europe. Water Quality Bulletin, Vol. 8, No. 3.

Young, O., 1989: The Politics of International Regime Formation: Managing Natural Resources and the Environment, *International Organization* 43, 3 Summer 1989.

Zaman, M., 1983: Ganges basin development; a long term problem and some short terms options, In; Zaman, M. et al (ed).

Zaman, M.., 1983: *River basin development*, Tycooly, Dublin.

Zartman, I.W., 1991: Regional Conflict Resolution, In; Kremenyuk ed. (1991).

ZACPLAN, 1989: *Zambezi River System Action Plan, ZACPRO 5 Development of a Basin-Wide Unified Environmental Monitoring System related to Water Quality and Quantity*, SADCC Coordination Unit, Soil and Water Conservation and Land Utilization Sector (SWCLU), Maseru, SADCC/ UNEP, 1991.

Ågren, C. 1990: Air, *Acid Magazine* No. 9.

Appendix 1

Extended Acknowledgements

The book is a product of extensive consultations and support given in various ways with resource people and institutions world wide. I am grateful for the advice received and for their thoughts. Below, some these people are listed. I apologize for any names which have been left out. The people listed are not responsible for any errors, statements (other-wise referred), or the perspectives taken in this book:

Attard, David	Foreign Office, Malta
Azimi, Nassarine	UNITAR, Geneva
Balek, Jaroslav	ENEX, Prague
Bartemus, Peter	DIESA, New York
Bugge, Hans Christian	Faculty of Law, University of Oslo
Hen, Susan	World Bank, Washington D.C.
Coles, Gervase	formerly UNHCR, Geneva
Coelho, Eduardo A.	SADCC/SECLU, Lesotho
Dalfelt, Arne	World Bank, Washington D.C.
Dokken, Karin	PRIO, Oslo
Dotson, Bruce	Institute for Environmental Negotiation, UVa.
Drake, Susan	U.S. State Department, Washington D.C.
Drammeh, Halifa O.	UNEP, Regional Office for Africa, Nairobi
Dukes, Frank	Institute for Environmental Negotiation, UVa.
Döös, Bo	IIASA, Environment Dept., Laxenburg
Eidheim, Idunn	The Norwegian Ministry of Environment, Oslo
Fort, Richard	The Norwegian Ministry of Environment, Oslo
Gebremedhin, Naigzy	Technology and Environment Branch, UNEP, Nairobi
Graham, Oddmund	The Norwegian Ministry of Environment, Oslo
Gucovsky, Michael	UNDP, New York
Hofseth, Paul	The Norwegian Ministry of Environment, Oslo
Ivars, Birte	The Finnish Ministry of Foreign Affairs, Helsinki (former)
Jeftic, Lyubomir	MAP, Athens
Johannessen, Lasse Bjørn	Norwegian Ministry of Foreign Affairs, Oslo
Johnsen, Hilde	Norwegian Ministry of Foreign Affairs, Oslo
Kjørven, Olav	Fridtjof Nansen Institute, Oslo
Klem, Gustav	NORAD, Oslo
Kohler, Larry	International Labour Organisation, Geneva
Kongsvik, Turid	Norwegian Ministry of Foreign Affairs, Oslo
Lavik Opdahl, Inger	Norwegian Ministry of Foreign Affairs, Oslo

Lauche, Barbra	World Bank, Washington, D.C.
Leiro, Jostein	Norwegian Ministry of Foreign Affairs, Oslo
Leleka, B.	SADCC/SWCLU, Lesotho
Lindsøe, Anne Britt	The Norwegian Prime Minister's Office, Oslo
Meneenly, Richard	Independent, Oslo
Molvær, Reidulf	PRIO, Oslo
Mugume, James M.	Uganda's permanent mission to the United Nations, New York
Munasinghe, Shira	University of Maryland
Nordby, Trygve	The Norwegian Refugee Council, Oslo
Nordbø, Eldrid	The Norwegian Ministry of Environment, Oslo
Quaterman, Mark	NIDR, Washington D.C.
Ofuso-Amah, Paati,	World Bank, Washington D.C.
Parra, A.	World Bank, Washington, D.C.
Pronove, Gao	UNITAR, Geneva
Rich, Bruce,	Natural Defense Fund, Washington D.C.
Rummel-Bulska, Iwona	UNEP, Geneva
Salewicz, Kazimierz A.	IIASA, Water Resources Project, Laxenburg
Salicath, Carl	Norwegian Diplomatic Delegation to CSCE, Vienna
Sand, Peter	UNCED, Geneva
Sand, Turid	The Norwegian Ministry of Environment, Oslo
Sandborg, Guri	The Norwegian Ministry of Environment
Schippers, Ashton	National Institute for Dispute Resolution, Washington D.C.
Shrigas, Diana	CMG, Harvard University, Boston
Sjostedt, Gunnar	Swedish Institute of International Affairs. Stockholm
Skogmo, Bjørn	The Norwegian Prime Minister's Office, Oslo
Spector, Bert	PIN, IIASA, Laxenburg
Stene-Johansen, Svein	NIVA, Oslo
Stevens, Yvette	UNHCR, Geneva
Street, Bill	Institute for Environmental Negotiation, UVa.
Søegaard, Pippi G.	The Norwegian Ministry of Environment, Oslo
Tråvik, Kim	The Norwegian Ministry of Foerign Affairs, Oslo
Vittani, Jurg	Federation of Red Cross Societies, Geneva
Wells, Michael	World Bank, Washington, D.C.
Wetland, Morten	The Norwegian Prime Minister's Office, Oslo
Wettestad, Jørgen	Fridtjof Nansen Institute, Oslo
Wilson, Stephen	Consultant in printing and publishing, Washington D.C.
Wright, Richard	NIVA, Oslo
Zillezen, Horst	University of Oldenburg
Aass, Svein	Norwegian Ministry of Foreign Affairs, Oslo
Aardal, Armand	The Norwegian permanent mission to UNEP, Nairobi

Appendix 2

Data Collection

Access to and collection of reliable information on potential and manifest international environmental conflicts have created methodological challenges. Literature reviews, fieldworks, and consultations have extensively been carried out over a two year period since I left the World Bank).

Although fieldworks are dating back to 1981 and throughout the years in Sub-Sahara Africa, Northern Africa, India, and in the Mediterranean region, more recently, my assistants have undertaken trips to the Zambezi River Basin in Southern Africa and to the Secretariat of the ZACPLAN (summer 1991), to Greece (to UNEP's secretariat for MAP, in summer 1991) and to Egypt (at the Ministerial Conference on MAP in Cairo, October 1991), to Oxford University (Refugee Studies), and to Refugee Policy Group (in Geneva).

Numerous consultations have been held at UNEP (Nairobi), at the UN (in New York and Geneva), and at the World Bank (Washington DC), Harvard University (Conflict Management Institute), International Institute for Applied Systems Analysis (IIASA in Laxenburg, Vienna) and Institute for Environmental Negotiations of Virginia (Charlottesville).

The data represent a diversity of sources ranging from physical measurements in the field to collection of tertiary sources (for example, UN statistical material). Some data are however, likely to contain uncertainties, particularly aggregated data at a regional and global level. Efforts have been made to express those concerns in the text (sometimes in the endnotes).

United Nations Institute for Training and Research
New York • Geneva

UNITAR was established in 1965 to enhance the effectiveness of the United Nations system through appropriate training and research. In the course of its existence, UNITAR has evolved as an institute dedicated to training with research functions limited to research on, for, and *cum* training.

The training activities of the Institute focus on two areas: training related to multilateral diplomacy, peace-keeping, peacemaking and peacebuilding; and training related to the promotion of economic and social development. The first category of training activities comprises programmes which have been closely identified with UNITAR since its very inception. They are usually addressed to diplomats accredited to the United Nations. In recent years, these programmes are also being conducted *in situ* in various countries. The second category of training activities are more varied and also involve close co-operation with other UN bodies and agencies. They have evolved to include training in environmental and natural resource management, debt management, disaster relief, and other areas which relate to the broad objective of promoting economic and social development. In all cases, however, these programmes aim at meeting specific needs of Member States and supporting the objectives of the co-operating lead agencies.

The views and conclusions in this book are the sole responsibility of the author and do not necessarily reflect the views of UNITAR or its Board of Trustees. Although UNITAR takes no position on the views and conclusions expressed in the book, it does deem it appropriate to be used as a pedagogical tool in its training programme on environmental negotiation and dispute resolution.

NIDR

National Institute for Dispute Resolution
Washington D.C.

NIDR is a non-profit organization based in Washington D.C. It promotes the use of creative, collaborative methods to resolve conflicts, including arbitration, mediation and negotiation, through grant-making, publishing, convening conferences and seminars, and providing technical assistance. NIDR's programmes focus on: public policy and governance, courts, community justice, education, innovation, and global information exchange.

This publication is the product of a joint WFED/UNITAR/NIDR initiative in international environmental negotiations and dispute resolution. However, the opinions expressed herein do not necessarily reflect the views of NIDR and no endorsement by NIDR should be inferred.

WFED

World Foundation for Environment and Development
Oslo • Washington D.C.

The World Foundation for Environment and Development (WFED) is an independent nonpartisan organization that has been established to promote international cooperation and conflict resolution initiatives in the field of environment and development around the world.

Despite growing international recognition of the importance of sound natural resource management, there is widespread disagreement as to just what should be done to address conflicting environment and development issues. The need for concentrated attention on these issues is particularly important as competition for natural resources and the economic aspirations of populations everywhere place ever growing demands on already burdened international institutions.

Through research, education, and conflict assessment assistance, WFED's programmes, activities, and services are designed to improve international understanding of environment and development issues and to contribute to the peaceful resolution of related international conflicts and disputes.

International Environmental Conflict Resolution: The Role of the United Nations reflects WFED's ongoing promotion of collaborative initiatives to improve international understanding of the critical environment and development problems now facing most of the world's populations. It also reflects WFED's commitment to explore innovative approaches to international environmental conflict resolution at many different institutional and geographical levels for the purpose of encouraging international cooperation and consensus building.

About the author

Dr. Jon Martin Trolldalen, who served as an Environmental Specialist at the World Bank between 1988 and 1990, is currently Director of the World Foundation for Environment and Development based in Washington and Oslo. He is a scholar at the Resource Geography Group, Department of Geography at the University of Oslo, and has served as an advisor to the Norwegian Secretariat for the 1992 UN Conference on Environment and Development since 1991.

Dr. Trolldalen holds degrees in Engineering, Human Geography, and a doctorate in Resource Geography from the University of Oslo.

While at the World Bank he worked in international environmental matters, and on policy/research on marginal lands (drylands). He also participated at the United Nations General Assembly as World Bank representative on environmental matters.

Prior to joining the World Bank, Dr. Trolldalen served as strategic planner of Norwegian Church Aid's worldwide international relief activities. He has worked in several African countries.

He has published widely in the field of environmental and development issues.

DATE DUE

DEMCO 38-297